The United States in the World

The
United States

A HISTORY OF

HOUGHTON MIFFLIN COMPANY   BOSTON   TORONTO

GENEVA, ILLINOIS   PALO ALTO   PRINCETON, NEW JERSEY

in the *World*

AMERICAN FOREIGN POLICY

H. W. Brands

Texas A& M University

VOLUME I

Sponsoring Editor: *Sean Wakely*
Senior Development Editor: *Fran Gay*
Senior Production/Design Coordinator: *Pat Mahtani*
Senior Manufacturing Coordinator: *Priscilla Bailey*
Marketing Manager: *Rebecca Dudley*

Cover credit: Salem Merchant Flags. *Courtesy, Peabody and Essex Museum, Salem, Massachusetts*
Cover design: *Dragonfly Design, Ron Kosciak*

Printed in the U.S.A.

Library of Congress catalog card number: 93-78669

ISBN: 0-395-62180-1

3456789-QF-02 01 00 99 98

Contents

Maps

Preface

This book adopts a global approach to the study of the history of American foreign relations. Two reasons motivate this approach. The first is historical: for the greater part of the existence of the American republic, the world has had a much larger impact on the United States than the United States has had on the world. Understanding relations between Americans and the rest of the world requires close attention to developments in the rest of the world.

The second reason is contemporary: at no time has an understanding of the foreign side of American foreign relations been more important than during the 1990s. The bipolar framework of international affairs that grew out of the Second World War has collapsed, and no compelling framework has emerged to replace it. Countries that did not exist in 1945 clamor to be heard. Nations leveled by the war have regained their former stature. Ancient rivalries suppressed during the Cold War have burst forth again. Economics and technology have evolved in ways unforeseen fifty years ago. The United States remains the single most powerful nation on earth, but Americans increasingly find themselves having to take account of the wishes and demands of people in other countries. Understanding America's present and shaping its future require understanding those wishes and demands.

The global approach of this book assumes the form, most obviously, of a more thorough treatment of developments in other countries and in the world at large than generally appears in texts on American diplomatic history. Where other books have planted their readers, so to speak, in Washington, or at least within the United States, and directed readers' attention outward to the world beyond American borders, this book conceptually locates readers somewhere above the earth, where they can see the entire planet; and while it keeps America always in the picture (a conceptual possibility if a geographical improbability), it allows them a much broader view.

Adopting, as it does, the world as its frame of reference, this book concentrates on large issues of world affairs. Sometimes this concentration comes at the expense of what might be called more traditional elements of diplomatic history. When, for example, considerations of space have dictated a choice between detailing the negotiations leading up to a particular treaty and sketching the evolution of the global balance of power, the latter has won out. Similarly, items often considered extrinsic to conventional diplomatic history—intellectual and technological developments, trends in the world economy, cultural influences on the actions of peoples and governments—receive substantial attention here. America's relations with foreign countries have reflected much more than what diplomats and governments said to each other, and histories of American foreign relations should reflect this fact.

Organization of the Book

The book is divided into two volumes to correspond to the typical two-semester course. The first volume covers the period from the colonial origins of the United States to 1914; the second volume (which overlaps the first by one chapter) covers the period from 1895 until the present. The first two chapters of Volume I lay out themes that have characterized American foreign relations for two centuries and place the creation and early evolution of the United States squarely in an international context. Subsequent chapters trace the conflicts between an expanding United States and the great powers of Europe, as well as between the United States and the lesser powers of the Americas and the aboriginal inhabitants of North America. The transformation of the American and world economies during the late nineteenth century, the emergence of nationalism and other ideologies in Europe and elsewhere, and the effects of these developments on American foreign relations are treated in the last three chapters of Volume I.

Volume II describes the rise of the United States to global dominance at the midpoint of the twentieth century and its relative decline since. Europe's two great wars play a central role, as do the long-running revolution in China, the emergence, eclipse, and re-emergence of Japan, and the transformation of large parts of the nonindustrial world. Several chapters discuss the assorted ideological reactions to modernization, particularly fascism, communism, and religious fundamentalism. The last chapters of Volume II chart the disintegration of the post-Second World War order, including the sudden and spectacular collapse of the Soviet Union and its Eastern European empire. The last chapter also covers the Persian Gulf war of 1991 and other recent developments.

Pedagogical Features

While the text of the book carries the story line and analysis, additional features of the two volumes provide guideposts to students. Each chapter contains a chronology of important events of the period in question; these often go beyond the narrative to lend additional context to the events described there. Maps orient students geographically; in keeping with the overall approach, the maps stress international and global developments. Each chapter concludes with numerous suggestions for additional reading, from broad-gauged surveys and synthetic works to detailed monographs. Reproductions of photographs, paintings, and cartoons convey images words cannot so easily capture.

Instructor's Resource Manual with Test Items

An *Instructor's Resource Manual with Test Items*, prepared by Donald Rakestraw of Georgia Southern University, provides teaching ideas and test questions as additional resource material for instructors. The manual includes for
each text chapter a chapter summary, lecture suggestions, classroom discussion
questions, class activities, term paper topics, approximately twenty-five mul-
tiple-choice questions, and five essay questions.

Acknowledgments

Although the title page of this book lists but a single author, no work of this
scope is really the work of one person. The book would not have been possible
without the assistance of those hundreds of historians, economists, political
scientists, and others who have investigated particular events in greater detail
than this author ever could have and who have recorded their conclusions in
books and articles (many of which are listed among the suggested readings).
Nor would this book have acquired its present form without the patient reading and careful commentary of the reviewers to whom earlier drafts were sent.
These include:

Richard A. Harrison, Lawrence University
Sandra M. Hawley, San Jacinto College
Lawrence S. Kaplan, Kent State University
Thomas R. Maddux, California State University, Northridge
Robert J. McMahon, University of Florida
Margaret R. Morley, Northern Arizona University
Donald A. Rakestraw, Georgia Southern University
William Stinchcombe, Syracuse University
William Stueck, Jr., University of Georgia

Finally, special thanks go to Frances Gay, Senior Development Editor at
Houghton Mifflin, for her work on the manuscript.

HWB

The United States in the World

Chapter 1

Legacies of the Past, Patterns for the Future

When the United States of America claimed membership in the world of nations at the three-quarter mark of the eighteenth century, it was a small and comparatively insignificant country. Its people huddled along the eastern shore of middle North America, far from the centers of European civilization and even farther from the much older centers of Asian civilization. Americans numbered about 3 million, of whom approximately one-fifth were black slaves, at a time when the largest countries of Europe counted ten times as many inhabitants and India and China comprised almost one hundred times as many. The country's armed forces sufficed—usually—to defend the Americans of European and African descent from attacks by the aboriginal Indian tribes, who constituted their closest foreign neighbors, but these forces suffered badly by comparison with the armies and navies of the great European states.

By the other principal measure of national strength, economic power, Americans fared little better. They were moderately prosperous as individuals— more prosperous, for example, than the people of Russia and far more prosperous than the peoples of India and China. But because Americans were so few, the aggregate economic power they could mobilize for national purposes was much less than that of Russia, India, or China—and perhaps a dozen other countries. In sum, Americans in the latter half of the eighteenth century were poorly positioned to exert major influence in world affairs.

During the course of the next two centuries, Americans would acquire such influence; this acquisition would be the central enduring theme of American international relations. For the first century of America's national existence, however, the country's influence grew only slowly, and for a long time the world influenced Americans far more than Americans influenced the world. But eventually the pace quickened, and by the middle of the twentieth century Americans were wielding power unmatched in world history.

Many Americans found this transition to international predominance unexceptional, for they considered themselves an exceptional people. This notion of American exceptionalism was a second important theme running through the history of American international relations. Americans liked to think of themselves as unique, as standing outside the ordinary course of human

Chronology

1492	Columbus lands in West Indies
1494	Treaty of Tordesillas between Spain and Portugal
1517	Martin Luther touches off Protestant Reformation
1543	Copernicus's *De Revolutionibus*
1588	Defeat of Spanish Armada
1607	Virginia colony established by English
1608	Quebec colony founded by French
1642–48	English Civil War
1687	Newton's *Principia*
1689–97	War of the League of Augsburg (King William's War)
1690	Locke's *Two Treatises* published
1702–13	War of the Spanish Succession (Queen Anne's War)
1729	China's Yongzheng emperor outlaws opium smoking
1743–48	War of the Austrian Succession (King George's War)
1752	British adopt Gregorian calendar (omitting September 3 to September 13)
1756–63	Seven Years' War (French and Indian War: 1754–63)

history. Often the idea of American uniqueness assumed religious connotations; sometimes it was cast in terms of theories of biological and social evolution. But whether religiously or secularly based, the conception that America was special placed a lasting mark on American relations with other countries and peoples.

To some extent the exceptionalists were right; America *was* different from other countries. But every country is unique in its own way, and in terms of relations with other countries the beliefs and attitudes Americans shared with other peoples were at least as important as those that set them apart. Like other peoples, Americans were very much creatures of their time and place. During the mid-eighteenth century, America's position in world affairs reflected conditions that had developed over hundreds of years. Long in the making, these conditions would continue to shape American international relations for an equally long time. For purposes of explanation and analysis, these conditions can be divided into five categories: politics, economics, intellectual activities, cultural concerns, and technology.

Politically, Americans on the eve of independence were subjects of the British empire, the current leader in the struggle for primacy among the European empires that had been under way since before Christopher Columbus's rediscovery of America in 1492. The struggle was as hot and furious as ever during the eighteenth century, and it would persist for another two hundred years. Americans would sometimes make active use of Europe's conflicts for their own benefit; sometimes they would attempt to stay clear. But always they would be strongly affected by the contests across the Atlantic.

Economically, Americans lived and labored under the regime of mercantilism, the dominant doctrine of international economics in the eighteenth century. Yet mercantilism was coming under challenge from the antithetical doctrine of free trade. In one form or another, the competition between the mercantilists and the free traders would last as long as international trade lasted—in other words, until the present day. Americans were among the most active of international traders; as a result, they constantly found themselves in the thick of the competition.

Intellectually, Americans were heirs of the Enlightenment, the European movement that since the seventeenth century had applied the principles of science to human affairs and insisted that government practices and institutions be based on reason rather than authority. As Americans related Enlightenment thinking to their own situation in the eighteenth century, they came to the conclusion that they ought to cut their ties to Britain and strike out on their own in international affairs. As they related Enlightenment thinking to the rest of the world in subsequent decades and centuries, they developed a characteristic approach to dealings with other countries—one that produced mixed results for both Americans and other peoples.

Culturally, Americans had been formed by their basically British background, although other European influences and some African influences (brought by slaves) occasionally surfaced as well. Even before independence, however, a recognizably American strain was developing in the Americans' Britishness; with independence, this strain grew increasingly distinct. Some foreigners thought American culture hardly merited the name of culture; they judged Americans crass and insipid. Others found American culture refreshing, free of pretense, and open to innovation. Matters of culture shaped American international relations by acting as a lens through which Americans perceived the world and through which the world perceived America. Sometimes this cultural lensing promoted international understanding, as in America's relations with Britain; sometimes it led to misunderstanding and worse, as in America's relations with many countries of Latin America and Asia.

Technologically, Americans of the mid-eighteenth century were poised several paces short of the Industrial Revolution. In certain activities they struggled with tools unchanged for centuries; in others the state of the art was undeniably modern. No single area of human knowledge can have such an immediate and decisive effect on international relations as technology—that is, the application of scientific knowledge to everyday life. Military power is commonly the final arbiter of international disputes, and from the age of sail and gunpowder to the age of intercontinental nuclear missiles the countries with the most advanced weaponry have usually managed to have their way. As America matured as a nation, it developed some of the most advanced technology in the world; this technology played a major part in America's rise to global influence.

Technology also shapes relations among countries in matters not intrinsically connected to war. Most obviously, technology defines what is possible in terms of communications and transportation. It is a truism of world history that the earth has grown effectively smaller with advancing technology. At times, Americans have considered this fact a blessing—namely, when they wanted to be in close contact with distant parts of the earth. At times, they have considered it a curse—when they wanted the world to leave them alone. But they have never been able to escape the implications of the planet's shrinking.

Americans of the eighteenth century did not dissect their lives into neatly labeled categories; they left such dissecting to future historians. Nonetheless, world developments in politics, economics, intellectual life, cultural affairs, and technology conspicuously affected American relations with other countries in the decades surrounding the birth of the United States and for more than two centuries thereafter.

The Politics of the Atlantic World

During the eighteenth century, the British colonies in North America occupied a position at the western edge of the Atlantic world. In geographic terms the Atlantic world consisted of those regions easily accessible to the Atlantic Ocean, including most of Europe, the northern and western portion of Africa, the eastern coasts of North and South America, and the islands of the Caribbean basin. In an era when people and goods traveled more easily by water than by land (and not at all by air), the Atlantic Ocean served as a highway connecting the communities and civilizations along its shores. Events—wars, famines, inventions—that occurred in one part of the Atlantic world soon reverberated in other parts as well.

But in human history geography never exists apart from political, economic, cultural, and technological factors. Politically, the Atlantic world was dominated by the imperial powers of western Europe, as had been the case for three hundred years. The relative ranking of those powers, however, changed dramatically over that time, and it was the struggle among the powers that gave birth, first, to the colonies that became the United States and, second, to the United States itself. During the great age of discovery in the fifteenth and early sixteenth centuries, Portugal and Spain took the lead in pushing Europe's political frontiers far to the west and south. The Portuguese coasted down Africa, eventually rounding the Cape of Good Hope and linking the Atlantic world to the world of South and East Asia. The Spanish forged west across the Atlantic, following the track of their hired Italian, Columbus. In 1494 the two Iberian powers signed the Treaty of Tordesillas, which granted Spain control of territories west of a mid-Atlantic dividing line and Portugal control of the discoveries east of the line (and accidentally laid the basis for Portugal's claim to Brazil, which bulged from South America back across the line). The inhabitants of the territories involved were not consulted; they rarely would be by either Europeans or Americans in similar treaty-making circumstances in the future.

For nearly a hundred years, the Portuguese and especially the Spanish exploited their head start in the race for global power, with Spain fashioning an empire extending from South America north all the way into Florida and New Mexico and reaching clear around the world to the Philippines. This empire brought the Spanish enormous wealth, notably gold and silver, which they used to build naval fleets, hire soldiers, and acquire the other chief instruments of power. Until late in the sixteenth century, Spain dominated the politics of Europe and the Atlantic world, but by the century's end the balance was beginning to shift. In 1588 Spain sent a formidable fleet—the Invincible (so the Spanish called it) Armada—against troublesome upstart England, whose pirate-princes Francis Drake and Walter Raleigh had been waylaying Spanish ship traffic, including the bullion-loaded galleons that regularly poured American gold and silver into the Spanish emperor's coffers. By a combination of good luck and bold tactics, the English defeated the Spanish and destroyed most of the Armada. While a great military victory, England's defeat of the Armada was at least as much a psychological triumph. It provided an enormous boost to English confidence and encouraged England to challenge Spain more vigorously than ever.

In one area of empire building—the founding of American colonies—the English could use the encouragement. In the late 1570s and early 1580s, the English sea dog Humphrey Gilbert had tried to construct a settlement in Newfoundland. But the cold, damp, and windy climate proved too discouraging and Gilbert gave up. In 1585 Walter Raleigh landed a group of colonists on Roanoke Island off the coast of Carolina. This colony did not last either, disappearing under circumstances never entirely explained. It did not help the Roanoke colony's chances that it required resupply just as the Spanish Armada was closing in on England. The English admiralty commandeered all available vessels to combat the invaders, and by the time the crisis ended and the supply ship got to America, the Roanokers had vanished.

Yet even though the defeat of the Armada may have helped doom the Carolina colony, it did persuade the British to keep trying. In 1607 a group called the London Company established a colony on the James River in Virginia. Like many business start-ups—and the London Company's Virginia colony *was* a business venture—Jamestown suffered from undercapitalization and underestimates of the hurdles to be overcome in making the enterprise work. Only the

The defeat of the Spanish Armada, shown here sailing for England, helped tip the balance of power in the Atlantic world from Spain to England. *The Granger Collection*

infusion of new capital and personnel after 1610 and the reorientation of the company away from gold seeking and toward the production of tobacco secured the venture's success. Although the founding London Company did not survive the shakeout, going bankrupt and delivering control of the colony to the English Crown in 1624, the idea that the world was an arena for winning profits soon took root in the American colonists' consciousness. No idea would outlive it in Americans' dealings with the world.

The establishment of the Virginia colony helped prompt the establishment of other colonies, settled farther north—albeit settled for different reasons. The English Reformation begun by Henry VIII in the sixteenth century had not quite played itself out three generations later; various groups complained that the Church of England remained too much like the Church of Rome. One radical sect, the Separatists, judged England beyond redemption and decided to relocate, first to Holland and then across the Atlantic to Plymouth on Massachusetts' Cape Cod. Another, larger group, the Puritans, initially intended to stay in England and purify Anglicanism from within, but the rise of staunch conservatives such as Archbishop of Canterbury William Laud convinced them that their only hope of salvation lay in fleeing the country. They would create a model church in New England, which would serve as an example of religious

Sir Walter Raleigh headed an early
English attempt to colonize North
America and later hunted for gold in
South America. After falling afoul of
James I, he was executed for
treason. *Brown Brothers*

righteousness and ultimately force the Anglicans to change their degenerately
popish ways.

The Puritan notion of setting an example for the rest of humanity—"We
must consider that we shall be like a City upon a Hill; the eyes of all people
are on us," said Governor John Winthrop—provided another lasting theme in
American relations with the world, a counterpoint to the theme of profit making and one that would live just as long. In the shorter term, it helped the
Massachusetts Bay Colony get off to a good start. The colony flourished, and
by the early 1640s more than twenty thousand English men, women, and children had arrived in Boston and were spilling over into the adjacent valleys.
Being naturally quarrelsome, the Puritans could not long sustain the consensus
that first followed their removal to the New World; some of the spillover, as
into Rhode Island, included individuals who had insisted on purifying Puritan-
ism and been thrown out of Boston for their efforts.

Just as the British had not allowed the Spanish to have the Western Hemisphere as their own colonial playground, neither did the French leave the
British alone in Atlantic North America. The year after the London Company established the Jamestown colony, the French planted their flag and a

settlement at Quebec on the St. Lawrence River. Earlier, during the 1560s, the French had attempted to settle in Florida, but the Spanish had thrown them out. Now they tried their luck in the north, and this time they succeeded. Yet French success differed significantly from British success. Where the British held that America was an opportune place for unloading religious dissenters, the French insisted on orthodoxy (Roman Catholic, in their case) among expatriates. This policy effectively shut the door to those groups—particularly the French Protestants, or Huguenots—who otherwise would have had the greatest incentive to settle in New France. As a result of this policy, as well as of the trying climate and recalcitrant soil of New France, the population of French North America grew very slowly during the seventeenth and eighteenth centuries. In 1763 the population of New France, exclusive of native Indians, was less than one hundred thousand. The population of British North America, by contrast, was thirty times as great.

But the slow growth of the population of New France did not prevent the French from waging a spirited contest with the British for predominance in North America. The stakes of the contest were much higher than North America; what the British and French were really fighting for was control of the Atlantic world. The fighting between the British and French went far back, at least to the Norman invasion of England in 1066. The Hundred Years' War, which actually lasted from the 1330s until the 1450s, was the single longest round of fighting between the two peoples, but even when they were supposedly at peace, each sneaked in a few blows against the other. The Reformation of the sixteenth century added a religious element to the contest—England went Protestant, while France remained Catholic—while the rise of aggressive merchant capitalists in each country contributed greed to the list of vices each side saw in the other. At the same time, the central government in each country was trying to consolidate its authority over rivals from the provinces, and directing hostile energies against foreigners, such as those across the Channel, helped galvanize nationalistic feelings. (William Shakespeare's Henry IV, first speaking at about this period, described the strategy of using foreign adventures to distract the common people from domestic troubles when he explained to his son how he had contrived to "busy giddy minds with foreign quarrels." The strategy, already old in Shakespeare's day, would never disappear from the practice of international affairs.)

By the seventeenth century, Britain and France had elbowed aside the other competitors for hegemony in the Atlantic world. Spain was definitely declining, coasting downhill on the momentum of former glory; Portugal and Holland (the latter having claimed the best harbor on either side of the North Atlantic, at the mouth of the Hudson River) after moments in the sun had run up against the limits that small size and narrow resources usually place on imperial ambitions.

The showdown between Britain and France might have begun sooner if not for internal difficulties in both countries during the early and middle seventeenth century. The British spent two generations debating whether political power ought to reside with the Crown or with Parliament. Their seventeenth-century arguing included a regicide, a civil war, a military dictatorship, and a revolution (albeit a relatively bloodless one). The parliamentary partisans won the argument, settling the question once and for all by extorting a promise from King William in 1689 to defer to Parliament in matters of substance. This outcome established important precedents not merely for Britain but also for America: in justifying revolt against the British Crown in the 1770s, the American revolutionists would stand on rights won from the Crown a century earlier.

The French arrived at the opposite answer to the issue of crown versus parliament largely because the French king, Louis XIV, was smarter, stronger, and more ruthless than any of his British counterparts. He also had a better constitution (personal, not political) and as a result reigned for seventy-two years, from 1643 until 1715. During that time, he tamed the French nobility, snuffed out the ambitions of regional warlords, and established himself as the model of the European absolute monarch. Britain's rulers, though despising Louis, could only wish for such power.

As part of his program for enhancing the power of France's central government, Louis bullied France's neighbors. By the end of the 1680s, he had antagonized an assortment of those neighbors, who formed the League of Augsburg against him. Britain joined the league after crowning William king in 1689. War soon broke out, called, in Europe, the War of the League of Augsburg and, in America, King William's War. The war lasted almost a decade, almost exhausted both sides, and settled almost nothing. The fighting ended with the essential question—Would France or Britain be leader of Europe and the Atlantic world?—unanswered.

After catching their breath, the French and British went at each other again, starting in 1702. Dubbed the War of the Spanish Succession in Europe (Queen Anne's War in America), this round concerned the disposition of Spain's tottering empire. The recently deceased Charles II of Spain had bequeathed his holdings to Louis XIV's grandson—a bequest that greatly alarmed the British because it would result in French control of an empire stretching from Manila to New Mexico and from the Mediterranean to the North Sea. The British would not stand for this, and they organized France's enemies to contest the will. The contesting—the war—lasted until 1713 and bled France badly. The British won control of Gibraltar from Spain (as durable a prize as Britain ever won from anyone) and Nova Scotia and Newfoundland from France.

Following the 1713 Peace of Utrecht, which ended the War of the Spanish Succession, Europe rested, albeit uneasily, for a quarter century. In 1740 Frederick II, the king of Prussia, laid claim to territory also claimed by the new Austrian heiress, Maria Theresa. Britain and France soon got involved in the War of the Austrian Succession (King George's War), which lasted until 1748. The high point of the war was a successful 1745 expedition of British American colonists against the French fortress of Louisburg on Cape Breton Island. The low point of the postwar settlement was Britain's agreement to return Louisburg to France in exchange for France's withdrawal from Belgium and the Indian entrepôt of Madras. The Americans, who had celebrated the costly

During Queen Anne's War, English soldiers attack the Spanish town of St. Augustine in Florida. *Brown Brothers*

capture of Louisburg as a tremendous victory, took the news of the trade hard. They resented being treated as pawns, their lives and fortunes sacrificed at the whim of a government in distant London for reasons that had nothing to do with America's welfare. The action rankled for years, especially in New England, which had supplied many of the fighters for Louisburg. It was no coincidence that Boston would become the hotbed of American radicalism within twenty years.

The Americans were not the only ones dissatisfied with the outcome of the War of the Austrian Succession: nobody liked it much. Scarcely a half decade passed before Britain and France were hitting each other again. Unlike the earlier bouts, the Seven Years' War (French and Indian War) began in North America (making it a nine years' war by the colonists' counting). Skirmishing began on the fuzzy frontier between British America and New France. For some time the British colonists had eyed the Ohio Valley covetously, hoping to claim its rich bottomlands for settlement—or, in the case of numerous land speculators, for resale at a profit. France thought the Ohio Valley ought to be under French control. Matters came to a head in the early 1750s when a group of Virginia militiamen commanded by Colonel George Washington built a fort not far from a rival French post on the later site of Pittsburgh. The French, acting in concert with Indian allies, attacked the Virginians in July 1754 and drove them away. During the previous rounds of fighting in America, various Indian tribes had allied with the French, while others had sided with the British. In the earlier cases, the influence of the Indians had not been decisive. But it threatened to be so during the French and Indian War. The strongest body of Indians in the Ohio Valley joined with the French, and when in 1755 the British sent a contingent of more than one thousand soldiers under General Edward Braddock to avenge Washington's defeat, the Indians and the French utterly annihilated them. Most of Braddock's force were killed or wounded; Braddock himself died in the battle.

Only after this defeat, in the spring of 1756, did the British get around to declaring war on France. The conflict that ensued was the first international embroilment that might reasonably be called a world war: the British and French fought around the globe and entangled lots of other people in their quarrel. In India both the British and French had been capitalizing on the disarray of the disintegrating Mogul empire to extract commercial concessions. The locals had been trying to play the foreigners off against each other, with variable success that depended on the relative cleverness of the locals and the agents of the European powers. When war broke out in 1756, such scant respect as the British and French had shown each other as fellow Europeans far from home evaporated. British troops led by Robert Clive of the British East India Company combined with British naval power to smash the French and France's (East) Indian allies. Clive's most conspicuous triumph occurred at Plassey in Bengal, where he routed the pro-French Muslim ruler Suraja Dowla. Clive proceeded to plant on the Bengal throne a more compliant replacement.

In Europe the Seven Years' War produced an alliance between Britain and Prussia against France, Russia, and Austria. The collaboration between long-time enemies France and Austria constituted part of what was called the "diplomatic revolution" of 1756 (the other principal part being the alliance between Britain and Prussia), and it reflected France's judgment that a rising Prussia posed a greater threat to French interests than did a falling Austria. The fighting went poorly at first for the British-Prussian side. But the losses mostly belonged to Prussia, which found itself surrounded by its enemies and unable to make good use of Britain's naval superiority. Prussia's Frederick refused to give in, however, and held on until British victories overseas caused the French to call it quits.

The most significant of those overseas victories, besides Plassey, occurred in America. In 1758 British forces recaptured Louisburg, effectively cutting New France off from contact with the old country. In 1759 General James Wolfe led a daring attack on Quebec, defeating the French and dying valiantly in the assault—while his French counterpart, the marquis de Montcalm, died, also valiantly, in the defense. Meanwhile British and colonial troops progressively evicted the French from the Ohio Valley. The British side met stiff resistance from an Indian coalition led by the Ottawa chief Pontiac, which in fact

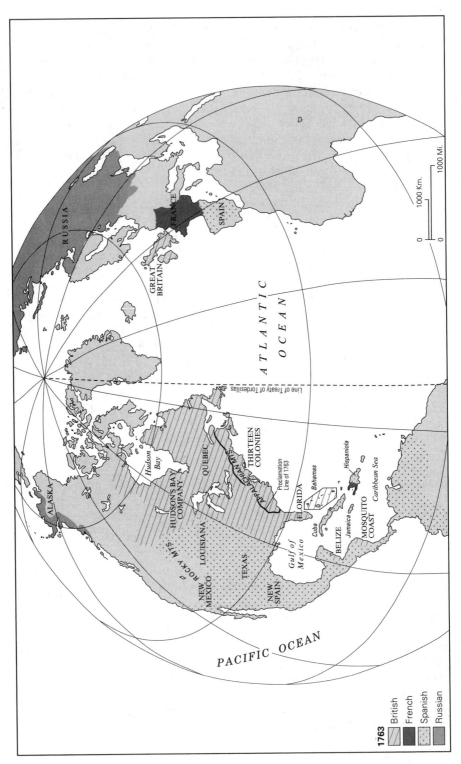

European Empires in 1763

mounted a counteroffensive that compelled the British to abandon several forts in the northwest. But as France's strength failed, so did the assistance the French were able to provide their Indian allies, and Pontiac had to fall back.

The British and American victories forced the French to the negotiating table. The Seven Years' War ended with the 1763 Peace of Paris, which confirmed the defeats France had suffered on the battlefield. The French ceded to Britain all their holdings on the North American continent east of the Mississippi River. France's western half of the Mississippi Valley—Louisiana—went to Spain, a late entrant in the war. The British allowed France to retain the Caribbean islands of Guadeloupe and Martinique, largely because British sugar interests wanted to keep those islands outside their protected imperial market.

The Peace of Paris left the British dominant in the Atlantic world. After seven years of fighting (counting only the latest war), or seventy years (counting the three previous wars), Britain had bested France, gaining control of the western half of North America, exercising naval supremacy in the Atlantic Ocean, and holding the balance of power in Europe.

Yet if France was down, it was not out. As far as the French were concerned, the contest with Britain was not over. France had been fighting against Britain for seven hundred years; there was no reason to stop now. When the opportunity arose, the French would try their luck against the British again.

The inhabitants of Britain's North American colonies shared in Britain's current dominance, at least indirectly and psychologically. Although they often chafed at their second-class treatment within the British empire, the American colonists recognized the important role they had played in the most recent British victory over France. Not surprisingly, they felt rather full of themselves.

Too full, as it turned out, for Britain's good, if not their own. The Americans soon found their place in Britain's empire confining. When they began agitating for change, they reopened some of the questions the peace treaty of 1763 was supposed to have settled. In the process, they challenged Britain's Atlantic hegemony and helped set in motion a chain of events that would prolong the contest between Britain and France for another half century—and embroil America thoroughly in European affairs for most of that period.

Economics: Theory and Practice

On the surface, the long struggle between Britain and France was about politics: about who would govern North America, India, and parts of Europe; but below the surface it was about economics: about who would exploit the possibilities for profit those regions presented. Politics and economics have always been closely connected to each other, and never was this more the case than during the mid-eighteenth century.

At that time the dominant theory of international economics was mercantilism, which explicitly linked the two realms. Mercantilism interpreted commercial relations between states as a form of warfare. This view was a holdover from the days when monarchs looked on their domains as their personal estates; the inhabitants were subjects, not yet citizens, and though they might enjoy privileges of trade and other economic activities, they could not claim much in the way of rights. Monarchs tended to identify national strength with their royal wealth—which made sense in an age of mercenary armies loyal to the highest bidder. These rulers usually equated wealth with gold and silver, the universally accepted forms of currency.

The object of foreign policy, in the mercantilist view, was to amass the greatest possible amount of gold and silver. One way to accomplish this object was to gain control of mines where the precious metals came out of the earth. The early blossoming of Spain's empire resulted directly from the country's good fortune in cornering the gold and silver supplies of the New World. The rise of Spain seemed to confirm the wisdom of the mercantilist approach.

A second way to accumulate gold and silver was to run a positive balance of trade, which meant that a country sold more goods to other countries than it purchased in return. Expanding exports while restraining imports would ensure that more money flowed into the country (to pay for the exports) than flowed out (to pay for the imports). To foster positive trade balances, governments placed numerous restrictions on commerce with other countries, specifying what could be exported and what imported and under what circumstances.

Mercantilism had the drawback that it treated international trade as a zero-sum game: what one country gained, another lost. There was only so much gold and silver to be dug from the ground, and those countries that were slow to grab the mines lost out—or resorted, as England did, to stealing from the swift. As for trade balances, because total world imports had to equal total world exports (what someone sold someone else had to buy), a positive trade balance for one country necessitated a negative balance for another (or others). International trade turned into a contest of beggar-thy-neighbor. Whether racing for gold mines or fighting for export markets, mercantilist nations inhabited a cruelly competitive world.

It was at least partly to shelter themselves from the harsh competition of a mercantilist world that the western European nations established overseas empires during the sixteenth through eighteenth centuries. Some parts of the empires, the imperialists hoped, would contain deposits of precious metals; other parts would furnish raw materials for imports and markets for exports. Each empire would approximate a closed economic system with trade arrangements designed to enhance the wealth of the imperial power.

Mercantilism was not the last word on international relations, however, and during the second half of the eighteenth century an alternative theory developed. The free trade school contended that commerce among different countries could benefit all. The wealth of a nation, the free traders held, consisted not simply in the gold and silver at the disposal of the sovereign but also in the prosperity of the people as a whole. (It was not coincidental that this notion won popularity as the peoples of various countries gained power at the expense of their monarchs.) And the best way to promote the prosperity of the people was to allow free trade among nations. If the English excelled at making cotton textiles while the French were best at producing wine, then the English ought to concentrate on textiles and the French on wine, and the two countries ought to trade the products of their expertise. Each would enjoy a higher standard of living—that is, greater prosperity—than if it tried to shut out the other. Any restrictions on trade, such as tariffs or quotas, would impede the flow of trade and diminish prosperity.

In the middle of the eighteenth century, the free traders remained a distinct minority tucked away on university faculties far from the corridors of power; mercantilism still occupied the high ground of orthodoxy and shaped government policies. It definitely shaped British government policies, and Britain's North American colonies bore the impress. London set narrow bounds within which the colonists could buy and sell: various "navigation" acts required that tobacco, sugar, cotton, rice, molasses, indigo, and other staple exports from America be sold only to British merchants; that imports to the colonies, almost without exception, had to come from Britain; and that cargoes bound to or from the colonies had to travel on ships of the British empire. Additional acts placed further strictures on colonial economic activities. One measure forbade the colonists from fabricating certain types of iron products, lest these displace exports from Britain; another levied a stiff tax on imports of molasses from foreign countries.

The Americans complained about these restrictions and would have complained more but for the fact that the British were better at passing laws than enforcing them. The colonists widely ignored bans on imports, developing smuggling into a national pastime and regularly bribing British customs officials. Molasses from the French West Indies supplied a lively distilling business in New England; outlaw iron makers in Pennsylvania forged contraband metal products, fearless of fines or jail.

The British government in London was not entirely unaware of the misdeeds of the Americans, but the king's ministers and the members of Parliament usually had other things to do than worry about minor infractions in the colonies. Between the English civil war of the seventeenth century and the anti-French wars of the first half of the eighteenth century, London could not be bothered. After 1763 it *would* be bothered—with results that would make it wish it had not been.

Through the cracks in Britain's mercantilist system the American colonists created for themselves a substantial place in the world economy. American trade with Britain constituted by far the largest portion of American overseas commerce, but trade with countries outside the British empire mattered greatly, too. American merchants sold foodstuffs and other farm products to the French West Indies. Their ships returned with sugar or derivatives such as molasses and rum, with cash or with slaves. Other slaves came directly from Africa. Either way the slave trade connected the American economy to the economy of Africa, which in turn was tied to the economies of the Mediterranean and the Indian Ocean. American trade with East Asia was confined to secondhand dealings through British middlemen; yet spices, silks, and other high-value items found their way to Boston, Newport, and New York. One product that would trigger riots on the way to the American Revolution—tea—also came from the East Indies.

Even before independence, Americans lived by international trade. When Parliament wanted to punish Boston for the Tea Party of 1773, the British lawmakers could think of no harsher penalty than closing Boston harbor. The Bostonians and other Americans recognized the closure as a threat to their economic existence; the consequence, within a year, was the American Revolution.

Americans would remain extraordinarily touchy on the subject of international trade for the next two hundred years. American merchants often acted as though they had a natural right to trade with whomever they pleased, regardless of the wishes of the governments of the countries their trading partners inhabited and irrespective of whatever troubles the traders got into. American governments usually—though not always—supported this view, forcing foreign markets open and waging wars to keep them that way. From the Revolutionary War of the 1770s and 1780s to the Persian Gulf War of 1991, no single issue figured more significantly in American international relations.

And no issue mattered more than economics in the evolution of America's position in the world. It has long been a fact of international life that countries get the foreign policies their economies earn for them. Countries with powerful economies become countries with powerful foreign policies; countries with weak economies become countries with weak foreign policies. The connection is not immediate, however; economic developments usually outpace changes in foreign policies. A country might maintain a modest foreign policy for a while after becoming an economic powerhouse; it might persist in an ambitious foreign policy for a while after its economy begins to slide. But sooner or later the discrepancy grows inescapable and adjustments become necessary. Both on the rise, as America's economy gained strength, and later on the decline, as it slipped relative to other economies, the United States would fit the pattern.

Intellectuals and the Universe of the Mind

At the time of its founding, the United States was the only country in history to be chartered explicitly on principles of human reason. There was a compelling cause for this. Thomas Jefferson wrote the American Declaration of Independence and the Continental Congress ratified it during a comparatively brief period—the Enlightenment—that elevated human reason to almost divine status. (The same era also witnessed the demotion of the divine to almost human status. Deists like Jefferson conceived of God less as an awesomely transcendent being who constantly hovered over humanity than as a clever old watchmaker who had long ago set the stars and planets spinning and subsequently retired.)

The rationalistic roots of the Enlightenment ran back at least to the publication of Copernicus's *De Revolutionibus Orbium Coelestium* (*On the Revolutions of the Celestial Spheres*) in 1543. For all the revolutionary tone of his title, Copernicus was not the revolutionary type, and the Polish astronomer allowed the release of his account of how the earth orbits the sun, rather than vice versa, only in the year of his death. To more combative natures such as Galileo Galilei, Copernicus left the hard fighting of defending the new sun-centered theory. But Galileo's courage ultimately failed, too, and under threat of eternal damnation (not to mention temporal penalties such as prison and torture) the great Italian scientist retracted his questioning of the Catholic church as the supreme authority on scientific matters.

Yet the rationalistic approach would not die, and eventually the Copernicans won their case; in doing so they prepared the way for the overarching genius of the age, Englishman Isaac Newton. Newton dabbled in most areas of scientific endeavor, but the work that made his reputation was the 1687 *Philosophiae Naturalis Principia Mathematica* (*Mathematical Principles of Natural Philosophy*), commonly called the *Principia*. Here Newton proffered, among other innovations, a universal theory of gravitation. The importance of this theory consisted not in its explanations—in fact it *explained* nothing, merely providing a closer *description* of phenomena already observed—but in its audacity. Newton convincingly contended that the same force of gravity that pulled an apple off a tree branch pulled the moon toward the earth. His opus drew immediate enthusiastic reviews (at least partly the result of the often demonstrated principle that people tend to be impressed by what they do not understand but feel they should); and its widespread acceptance cut the last of the ground from under the belief dear to the hearts of classical and medieval philosophers that the earth was essentially different from the heavens. To Newton and to all who came afterward, the universe was basically like the backyard. After Newton, no self-respecting theorist of physical or human affairs would rest content without trying to universalize his or her insights. Thomas Jefferson was a devoted Newtonian; his Declaration—the first official act of American diplomacy—spoke of the inalienable rights of *all* men, not just Americans. Americans for two centuries followed Jefferson's example in following Newton: whenever they became convinced of the validity of some principle of politics or economics, they felt an overwhelming temptation to apply it to the rest of humanity.

Francis Bacon and René Descartes also wielded wicked hatchets in the attack on received prejudice. Bacon, an Englishman of the early seventeenth century, demanded putting conventional wisdom to the test by experiments. To modern minds this approach might seem obvious—but its modern obviousness is due to Bacon's success (and others') in making precisely this point. Before Bacon, speculation regarding the nature of the world often stopped with a quotation from Aristotle: if "the Philosopher" said something was true, then true it must be. Bacon reminded people that Aristotle was human and might err; the only way to know was to try out his statements empirically. Bacon went so far as to describe a "House of Solomon," an investigative think tank much like those that would sprout in America and elsewhere three and a half centuries later.

René Descartes, a Frenchman who did his best pondering while lying in bed until noon (and who fell ill and died when the queen of Sweden hired him to rise early for private tutorials), carried Bacon's skeptical attitude still further. Where Bacon advocated questioning the conclusions of earlier philosophers, Descartes insisted on questioning everything. Descartes even questioned his own existence—until he realized that the very process of questioning confirmed his existence. "Cogito ergo sum," he concluded. ("I think; therefore I am.") From this starting point Descartes proceeded to reconstruct the physical world on what he deemed a rigorously logical basis. He got so far as to prove, to his own satisfaction at any rate, the existence of God. Yet Descartes' method almost made God the creation of man rather than the other way around. His unrelenting rationalism challenged the authority of religious leaders to tell people what to believe, and it implicitly called into doubt any institution that could not justify its existence on logical grounds. Descartes was not a favorite among the American intellectuals who launched the American ship of state into the ocean of world affairs; he was too Catholic for their tastes. But the American intellectuals who defended revolution and independence were Cartesians all.

In contrast to their tepidity toward Descartes, the American revolutionists warmly embraced the writings of John Locke and cited him endlessly. Locke was not quite the system builder that Descartes was, but he was equally impatient with intellectual constructs that rested on authority rather than reason. Locke, who lived in England during the late seventeenth century, applied the rationalist approach to the study of human beings in society and particularly to an examination of their relationship to government. Locke argued that governments exist to serve the interests of the people. So long as a government does so, guaranteeing their rights to life, liberty, and property, the people owe it their allegiance. But if a government fails to serve their interests, if it begins to oppress the people and deny their rights, it thereby breaks its part of the "social contract" that binds society together, and the people might—indeed must—change the government. This justification for revolution, enunciated in Locke's 1690 *Two Treatises on Government* and other essays, would ring for centuries in the ears of discontented individuals all around the world who felt that government was shortchanging them. Locke's theory provided the intellectual underpinning for the American revolution; Jefferson, Benjamin Franklin, Thomas Paine, Samuel Adams, and John Adams knew their Locke forward and backward.

The American revolutionists were less familiar with the work of another social-contract theorist, Jean-Jacques Rousseau. The French Rousseau was a contemporary of the Americans (he died in the third year of the American Revolution); his writings had not had time to acquire the reputation Locke's

John Locke embodied Enlightenment thinking on the reciprocal obligations of governments and citizens. His writings furnished philosophical underpinning for the American and French revolutions. *The Bettmann Archive*

had. Besides, Rousseau was ahead of his day, appealing as much to the hearts of his readers in the manner of nineteenth-century romantics as to their heads. Rousseau described humans who lived in a primitive state of nature as being essentially noble and good; but with the development of society and civilization, inequality and oppression set in. Although governments often functioned to further this inequality, they need not do so; they might operate to lessen inequality and correct civilization's deficiencies. Socialists of the nineteenth century and after would find Rousseau quite congenial.

What Rousseau knew of the work of Locke and other thinkers of the English Enlightenment he owed chiefly to François Marie Arouet, called Voltaire. As confirmed a skeptic as Rousseau was a romantic, Voltaire despised the arrogant closed-mindedness of French absolutism even as he found it entirely understandable. Voltaire never learned to keep his gifted but opinionated pen in check, and he landed in jail twice before being banished to England in 1726. Compared to France, England was a liberal paradise, and when he eventually returned to France, Voltaire did his best to disseminate the progressive ideas of Locke and the others. France was not quite ready for such ideas, and after several years Voltaire departed for the Prussian court of Frederick the Great. But two strong-headed types such as Voltaire and Frederick were bound to fight, which they did, and Voltaire wound up back in France. He built a house on the border between France and Switzerland so that when he provoked the authorities in either country he could dodge across the line into the other for safety. Voltaire especially decried the stifling influence of established religion on the life of individual minds—an influence that buttressed monarchy and associated institutions. In *Candide* and other works, he skewered the churchmen and their allies with venomous zest, and he adopted as his battle cry the antichurch slogan *Écrasez l'infâme!*—"Crush the loathsome thing!" Voltaire was no revolutionary, being almost as distrustful of enthusiasm for change as of enthusiasm for the status quo; the famous closing advice of *Candide*, that one should cultivate one's own garden, summarized his view on individuals' limited obligations to the remaking of society.

All the same, by adding his influence to the attacks on the established order, Voltaire helped knock the props out from under that order. Shortly before his death in 1778, he met another individual engaged in overturning an established order, Benjamin Franklin. At the theater in Paris one evening, the two came face to face and fell with great enthusiasm into each other's arms, to the loud applause of the theater audience. The American Revolution was currently the cause célèbre of French intellectuals, and Franklin was the darling of the Paris salons. For his part, Franklin recognized and acknowledged the debt he and his fellow American revolutionists owed Voltaire for hammering away at the idea that governments could rest on authority rather than reason. Franklin, Jefferson, and others were busy completing Voltaire's work in America; Voltaire's French followers would deliver the coup de grâce to the established order in France a dozen years later.

The Enlightenment tradition that provided the intellectual foundation for the American Revolution included thinkers beyond Voltaire, Locke, Bacon, and the others just mentioned. Jefferson, Adams, Franklin, and their contemporaries read the Italian jurist and economist, the marchise di Beccaria, on legal reform. They consulted the French judge and philosopher, the baron de Montesquieu, on the advantages of separating and balancing powers within government. (They consulted Montesquieu even more closely after they won their independence and were sitting down to write a constitution for their new nation.) The Dutch humanist Hugo Grotius instructed them on the connections between natural law and international law.

The British Whig school of political thought, noted for its skepticism regarding the overweening ambitions of governmental authority and explicated in the writings of such dissenters as Algernon Sidney, John Trenchard, Thomas Gordon, the viscount Bolingbroke, and Francis Hutcheson, demonstrated less originality and reach than the better-known exemplars of the Enlightenment, but it provided examples and illustrations more immediately relevant to the circumstances of the American colonists. When the American revolutionists wanted to complain about the tyranny of the British monarchy, they often found that Sidney and the others had already complained for them. Josiah Quincy, an associate of John Adams, specified in his 1774 will that his son should receive his copies of Locke, Bacon, Sidney, Trenchard, and Gordon. "May the spirit of liberty rest upon him!" the father added.

Wine and Water: The Culture Americans Inherited

Mark Twain once likened the writings of renowned authors such as Voltaire and Rousseau to fine wine; his own work, he said, was like water. But, he noted, "Everyone drinks water."

Crucial as the musings of Locke, Voltaire, and the rest of the beaconship of the Enlightenment were in molding the outlook of Americans and other inhabitants of the eighteenth-century Atlantic world, most souls then living got their enlightening only secondhand. Historians have often marveled at the learning and intellectual competence of the generation that fought the American Revolution and fashioned the federal constitution of 1787; they have argued quite credibly that no preceding or subsequent generation in American history could have accomplished what the generation of Jefferson, Franklin, James Madison, and Alexander Hamilton did. But if learning ran deep in the upper classes of eighteenth-century America—far deeper than the Enlightenment, to the classical Greek and Roman authors and all the philosophical authorities in between—it ran considerably shallower among the American people as a whole. Public education had yet to catch on in a big way; children of ordinary people usually learned their letters at home from the Bible and John Milton's *Paradise Lost*. Girls had it worse than boys, being expected to concentrate on the affairs of the home rather than those of the world at large. The most compelling argument for educating everyone—that a democracy requires educated voters for its effective functioning—did not move many people because the colonies were not democracies.

Books were expensive and otherwise hard to come by. Benjamin Franklin's recent good idea—lending libraries—had yet to gain broad acceptance. Newspapers cost comparatively little but consisted largely of articles and notices lifted from other newspapers. Even though this did not necessarily diminish their educational value, it did guarantee that most of the news people read was old—weeks old in the case of information pulled from other American papers, months old for news drawn from British and, rarely, continental European sources.

All the same, if the fishing families of Maine, the blacksmiths of Philadelphia, and the tobacco farmers of backcountry Virginia did not know Locke by heart, they did imbibe the general cultural milieu of the Enlightenment. They tended to be more traditional in their religious ideas than freethinkers like Jefferson, who took up scissors and cut the miracle stories out of his personal copy of the Gospels, treating Jesus as nothing more than a wise and convincing teacher. The Great Awakening, the series of religious revivals that swept through the American colonies in the 1730s and 1740s, demonstrated the continuing appeal of hair-raising, heart-rending evangelism; to a large degree the Awakening represented an anti-Enlightenment backlash by those who felt that the incessant questioning of received values had gone too far. Yet even as tens of thousands of Americans endorsed the religious principles of the Awakening—which, like the Enlightenment, was a transatlantic phenomenon, imported to America by the English Calvinist George Whitefield, among others—nearly all rejected the unquestioning appeals to authority that had buttressed monarchies and other traditional political institutions. (Indeed, the Awakening itself signified a rejection of certain kinds of authority, in particular the authority of the established churches and the political regime that supported them.) Americans might disagree with Jefferson on the precise attributes of God, but they accepted the argument of the author of the Declaration of Independence that God had endowed men with unalienable rights to life, liberty, and the pursuit of happiness. Americans might be emotionalists in matters of the hereafter, but they were hardheaded rationalists in matters of the here and now.

Anthropologists studying the prehistoric spread of agriculture have long debated whether it was agriculture that spread or agriculturalists. Did the knowledge of farming spread from farmers to their nonfarming neighbors, or did the farmers invade their neighbors' territory and push the backward ones aside? Evidence unearthed in the early 1990s indicated that it was the farmers who spread, that cultural transmission in this case operated most efficiently (if maybe brutally) through the migration of the people possessing the culture that eventually won out.

So it was with the spread of the dominant culture of the Atlantic world from the fifteenth through the eighteenth centuries. The values and practices of western Europe gained ascendancy in the Americas, not because the indigenous inhabitants of the Americas voluntarily accepted those values and practices, but because western Europeans traveled to the Americas and pushed the natives aside. Many of the native Americans died of diseases exotic to the Western Hemisphere; a relative few died in battle against the European invaders; undeterminable numbers retreated to the hinterland beyond the frontier of European settlement. (When that frontier advanced, their descendants retreated still farther.)

The migration of Europeans and European culture to the Americas after 1492 was one of the landmark developments in world history. The migration pulled the two continents of the Western Hemisphere into the Atlantic world; ultimately it would lead to the rise of the foremost international power of the twentieth century: the United States. In time Euro-American culture would spread across the globe, becoming by the end of the second millennium of the modern era the closest thing to a world culture the planet would see—which admittedly was still not very close.

In the middle of the eighteenth century, the westward—and westernizing—migration had only just begun. Europeans and their descendants in the Americas totaled but a few million; the indigenous Americans still far outnumbered them. Although European culture predominated in those regions where the Europeans had planted communities, in large tracts of North and South America Europeans and their ways of living were only vague rumors.

Another, simultaneous migration had a smaller impact on the culture of the Western Hemisphere but one that was still substantial. Since the sixteenth century, Europeans had been transporting Africans to the Americas as slaves. The slave trade formed a vital part of the economy of the Atlantic world, and it peopled the Western Hemisphere with millions of persons speaking languages never before heard there, worshipping deities never known there, raising children according to unfamiliar customs, and generally living their lives along strange lines. In a few Caribbean islands the culture of the Africans, modified by American contacts, eventually would become the dominant culture. Elsewhere, as in North America, it would become a subculture, less influential than the primary Europe-based culture but significant all the same.

The importance of cultural factors in international affairs lies chiefly in the contribution culture makes to the world views of the inhabitants of various countries. Inhabitants of the United States, for example, as children of the rationalistic Enlightenment, have often had difficulty dealing with the deeply emotional quarrels that vex much of the world. Why do Greeks hate Turks so? What accounts for the persistence of caste antagonisms in India? Why cannot Israeli Jews and Arab Muslims sit down together (in a "true Christian spirit," as one amateur American diplomat inaptly put it) and negotiate a settlement of their troubles? Such quarrels, rooted in animosities that long predate the Enlightenment and often defy Cartesian logic, have frequently been beyond the ability of Americans to comprehend.

And the knife of cultural misunderstanding has cut both ways. Just as Americans have found other peoples difficult to understand, so other peoples have found Americans hard to fathom. Many foreigners have been put off by the materialism of American culture; many have thought Americans rude and abrasive. By no means have all America's difficulties with countries outside the milieu of Euro-American culture resulted from cultural misunderstandings, but many have been exacerbated by them.

Technology: The Instruments of Power

One reason, perhaps the most important, for the expansive power of Euro-American culture was its ability to harness the forces of nature to human ends. Europeans exploring the Americas had at their disposal devices—steel knives, iron cookpots, rifles—that made the business of daily life much easier than it was for individuals and groups without them. Most of the people the Europeans encountered leaped at the opportunity to acquire these inventions, even if they did not always leap at the chance to acquire the rest of the culture that produced them. For better or worse, Indian tribes soon found themselves tied into the economy of trade that brought the knives, pots, and guns to America; in exchange the Indians delivered furs and other items the Europeans valued.

Just as exploration facilitated the spread of technological innovation, so technological innovation facilitated exploration. In the mid-eighteenth century, accurate knowledge of the earth remained spotty. Cartographers no longer pleaded "Here be monsters" in sketching remote areas, but maps of most of

Trade was the incentive for much exploration of the Americas. Here Dutch merchants do business with their Indian counterparts. *The Granger Collection*

the southern Pacific, of the entire interior of Australia, of the bulk of Africa and South America, of sizable portions of North America, and of both the polar regions were either fanciful or blank.

Some of the basic problems of global geography still bested explorers and cartographers. When Spain and Portugal in the 1490s divided up their recent discoveries, they accepted as the dividing line a meridian of longitude located one hundred leagues west of the Azores. The pact suffered from two deficiencies beyond the failure to consult the people native to these areas and the refusal of other countries to accept it. (King Francis of France asked to see the clause in Adam's will that reserved the new territories to the Iberians.) First, experts disagreed on how long a league was; second, no one knew how to measure a league at sea. Of course, the whole business of exploration in the western Atlantic had begun with a colossal underestimate of distance at sea: Columbus sailed from Spain thinking China was only about four thousand miles away when the true distance was three times as great. Had he known this, not even the intrepid Italian would have hazarded the voyage, and gifted salesman though he was, he would not have been able to talk Ferdinand and Isabella into underwriting it.

At the root of the trouble was an inability to calculate longitude. Latitude— the angular distance north or south of the equator—was easy; the Mesopotamians, Greeks, and other ancients had learned to determine latitude with impressive accuracy. (Eratosthenes' estimate of the earth's circumference, based on his measurement of latitude, should have informed Columbus how large the earth really was. Unfortunately, the aspiring admiral preferred other, wishful estimates.) Longitude was harder since on a spinning planet it required comparing local time to some fixed standard time far away. In the early seventeenth century, Galileo proposed watching the moons of Jupiter rise and set—a phenomenon that would occur at nearly the same time for all earthly observers; but technical difficulties, such as how to operate a telescope on a pitching ship, as well as the theological difficulties that got Galileo into trouble with the Catholic church, limited the appeal of his theoretically sound plan.

During the next century and a half, the governments of Holland, France, and Britain offered large prizes to the first person to develop a practicable method for calculating longitudes at sea. One would-be winner proposed a picket line of lightships anchored across the northern Atlantic, with each ship to fire signal flares at predetermined intervals of time. Ships in the area could calculate their distance from the flare shooters, and hence their location, by timing the lag between the flash of the flares and the sound of the explosions they made. This plan failed to solve the general longitude problem; it also ran aground—or rather the opposite—when no one could figure out how to anchor ships in midocean. (The authors of the proposal thought the depth of the north Atlantic never exceeded three hundred fathoms—an error in excess of three vertical miles.)

A more imaginative scheme was based on a nostrum known as the "powder of sympathy," which purportedly produced a sympathetic reaction in wounded persons and animals when applied, not to the injury, as one might have expected of a run-of-the-mill potion, but to the weapon that caused the injury. Under this plan ships about to undertake sea voyages would be provided with cut-to-order dogs; at regular and agreed intervals the powder would be applied to the wounding knives, which would be kept in the home port. At precisely the same moments, the dogs on shipboard hundreds or thousands of miles distant would give happy barks.

In the end the longitude problem yielded to a much more mundane solution: pendulum clocks that could keep accurate time aboard ships over many months. The perfection of such clocks occupied the middle of the eighteenth century; only on the eve of American independence did the British Board of Longitude award its prize and declare the problem solved. The new clocks, and the greater accuracy in navigation they allowed, gave the British navy an edge over its rivals in the War of the American Revolution—but not quite a decisive edge, as events turned out.

The lack of knowledge about the earth's surface and the inability to tell just where one was on the surface made long-distance travel and long-distance communication—the latter in those days requiring the former—hazardous and uncertain during most of the eighteenth century. British explorer James Cook in the 1760s needed three years to circumnavigate the globe—traversing, to be sure, not the shortest route. A subsequent attempt proved more hazardous and uncertain still, culminating for Cook in his death in the Hawaiian Islands. (In

1789 one of Cook's former junior officers, William Bligh, encountered hazards of another kind while commanding the *Bounty*. But in its own way the famous mutiny on the *Bounty* similarly attested to the difficult physical and psychological conditions that inevitably accompanied long-distance voyages during the eighteenth century.)

In the middle of the eighteenth century, America was not so far off the beaten track as the tropical Pacific, but under the best of circumstances it was several weeks from Europe. Under more normal and less favorable circumstances, sending a message from America to Britain and awaiting a reply could consume several months. Communication was improving, the result of more artful sail rigging, which allowed vessels traveling west to tack closer to the prevailing headwinds, and better knowledge of weather and current patterns. Even so, Americans could be forgiven for feeling themselves on the far edge of civilization.

By the mid-eighteenth century, the Atlantic held no important undiscovered secrets for mariners, and reductions in travel time from America to Europe would await further improvements in maritime technology; but travelers from the American colonies to Asia could still hope for a geographic breakthrough that would shorten their journey considerably. For two hundred years, explorers of all nationalities had searched for an easy water passage from the Atlantic to the Pacific. By the eighteenth century, it was apparent that no such passage existed in any convenient latitude. Magellan's strait in South America lay much too distant south; to the north, ice blocked whatever channel might link the two biggest oceans. As far as any American colonist or European knew, however, there remained the possibility that the headwaters of one or more of the rivers of Atlantic North America might mingle closely with the headwaters of one or more of the rivers of the Pacific slope of the continent. Explorers might find an interlocking system of headwaters such as that which made Russian rivers flowing into the Baltic Sea readily accessible by portage from those flowing into the Black and Caspian seas and which for centuries had provided the basis for a thriving eastern European trade. With greater luck they might even find the sort of natural canal that connected the Orinoco and Negro rivers in South America, rendering portages unnecessary.

Early explorers of North America had labored under the Balboan delusion: that the continent in temperate latitudes was not much wider than it was farther south, where Vasco Núñez de Balboa had crossed from the Atlantic to the Pacific. When the charters of the early British colonies had granted to their new owners title to territory stretching from sea to sea, no one suspected how unrealistically generous such charters were. Nor did the individuals who ascended the Potomac, Hudson, and other eastern rivers recognize how futile were their efforts to blaze a watery trail to the Pacific. They eventually learned, however, and by the first half of the eighteenth century there was no denying the great width of upper North America.

Yet before anyone actually traveled overland across the continent, and in the absence of reliable methods of calculating longitude (which would have allowed captains cruising the Pacific coast of the continent to determine its width), cartographers could only guess at just how much land separated the Atlantic from the Pacific. From the early seventeenth century until the late nineteenth, Americans often thought of the American West as a land of illimitable horizons and equally illimitable opportunities. One important early cause of this view—at least as it involved the horizons—was Americans' woeful geographic ignorance.

As to what kind of land separated the Atlantic from the Pacific, that question had been half-answered. French explorers had been up and down long stretches of the Mississippi River; Spanish explorers had crossed the deserts of northern Mexico and New Mexico. But no European had seen the headwaters of the chief tributary of the Mississippi, the Missouri; and none had sighted any part of the largest river running into the Pacific, the Columbia. With so much unknown, the possibility of a river road across the continent, a shortcut to the Orient, continued to tantalize.

In the meantime, travelers from the Atlantic to the Pacific went by sailing ship, as did most long-distance travelers in the eighteenth century. The design of ships was caught in a doldrums at that period, owing to the fact that shipbuilders had accomplished about all they could with the materials available. The biggest ships were not much larger than two thousand tons, mostly because wooden ships bigger than that were not structurally or economically feasible. The best merchant ships, such as those of the British East India Company, were on the order of six hundred or seven hundred tons. Some smaller ocean-going vessels—for example, frigates built for speed to outrun pirates—still carried oars for use when the wind failed or when the ship was maneuvering within a harbor.

The first part of the eighteenth century had seen the introduction of the steering wheel, which was easier to control in heavy weather than the previously favored whipstaff. Further refinements in rigging took place about the same time; the British Royal Navy adopted the jib in 1702 and abolished the spritsail topmast on its biggest ships in 1715. One measure of the success of the architects of the wooden sailing ships of the eighteenth century would be the fact that when steam and steel fundamentally changed the nature of ship design in the nineteenth century, sailing ships built on essentially eighteenth-century lines would remain competitive for many decades.

Ships not only served commerce; they were also the most important military weapons of the day. Since the battle of the Spanish Armada in 1588, naval warfare had consisted principally of bringing ship-mounted cannons to bear against enemy vessels and attempting to pound the enemy craft into submission. The cannons did not have the accuracy to hit targets at a distance, so the preferred tactic was the broadside, normally delivered at pointblank range. The method lacked imagination, yet for almost two hundred years no one had managed to improve on it. (The range of eighteenth-century cannons played a role in international affairs that long outlasted the cannons: until modified in the second half of the twentieth century, international law normally specified that the territorial waters of a country extended three miles out from land—roughly the waters that could be covered by cannon fire from shore.)

The American colonists developed thriving industries, some legal and some not. One of the legal industries was shipbuilding, practiced here, which provided vessels for Britain's fleet. *National Archives*

The techniques and technology of land warfare likewise had plateaued. Gunpowder had revolutionized organized killing during the fifteenth and sixteenth centuries, but by the end of the seventeenth the revolution had ended. The invention around 1690 of the ring bayonet allowed armies to dispense with pikemen, who until this time had been required to defend musketeers from cavalry charges. On the strength of this invention, on the stagnation of applied chemistry and metallurgy, and on the bureaucratic inertia that afflicts all military establishments, personal-arms technology essentially stood still for a century and a half. From 1690 until 1840 the standard infantry weapon of the British army was a musket dubbed affectionately, and sometimes otherwise, "Brown Bess," which remained basically unchanged during this time.

In bigger guns the early eighteenth century saw no quantum leaps either. Most cannon barrels were cast, rather than bored, following the practice common since before the Turks took Constantinople in 1453 with the aid of cast bronze cannons weighing thirty tons apiece. The Turkish experience demonstrated that though cast barrels might be large, the imprecisions inevitable in casting prevented them from being very accurate. Nor were these cannons very rapid in firing, because most were muzzleloaders. Effective breechloaders would await further advances in metals science and machining techniques, as would precision-milled barrels.

America stood near, if not quite at, the forefront of eighteenth-century technological progress. Despite Britain's imperial restrictions, American iron manufacturers produced one-seventh of the world's annual output of iron. American shipbuilders, blessed with abundant supplies of wood and other necessary raw materials, constructed some of the best vessels afloat. Gunsmiths kept busy throughout the colonies, and even though they did not turn out the heavy ordnance required by regular military forces, they rendered the colonies largely self-sufficient in small arms.

While the ability to produce iron, ships, and guns would be essential when the Americans decided to break with Britain, of greater importance in precipitating the break was the wide dissemination of printing technology among the colonies. On the eve of the troubles that led to the American Revolution, American printers operated approximately forty presses, which published more than a dozen newspapers and could just as easily crank out broadsides and pamphlets by the hundreds and thousands. Benjamin Franklin, while busy in the politics and diplomacy of the era, played no less a role in the crucial technology of propaganda. Beyond personally training and financing apprentice and journeyman printers, Franklin established a network for collecting linen rags and recycling them into paper. At the same time, he owned and operated several lampblack houses, which produced the blacking used in ink. A Franklin pamphlet was truly a Franklin product: written by Franklin and printed by the author on his own printing press using paper and ink of his own manufacture.

*   *   *

Americans on the verge of independence reflected a century and a half of their own colonial experience and centuries more of the experiences they shared with other inhabitants of the Atlantic world. Together these experiences had prepared the Americans to strike out boldly into the world of sovereign nations and would continue to shape America's relations with other countries for many years beyond independence.

Politically speaking, the American colonies occupied a prominent place in the British empire, which itself held the dominant position in the Atlantic world, but one that remained under challenge from France. Economically, the colonies slaved—as many Americans interpreted things—under a mercantilist philosophy that placed their welfare behind that of Britain. Intellectually, most Americans embraced the attitudes and beliefs of the European Enlightenment, including distrust regarding received wisdom and a disposition to value reason over authority. Culturally, the dominant class of Americans shared the values of their British cousins, although a sizable minority had ties of ancestry and affinity to Africa. Technologically, Americans enjoyed most of the benefits and suffered under most of the limitations that characterized Europe on the brink of the Industrial Revolution.

For few people on earth in the mid-eighteenth century was life as good as it was for the Americans. But they soon decided that good was not good enough, and they determined to make it better—demonstrating yet another trait that would long color their approach to the world.

Sources and Suggestions for Further Reading

A recent best-selling examination of the contest for control of the Atlantic world (and much else), is Paul Kennedy, *The Rise and Fall of the Great Powers: Economic Change and Military Conflict from 1500 to 2000* (1987). Earlier works, more tightly focused on the Atlantic world and the European colonial empires, are John B. Wolf, *The Emergence of the Great Powers, 1685–1715* (1951); G. Williams, *The Expansion of Europe in the Eighteenth Century* (1966); Kenneth G. Davies, *The North Atlantic World in the Seventeenth Century* (1974); Max Savelle, *Empires to Nations: Expansion in America, 1713–1824* (1974); and J. H. Parry, *Trade and Dominion: The European Overseas Empires in the Eighteenth Century* (1971). Winston S. Churchill's monumental (and triumphal) *History of the English-Speaking Peoples* (1956–59) gives the distinctive view of the great British statesman and Nobel-prize winning historian. The same topic motivates Angus Calder, *Revolutionary Empire: The Rise of the English-Speaking Empires from the Fifteenth Century to the 1780s* (1981). Derek McKay and H. M. Scott, *The Rise of the Great Powers, 1648–1815* (1983), looks beyond the English-speaking world. Fernand Braudel's three-volume *Civilization and Capitalism: 15th–18th Centuries* (1981–84), covers an enormous amount of material, much relevant to the rise and transformation of the European colonial empires.

Braudel's volumes trace the development of the Atlantic and Mediterranean economies; even broader-gauged economically and chronologically is Rondo E. Cameron, *A Concise Economic History of the World: From Paleolithic Times to the Present* (1989). Nathan Rosenberg, *How the West Grew Rich: The Economic Transformation of the Industrial World* (1986), is narrower but more to the point of the development of the Atlantic world. Ralph Davis, *The Rise of the Atlantic Economies* (1975), is more tightly focused still. Robert Heilbroner, *The Worldly Philosophers: The Lives, Times, and Ideas of the Great Economic Thinkers* (1986 ed.), is a very readable introduction to the history of economic theory.

An accessible introduction to the European Enlightenment is Peter Gay, *The Age of Enlightenment* (1966). Ernst Cassirer, *The Philosophy of the Enlightenment* (1951), is more sophisticated. Norman Hampson, *The Enlightenment* (1968), is succinct. Henry S. Commager, *The Empire of Reason* (1977), explains the transatlantic connections of the Enlightenment. Henry F. May, *The Enlightenment in America* (1976), concentrates on events on the western shore of the ocean. On the impact of English Whig thought in America, see Bernard Bailyn, *The Ideological Origins of the American Revolution* (1967), and Gordon S. Wood, *The Creation of the American Republic, 1776–1787* (1972 ed.).

A concise and eminently readable description of American culture and social life during the mid-eighteenth century is Richard Hofstadter's posthumous *America at 1750: A Social Portrait* (1973 ed.) Also useful are Roy Porter, *English Society in the Eighteenth Century* (1982), and David H. Fischer, *Albion's Seed: Four British Folkways in America* (1989). Bernard Bailyn, *Voyagers to the West* (1986), describes how the bearers of English culture (and other cultures) got to America.

An introduction to the history of technology can be found in such surveys as Thomas Parke Hughes, *The Development of Western Technology since 1500* (1964); and George Basalla, *The Evolution of Technology* (1988). Michael Adas, *Machines as the Measure of Man: Science, Technology, and Ideologies of Western Dominance* (1989), provides a stimulating view of the connections between material advancement and intellectual and cultural affairs. J. Needham, *The Grand Titration: Science and Society in East and West* (1969), likewise links material and cultural concerns, and compares the European and Asian traditions. A. Wolf, *A History of Science, Technology and Philosophy in the Sixteenth and Seventeenth Centuries* (1935) deals with an earlier period.

On the connection between technology, warfare, and imperialism, see L. H. Addington, *The Patterns of War Since the Eighteenth Century* (1984); John F. Guilmartin, *Gunpowder and Galleys: Changing Technology and Mediterranean Warfare at Sea in the Sixteenth Century* (1974); and William H. McNeill, *The Pursuit of Power: Technology, Armed Forces and Society Since 1000 A.D.* (1983).

Chapter 2

The Age of Revolution, 1763–1800

A s with many glorious victories, Britain's triumph over France in the Seven Years' War proved less complete and permanent than it first appeared to be; and as with some other such victories, it turned out to contain the seeds of its own undoing. The British triumph reinforced the self-confidence of the Americans, rarely in short supply anyway, and made them more inclined to fend for themselves. At the same time, the triumph and the cost of securing it convinced the British government in London of the need to tighten imperial control over the colonies. Finally, the British triumph left France wounded but not mortally—a dangerous condition, as Machiavelli had noted hundreds of years earlier, to leave an enemy in. The French were aching for an opportunity to strike back at the British; as soon as they discovered the opportunity, they did.

The structure of international politics established by the 1763 Peace of Paris dissolved during the succeeding generation, the victim of the two great revolutions of the eighteenth century. The American Revolution came first, and it reopened the contest between Britain and France for hegemony in the Atlantic world. During the War of the American Revolution, France attempted to make up for its recent defeat at Britain's hands; though it did not succeed completely, it succeeded (with help from others of Britain's many rivals) sufficiently for the Americans' sake, hitting Britain hard enough to knock the American colonies free of London's control.

Yet the recoil from the blow had a strong impact in France itself. In the same way that Britain's need to pay for the long series of Anglo-French wars helped trigger the American Revolution, so France's need to pay for its part in those wars helped trigger the French Revolution. The expense of the wars added to the burdens the French middle and lower classes were bearing, and it intensified their growing insistence that things change. This insistence finally exploded into revolution in the summer of 1789. Like the American Revolution, the French Revolution was premised on the Enlightenment's reverence for reason—in particular on the social contract ideas of Locke and Rousseau that people owe allegiance to government only so long as government serves their interests. But far more than the American revolutionists, the French revolutionists carried the reasonable premises of their revolution to unreasonable conclusions. In doing so they set all Europe aflame. Many Americans had hoped that by breaking free of Britain, they might spare themselves embroil-

George Washington breathes a silent and inconspicuous sigh of relief upon the arrival of Lafayette and French reinforcements. Over the horizon (out of the picture), Washington can see victory. *The Bettmann Archives*

ment in Europe's troubles; the wars of the French Revolution demonstrated the futility of such hopes and touched off the first international crises in the history of the new American republic.

Loosing the Torrent: Britain Reorganizes Its Empire

According to mercantilist theory, empires are supposed to make money for the imperial power. If instead they lose money, then something must be wrong either with the general theory or with the management of the specific money-losing empires. During the 1760s, mercantilist theory remained sufficiently entrenched that George III's accountants, observing the red ink that increasingly filled the British king's ledgers, assumed that the problem had to lie in the management of the British empire. (They were partly right, partly wrong.) They informed the king and his ministers that if the imperial government intended to rectify the situation, it had to cut expenses, increase revenues, or do both. An obvious place to start was to reduce the size of the army. Now that the war with France was over, much of Britain's large army was wasteful. By

Chronology

1763	Proclamation barring settlement west of the Appalachians
1764	Sugar Act
1765	Stamp Act
1766	Declaratory Act
1767	Townshend Acts
1770	Boston Massacre
1773	Boston Tea Party
1774	Coercive Acts (Intolerable Acts); First Continental Congress convenes
1775	Skirmishes at Lexington and Concord; Second Continental Congress convenes
1776	*Common Sense*; Declaration of Independence
1777	Battle of Saratoga
1778	American alliance with France; France and the Netherlands join war against Britain
1779	Spain declares war on Britain, besieges Gibraltar
1781	British defeat at Yorktown
1783	Peace of Paris
1784	First American ship to China, *Empress of China*, reaches Canton (Guangzhou)
1787	Constitutional Convention
1789	Federal government begins operation under new constitution; French Revolution begins
1792	Outbreak of war in Europe
1793	George Washington proclaims American neutrality; Genêt affair
1794	Battle of Fallen Timbers; Jay's treaty
1795	Treaty of Greenville; Pinckney's treaty
1796	Washington's farewell address
1798	XYZ affair; Alien and Sedition acts; Quasi-War with France begins
1799	Napoleon assumes power in France
1800	Convention of 1800 ends hostilities with France; Louisiana returned to France by Spain

mustering out many of the soldiers, the government could save the cost of their pay and provisions.

George, a strong-willed but unstable individual (his recurrent bouts of mental illness dismayed his advisers and disrupted the governance of the empire), had different ideas. He enjoyed having a big army, which gave him a feeling of security in the ever-uncertain realm of European and world politics, and he determined to keep the bulk of the troops on. Others in England also resisted the idea of cutting defense spending, for various economic and political reasons. George told his ministers to find other places to save money and to work harder on the income side of the budget. The ministers and Parliament accepted the advice.

Both decisions—to retain the army and to raise new revenues—upset the Americans. The decision on the army seemed suspicious since some ten thousand of the troops were to be stationed in America. This was half again as many as even the British commander in America thought necessary for the principal remaining avowed purpose of the soldiers: to protect the colonists from Indian tribes. American suspicions increased when it turned out that the troops were to be stationed, not on the frontier where they were needed, if they were needed at all, but in port cities such as New York. The British explanation—that maintaining the troops within easy reach of the Atlantic was cheaper—struck many Americans as too pat.

Americans became still more suspicious and upset when in 1763 the British government announced the closing of the trans-Appalachian west to settlement. From London's perspective the move made sense: the Americans who settled beyond the mountains caused endless troubles with the Indians, thereby raising the possibility of a costly frontier war. But from the American perspective the ban on settlement was a disappointment and an insult. A major purpose of the French and Indian War, in American thinking, had been to open the West to settlement. The war had been won with the active participation of the Americans, but now London appeared to be surrendering to the Indians after the fact and in the process denying those who had fought the war the fruits of their victory—in particular, the lands in the Ohio and Mississippi valleys they coveted.

Even if the no-settlement policy had affected only ordinary farm families looking for a piece of land on which to live, the resistance to it would have been substantial. Most Americans took for granted their right to spread across the continent, creating homes and livelihoods for themselves in the process. If this process involved displacing Indians, most Americans believed that the Indians occupied more land than they needed. Besides, many Americans thought, as heathen nomads the Indians held a poorer claim to the land than did the Christian farmers who desired to displace them. That many of the Indian tribes practiced agriculture was conveniently overlooked by the colonial expansionists.

The no-settlement policy, however, also offended another influential class: land speculators. For a generation well-heeled investors had taken chances on western lands. With the British victory over France the value of their investments had soared—only to be shot down by the no-settlement policy. The speculators were often as well connected as they were well heeled, and their frustration soon surfaced in American politics.

In the meantime—a meantime extended by the slow pace of transatlantic communications in those days—the British devised new methods of raising revenues from the colonies. Chief minister George Grenville, whose bottom-line approach to governing betrayed his background as George's finance minister, pushed a bill through Parliament levying higher taxes on sugar, particularly molasses. Grenville was not without imagination: he sought his objective of higher taxes by actually *lowering* the tax *rate*. The current rate of six pence per gallon was so high that only the most scrupulous paid up: it was cheaper for merchants to bribe customs agents to be at lunch when the molasses landed. At the new rate of three pence per gallon, smugglers could do better by turning honest and paying the tax than they could by suborning the tax collectors.

The colonial merchant-smugglers found life on the right side of the law strange and uncomfortable. Who knew what schemes Grenville and his minions might hatch next? The worst of the new law was the bad example it set: if the colonies acquiesced in the notion that London could raise or lower import taxes at will—London's will, not the colonies'—there would be no safety for American commercial and property interests. James Otis, Jr., a young Massachusetts attorney, employing the language of Locke and Rousseau, declared, "In a state of nature, no man can take my property from me without my consent; if he does, he deprives me of my liberty and makes me a slave." But this was precisely what London was doing, and it boded ill for American rights.

Whereas the 1763 ban on trans-Appalachian settlements had antagonized western farmers and land speculators, and the 1764 Sugar Act had alienated merchants, a new measure passed in 1765 sparked opposition from two other influential groups: lawyers and newspaper editors. The Stamp Act required the purchase of special stamps for legal documents and newspapers. The act hurt the law business by raising the price to clients of the lawyers' services; it threatened newspaper sales by raising their price as well. And even more directly than the Sugar Act, critics asserted, it overstepped parliamentary boundaries by contradicting the principle that Englishmen could be taxed only with the consent of their elected representatives.

In raising the question of Parliament's authority to tax the colonies, the American resisters opened a can of constitutional worms. The supporters of Grenville and the British government (including a fair number of Americans) contended that the colonists *were* represented in Parliament by virtue of the fact that members of Parliament took account of the interests of all British subjects, not simply those residing in their districts. Nonsense, replied the objecting Americans (and their not inconsiderable band of British backers). The essence of representative government was the ability to throw the rascals out; if Americans could not vote against them, they did not represent Americans.

Radicals among the colonists, ignoring the niceties of constitutional debate, took matters directly into their own hands. They organized a campaign of economic warfare against the British, forswearing the purchase of British merchandise and browbeating those less determined than themselves into joining the boycott. They also launched an offensive against the agents of the British government in America. They sacked the house of the royal lieutenant governor of Massachusetts, Thomas Hutchinson, and terrorized officials designated to distribute the stamps into resigning their posts.

The violence of the American reaction shocked the British government—just as it was intended to do. At the behest of British merchants, who feared major losses from the American boycott, Parliament repealed the Stamp Act. But to reaffirm the principle of parliamentary sovereignty, the legislature linked repeal to the passage of the Declaratory Act of 1766, which asserted Parliament's right to legislate for the colonies "in all cases whatsoever."

Although the repeal of the Stamp Act temporarily eased the tension between the American colonies and London, the essential cause of the tension remained. The British government wanted to squeeze more revenue out of the colonies; the colonists refused to be squeezed. While nobody important was yet calling for American independence from Britain, Americans increasingly felt their interests to be different from those of the British across the sea. As this feeling grew, independence became a more inviting prospect.

Not many people in Britain recognized the depth of Americans' conviction on this subject. Had the responsible officials in London seen that their insistence on raising less than one hundred thousand extra pounds in taxes each year would result in the rending of the British empire, they surely would have

The art of political protest has deep roots in America. Here colonists demonstrate against the Stamp Act. *The Bettmann Archives*

acted differently. But they could not tell the future any more than the losers of most wars can before the wars start.

In their ignorance George's ministers and Parliament imposed additional heavy-handed measures on the colonies during the next several years. The 1767 Townshend duties laid new tariffs on a scattershot collection of imports, among them paper, glass, lead, pigments, and tea. These provoked a new outcry in America and prompted renewed boycotts of British imports. Agitation in New England led to the 1770 Boston "massacre," in which five Americans were killed by besieged British soldiers. The Tea Act of 1773 granted the struggling but influential British East India Company the privilege of bypassing colonial wholesalers and selling tea directly to American retailers. The Tea Act provoked the Boston "tea party" of 1773, in which a mob seized and destroyed a cargo of East India Company tea. Parliament responded with the 1774 Coercive Acts—the American name for them, used interchangeably with Intolerable Acts—which closed the port of Boston, curtailed popular government in Massachusetts, transferred some criminal trials to Britain, and authorized the quartering of British troops in buildings owned by American civilians, even against the owners' will.

The Coercive Acts galvanized American opposition as nothing had so far. American leaders convened the First Continental Congress to coordinate resistance to the laws, which seemed to them a clear case of imperial vindictiveness. Colonial militias prepared to defend the rights of the colonists, by force of arms if necessary.

John Adams was a brilliant lawyer, a distinguished diplomat, a modest vice president, and a mediocre president. *Boston Athenaeum*

Nothing in international relations is inevitable until it actually happens, but by the spring of 1775 some sort of violent clash between the imperial government and the colonies had become quite likely. Earlier the dispute had hinged on the matter of balancing Britain's imperial books; at that time compromise had been possible. But during the ten years since the passage of the Stamp Act, the dispute had become a test of wills, a contest of uncompromisable principles. King George and Parliament insisted that Americans bow their heads to British authority; the colonists stood on their right to resist illegitimate actions by London—and to decide for themselves what constituted illegitimacy. As John Adams later remarked to Thomas Jefferson, by 1775 the die had been cast. "What do we mean by the Revolution?" Adams rhetorically asked Jefferson. "The war? That was no part of the Revolution; it was only an effect and consequence of it. The Revolution was in the minds of the people, and this was effected, from 1760 to 1775, in the course of fifteen years before a drop of blood was shed at Lexington."

The War of the American Revolution

Regardless of whether the revolution had been accomplished by 1775, the war that made the revolution a success started in the spring of that year. In mid-April a squadron of British troops marched from Boston to seize a cache of arms reported to be hidden outside the city. A local militia unit at Lexington blocked passage of the British force, an exchange of shots followed, several colonials died, and the war was on.

Once difficult political disputes lead to bloodshed, compromise becomes more difficult than ever. Tempers run hot, and no one wants to admit that lives lost might have been lost in vain. So it was with the American Revolution. At the time of the first fighting, most Americans would have accepted recognition by Parliament of their rights under the British constitution (the largely unwritten body of precedents and traditions that guides the British political and legal system). But the commencement of fighting radicalized American opinion. An increasing number of Americans came to believe that their rights would never be secure under British rule and that their only recourse was to separate themselves from Britain.

Several considerations helped them arrive at this conclusion. First, the social contract philosophy of Locke and other Enlightenment thinkers provided ready intellectual justification for breaking away from Britain. By failing to honor American rights, by treating those rights as nonexistent, the British government had broken its part of the social contract binding Americans to London. Once broken, the contract no longer had any moral authority over American actions. "A government of our own is our natural right," wrote Thomas Paine; and with each passing month more Americans agreed.

Second, the American colonies clearly had the makings of a successful independent country. Attached to Britain, they had grown to include between 2 and 3 million people. Their economic enterprises, from the fisheries of New England to the metal shops of Pennsylvania and the plantations of Georgia, nicely complemented one another; and what the colonies could not produce themselves, their active and ingenious merchants could procure overseas. Their militias had shown spirit and ability in the war against France (a lesson lost on the British editorialist who asserted contemptuously of the Americans, "These yellow shadows of men are by no means fit for a conflict with our troops"). Their politicians had to date demonstrated leadership and organizational skills in the dispute with Britain. With a great continent at their backs, the Americans had a great future before them.

Third, in a war against Britain the American colonies would enjoy a tremendous political and psychological advantage. The Americans would be fighting on their home turf for something that meant very much to them: the opportunity to run their own affairs. The British would be fighting far from home for something that meant relatively little to *them:* the right to run the Americans' affairs. Further, in such a war Americans did not have to win; they only had to avoid losing. Sooner or later the British would tire of the war and go away.

Finally and crucially, the political configuration of the Atlantic world in the 1770s was favorable to an American breakaway from Britain. The Americans could confidently expect help from France and perhaps other countries in a war against Britain. European politics had been simmering since 1763, and peace did not appear an indefinite likelihood. "It is by no means probable that Europe will long remain in a state of peace," wrote Silas Deane, an envoy sent to Europe by the Continental Congress, during the summer of 1776. The French had been observing Britain's imperial difficulties, receiving dispatches from secret agents placed in America expressly for the purpose. Though Paris refused to give any commitments to the Americans ahead of time, the French government could be counted on to make trouble for Britain. Exactly what form such troublemaking would assume was uncertain. At the least it would include assistance to Americans in obtaining weapons; at the most, a declaration of war against Britain and the commitment of French ships and troops to battle.

The French had already given the Americans a clue as to what to expect. In late 1775 members of the Committee of Secret Correspondence of the American Continental Congress met clandestinely in Philadelphia with a representative of the French government of Louis XVI. The members asked Julien-Alexandre Achard de Bonvouloir if the French government wished the Americans well. More pointedly, they inquired whether France would help the Americans acquire guns and other military supplies. Bonvouloir responded cautiously, but he indicated clearly that France did indeed wish the Americans well and would do what it could to assist them.

Bonvouloir passed the Americans' query along to the French foreign minister, Charles Gravier, the comte de Vergennes. Vergennes believed that France must not waste this opportunity to harass Britain. If Britain got bogged down in a war with the American colonies, it would lose much of its freedom of maneuver in Europe. If Britain thoroughly bungled the affair and lost the colonies, it might subsequently watch its entire empire unravel. The prospect naturally pleased France.

Vergennes did not think France ought to enter the Anglo-American struggle openly just yet; after all, the Americans still had not summoned the nerve to declare independence. But they probably would, probably soon, and they ought to receive France's support. Vergennes recommended sending Americans a large shipment of covert military aid. The weapons and other equipment would keep the Americans fighting; the aid should be covert to prevent Britain from feeling obliged to declare war on France, which was not quite ready for another fight with its long-time antagonist. In May 1776 Louis approved Vergennes's proposal. The French government established a trading company as a front, secretly funneled one million livres through it, and allowed it to purchase on behalf of the Americans as much in the way of guns, bullets, and boots as that amount would buy.

Bolstered by this assistance, the Americans made the leap to independence. After fifteen months of fighting, the Continental Congress in July 1776 adopted Thomas Jefferson's statement declaring that "these united colonies are, and of right ought to be, free and independent states" and that they had "full power to levy war, conclude peace, contract alliances, establish commerce, and to do all other acts and things which independent states may of right do."

By declaring independence, the Americans changed dramatically the character of their contest with Britain. Until this moment London had been able to look on the troubles across the ocean as hardly more than a disturbance in the provinces; now these troubles threatened the very existence of the British empire. For two hundred years the British had struggled to attain preeminence in the Atlantic world. Having recently confirmed this preeminence by their victory over France, the British were loath to let some fractious colonials jeopardize it. If compromise had been even slightly possible before July 1776, it was impossible afterward. The outcome had to be decided by war.

The American Declaration of Independence converted the Americans from being disturbers of Britain's imperial peace to being perpetrators of outright treason—and monstrous illogic, in the minds of those many English who agreed with Lord North when he said, "I can never acquiesce in the absurd opinion that all men are equal." The penalty for treason was ghastly even to contemplate: it began with drawing and quartering (being disemboweled and cut into four parts) and got more horrid from there. George III was not the forgiving type, and the leaders of the rebellion had to expect the worst should their effort at independence fail.

The American declaration piqued the interest of other European powers besides France in the conflict within the British empire. However tragic wars may be for the individuals directly involved, they are often good business for countries on the sidelines. The belligerents pay top dollar (or pound or livre or mark) for the supplies they need, and they are not usually finicky about who provides them or how. The Netherlands, less a world power than formerly—

though still master of an empire that included the Dutch East Indies (Indonesia), Ceylon (Sri Lanka), and part of southern Africa—retained the aggressive attitude toward trade that had won the Dutch influence that went far beyond their numbers. Dutch merchants immediately perceived the war between the British and the Americans as an opportunity to pick up some quick profits in the short run and to steal some of Britain's American market in the long run. If the Americans gained independence, Britain would lose its favored—in some cases exclusive—position in the American market; Dutch businesses could only stand to gain. Eventually the Dutch would join the French in actively aiding the Americans; for the moment, however, Holland's burghers held back, not wishing to provoke Britain into declaring war on Holland, which would be disastrous for business.

Spain also cheered the American rebels. The Spanish did not have any great love for the Americans, and the Spanish crown certainly did not accept the republican ideas of the American Declaration of Independence; but Spain resented its loss of Gibraltar and, more recently, Florida to Britain. Moreover, Spain's King Charles II was the closest ally of France's Louis, a distant relative. In addition, Britain had recently sided with Spain's old enemy, Portugal, in a boundary dispute in South America. As a consequence, Charles was happy to join Louis in contributing to the American revolutionary effort.

For the first thirty months of the fighting—from April 1775 through the autumn of 1777—European backing for the American cause remained diffident and covert. Covert did not mean the same thing as secret; however: the British had infiltrated America's diplomatic establishment (Benjamin Franklin's private secretary, Edward Bancroft, was a British spy) and knew at least in general terms of the French and perhaps Spanish aid. But by refusing to acknowledge the aid, the French and Spanish made it easy for the British to ignore that aid, which for their own reasons and for the time being they did.

The big question in the minds of the continental Europeans was whether the Americans possessed the capacity to succeed in seizing independence from Britain. If the Americans could not complete what they had started, France and Spain would be foolish to antagonize Britain. The last thing they wanted was to side with the Americans only to have them collapse, leaving Spain and France vulnerable to British reprisals.

This question remained open through the middle of 1777. After a respectable showing at the early battle of Bunker Hill at Boston, the colonial armies had suffered a series of bruising defeats in New York and New Jersey. Commanding general George Washington spent as much time squabbling with his own political leaders as fighting the British, and on more than one occasion the American forces seemed on the verge of dissolution.

The skies brightened, however, in October 1777. The British, hoping to sever New England from the lower colonies, arranged for two armies, one moving south from Canada and the other pushing north from New York City, to meet in the Hudson Valley. The plan went awry when American units ambushed the redcoats in the thick forests between Lake Champlain and Albany. After flailing haplessly in the woods for weeks, British general John Burgoyne surrendered nearly six thousand troops to the American general Horatio Gates at Saratoga on October 17.

Reports of the battle of Saratoga reached Europe in December 1777. The news of the British defeat made it easier for France to decide what Vergennes and Louis might have decided anyway: to sign a treaty of alliance with the Americans and openly join the war against Britain. One reason, beyond concerns about the Americans' potential for success, for France's decision to hold back until now was that the French armed forces, particularly the French navy, had needed the time to get in shape for another war against Britain. By the end of 1777 the French rearmament program was nearing completion; the navy appeared ready to fight come sailing season the following year.

The French still feared that the British might offer a compromise settlement to the Americans. Whether the American victory at Saratoga made a negotiated peace more likely or less was hard to say. Presumably the British people, if not the British government, would find the outcome disheartening; they might support a settlement that ended the war on terms not too damaging to British prestige. On the other hand the Saratoga result would encourage the Americans to resist compromise with the British. The momentum in the war was shifting the Americans' way. Why should they settle for less than their full agenda?

Not wishing to see an early end to the war, France notified the Americans that it wished to sign a treaty of alliance with the United States. In fact, Paris signed two treaties. The first was a commercial pact promising reciprocity in trade relations between the two countries: each would treat the other's products as the other treated its products. This document was not especially remarkable, but it did provide a model for American commercial diplomacy that persisted into the twentieth century (and, appropriately, was itself based on the so-called Model Treaty of 1776, drawn up by John Adams as a guide to American relations with foreign powers).

The second treaty was the treaty of alliance itself. Vergennes's representative drafted the document; American commissioners Benjamin Franklin, Silas Deane, and Arthur Lee accepted the French draft largely unchanged. The most important provision of the treaty pledged the two sides to continue fighting until both agreed to quit. Neither wanted to risk being left to fight the British alone in case the other tired of the war.

The treaty of alliance with France, signed in Paris in February 1778, seemed a tremendous boon to many Americans. "France is the natural defense of the United States against the rapacious spirit of Great Britain," John Adams wrote to Samuel Adams. "France is a nation so vastly eminent, having been for so many centuries what they call the dominant power of Europe, being incomparably the most powerful at land, that united in a close alliance with our states and enjoying the benefit of our trade, there is not the smallest reason to doubt but both will be a sufficient curb upon the naval power of Great Britain."

Yet the Franco-American treaty of alliance involved two drawbacks for the United States. The first would show up within a few years; the second would take longer to surface. The short-term deficiency was the treaty's failure to specify war aims. By saying simply that the United States would fight as long as France desired to fight, the treaty handed the French a blank check on American military cooperation. The French could reply that the obligation was reciprocal, in the spirit of the treaty of commerce; but the American aims were fairly obvious, centering on independence, while French aims might include any number of designs for restructuring the Atlantic balance of power. The long-term deficiency was the open-ended character of the alliance. Containing no provision for review or termination of the treaty, the document wedded the United States to France indefinitely.

The Winding Road to Paris

The unspecified nature of French war aims soon entangled the United States more deeply in the thicket of European politics than Americans ever intended. Since the first days of the war, Spain had gradually cooled to the American colonials. During the spring and summer of 1777, Madrid settled its dispute with Portugal, removing a chief bone of Spanish contention with Britain, Portugal's ally. A bigger bone, Gibraltar, remained, but the government of Charles III needed to be convinced that war was the best means of reclaiming the rock. Should France declare war on Britain, as appeared increasingly likely, Britain might choose to buy Spain's neutrality, perhaps by giving up Gibraltar. Or Britain might not. But there was no reason to rush to a decision for war.

The French felt exposed while the Spanish delayed. Vergennes pressed Charles to come out openly against Britain, offering to fight at Spain's side until the British evacuated Gibraltar. Charles liked the idea of being wooed by both Britain and France, and he procrastinated the more. In the end, however, the British declined to give the Spanish the guarantees Charles desired, and in April 1779 Spain signed a treaty of alliance with France. Under the terms of this treaty, France promised to keep fighting against Britain until Spain won back Gibraltar.

The terms of the Franco-Spanish treaty were closely held—with reason. The French would have been embarrassed to reveal that they had committed the United States, by virtue of this treaty and the French treaty, with the Americans, to the reconquest of Gibraltar. The French treaty with America did not explicitly rule out French commitments to third parties—but neither do marriage vows explicitly mention bigamy. The plain fact of the case was that the French were two-timing the Americans. Like many of those two-timed, the Americans did not know right away exactly what was going on, but they caught on quickly enough that *something* was afoot, and the knowledge tended to sour their relationship with France.

Beggars cannot be choosers, however, and the Americans needed French help. Saratoga demonstrated that the Americans could hold their own on land—at least in the woods—against the British, but other campaigns indicated that without help at sea Americans could find themselves in serious trouble. When British general William Howe decided to drop his siege of Boston, he was able to transport his troops via ship to New York with an ease George Washington and the Americans could only envy. So long as the British controlled the waves, they would be able to prosecute the war at relatively small expense, moving troops here and there as needed and bottling up American coastal and foreign trade.

The greatest asset France could bring to America's side of the war was a navy that would help even the odds. The French navy was smaller than the British navy, but at a time when the American navy was nearly nonexistent, every ship counted. Besides, as events proved, the American side did not require overall superiority at sea; it needed only superiority at certain crucial times and places. This the French fleet could provide.

But France could not do so without help, which was where Spain came in. Although Britain's fleet outnumbered and outgunned that of France, Spain's fleet was almost as big as France's, and together the French and Spanish fleets overmatched the British. Even if Spain committed no ships to the American theater of fighting, the Spanish presence in the Mediterranean and eastern Atlantic would tie down many British vessels. In league with the French, the Spanish might even contemplate an attack on Britain itself—an effort called for, in fact, by the 1779 treaty between France and Spain. Such an attack would have little chance of success, if success meant repeating the Norman conquest. But even an unsuccessful attack would remind the British people quite graphically of the hazards and expense of the war. Britain had not had a serious scare since 1588, and a reappearance of the Armada, this time including French ships, might dispose the British government toward a peace on terms favorable to Spain and France.

The American alliance with France, together with France's alliance with Spain, guaranteed the victory of the American Revolution. Perhaps the rebels would have won anyway, for they grew better at fighting as the war grew older. The fundamental question remained as before: Who would tire of the struggle first? As before, the Americans had more at stake and therefore greater cause to keep fighting than the British did. But the victory would have taken far longer had the Americans not received the aid they did from the Europeans. The French provided soldiers to complement French naval vessels; the Spanish sent a few ships to the western Atlantic and harried the British elsewhere; the Dutch floated some needed loans as well as a modest fleet that helped distract the British in the North Sea at the climax of fighting in America.

American diplomats also sought help from Russia. Success in the effort was improbable: in the constant jostling for power in Europe, Catherine the Great's government had generally looked to Britain for assistance in containing France and Austria. If Russia became involved at all, it likely would side with Britain rather than America. As matters happened, Catherine chose not to get involved on either side. Russia had problems closer to home with the Turks and the Poles, and a fight in the Atlantic did not hold much attraction.

Catherine the Great didn't help the Americans much during the Revolutionary War, but the principles she laid down regarding neutrality in wartime served the United States until the twentieth century. *The Bettmann Archives*

But Catherine wanted Russia to be considered a great power, and great powers had to take positions, if not sides. In 1780 Catherine announced the formation of something new in world politics: the League of Armed Neutrality. The purpose of the organization was to define and defend the rights of neutrals in wartime. The most important of these were the rights to travel between ports of belligerent nations and to transport noncontraband goods owned by belligerents. To prevent would-be molesters from broadly construing contraband, Catherine specified a narrow list restricted to materials directly related to warmaking and not including, for instance, generic shipbuilding materials. Belligerent nations would be allowed to blockade specific ports, thereby keeping neutrals out, but the blockade had to be short range. Cruising shipping lanes at sea and scooping up enemybound neutrals did not qualify.

The Russian initiative appealed to several other European nations that did not wish to join the fighting at this time; it also initially pleased the Americans, who took Catherine's refusal to join with Britain as a sign that Russia might be favorably disposed to their efforts to throw off the British yoke. American representatives went so far as to suggest that the United States be admitted to the League of Armed Neutrality. But Catherine rebuffed this strange suggestion—after all, the United States was one of the principal belligerents in the war—and made plain that she did not intend to go any further toward supporting revolution and the overthrow of legitimate government.

In the short term Russia's policy of neutrality had only a modest effect on the course of the war—though a neutral Russia was certainly better for America than a Russia allied to Britain would have been. The longer-term significance of the Russian policy lay in the precedents it set on issues of neutral rights in wartime. During the next century and a half, Americans would find themselves repeatedly defending neutral rights; the example of the League of Armed Neutrality would give them a useful point of reference.

The assistance the Americans did get from the Europeans shortened the war, but the United States still required six years after the battle of Saratoga to persuade the British to admit defeat. The decisive break came in the autumn of 1781. After a series of victories in the American South, British troops under General Lord Cornwallis headed north into Virginia. The British commander could hardly have chosen worse terrain for a major battle with the Americans, for the tidewater territory he entered was the home turf of George Washington. The American general let Cornwallis march himself into a bottle at Yorktown on a peninsula between the York and James rivers. Then with the French fleet momentarily superior to the British fleet in the area, Washington corked the bottle. His own Continental army and several thousand French troops trapped Cornwallis and forced the surrender of the British army.

Wars are fought on battlefields, but won or lost in the political arena. Political leaders responding to political pressures decide whether to continue fighting or sue for peace. Cornwallis's surrender at Yorktown scarcely signaled the end of Britain's military power in America: had the British people so desired, the British government could have treated Yorktown as a temporary setback and carried on. British forces still controlled New York City, the hub of mid-America, and Charles Town (Charleston), the gateway to the South.

But after five and a half years of combat by arms and after almost two decades of political and economic warfare against the Americans, the British chose to have done with the American troubles. The conflict had become a liability for the government, which could not win the war at a cost acceptable to British taxpayers but which until now had refused to admit that fact. The loss at Yorktown demonstrated undeniably that victory was farther away than ever. Early in 1782 a new government took office in London, a circumstance that made the liquidation of the war—the work of those incompetents who preceded us, the new officials could say—that much easier.

Peace negotiations went slowly. Part of the slowness resulted from a lack of coordination and trust among the American diplomats in Europe. Benjamin Franklin repeatedly scandalized his American associates; Arthur Lee reported to the Continental Congress, "The truth is that Dr. Franklin is now much advanced in years, more devoted to pleasure than would become even a young man in his station, and neglectful of the public business." But the Congress had more faith in Franklin than in Lee—whom Franklin called "the most malicious enemy that I ever had"—and recalled Lee from Europe before the serious negotiating started. John Adams, who joined Franklin in Paris, found Franklin's behavior almost as scandalous as Lee did and refused to confide in him. Franklin thought Adams a prig. In one of Franklin's friendlier moods, he called Adams "an honest man, even a wise one, but sometimes and in some things absolutely out of his senses." On another occasion, when he was feeling

Benjamin Franklin caused a sensation in Paris. Here he is impressing Louis XVI and Marie Antoinette. *The Granger Collection*

less charitable, he labeled Adams a "mischievous madman." John Jay, the third member with Franklin and Adams of the team that negotiated the final peace settlement, thought Franklin had been in Paris too long. Not only had Franklin become enamored of French ladies, Jay judged, but he had also come to mistake French interests for American. Jay deeply distrusted the French. "He says they are not a moral people," John Adams noted in his diary. Distrusting the French, Jay, like Adams, was wary of Franklin.

Personal idiosyncracies often matter in international relations, as they did in this case; but national interests usually matter more, as they also did in this case. The major reason for the delay in achieving an end to the war was that the Spanish still hoped to regain Gibraltar. This hope was vain, but the Spanish required time to recognize it as such. The French, desiring to retain Madrid's friendship, declined to assist in the recognition, despite the urgings of the Americans to do so. France's unwillingness to pressure Spain confirmed Adams's and Jay's suspicion of French intentions; eventually even Franklin grew annoyed. Finally Franklin hinted that the United States might abrogate its treaty with France and sign a separate peace accord with the British. Franklin went so far as to talk of an Anglo-American alliance.

Vergennes reacted indignantly, but American impatience actually suited the French well enough. Vergennes was weary of the war, and he used the American threats as leverage against the Spanish, to illustrate to Madrid the dangers of carrying on too long. In the end, however, the Spanish had to learn for themselves, and not until the British repulsed a last-ditch Spanish assault on Gibraltar did Spain acquiesce in a peace settlement.

That the Americans would achieve their principal war aim—recognition of the independence of the United States—went without saying. What else they would get depended in large part on how generous the British were—or, rather, on how generosity toward the Americans served Britain's postwar interests. Despite grave suspicions in Britain regarding Benjamin Franklin (George III declared, "The many instances of the inimical conduct of Franklin towards this country makes me aware that hatred to this country is the constant object of his mind"), British colonial secretary Lord Shelburne understood that it might be wise to let bygones be bygones. The United States had allied with France against Britain from fear of Britain; but of the two countries, France represented a far greater threat to British interests than the United States did. Prudence therefore recommended a generous peace with the Americans to prevent the Franco-American wartime alliance from solidifying into a permanent fixture of Atlantic diplomacy.

Exactly how generous the peace should be was the crux of the negotiations. Franklin, especially, bargained hard and skillfully. He blandly declared that the United States ought to receive Canada, pointing out that British cession of the northern territories would prevent future friction between the two English-speaking nations. Canada was more than the Americans had earned on the battlefield, and more than they had any reasonable hope of getting; Franklin knew this, but he was using Canada as a bargaining chip. For their part the British demanded reparations for the Loyalists who had left America during the fighting—often a step ahead of angry rebel mobs—and had suffered personal and property losses. London also insisted that Americans who owed debts to British merchants be required to repay the debts.

After much haggling, punctuated by reminders from the Americans that they could always fall back on their alliance with the French in the event the British refused to bend, the American peace commissioners and Shelburne's government agreed on terms of a treaty in September 1783. The British recognized the independence of the United States, with a domain that stretched from the Great Lakes in the north to Florida in the south and from the Atlantic in the east to the Mississippi in the west. In exchange for these provisions as well as for fishing rights off Newfoundland, the Americans agreed not to block the efforts of British merchants to collect debts owed by Americans and to assist in restoring the property of the Loyalists.

The Americans could hardly have desired a better outcome to their war for independence. They had won their independence; they had gained a country far bigger than they had any right to expect; they were becoming an object of competition among the great powers. Although the peace settlement had more to do with the state of Atlantic affairs than with the importance of America, many Americans interpreted it as confirmation of the latter. From the time of the Puritans and the establishment of the "city on a hill," Americans had tended to see themselves as special. The outcome of the Revolutionary War strengthened that tendency.

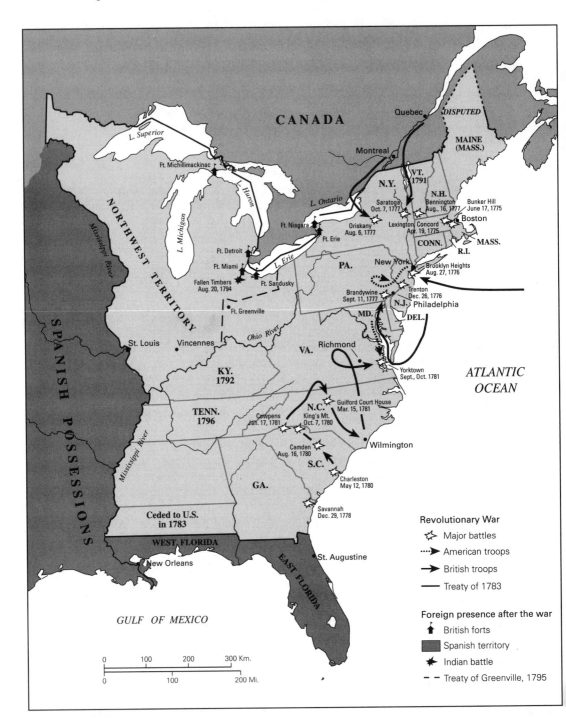

The United States and Foreign Territories in the Late 1700s

Tinkering with the Machinery of Foreign Policy:
The Constitution of 1787

Yet the more reflective among the Americans should have seen that what Europe could give Europe might take away, or try to. It was America's fate during the first half century of its national existence—as it has often been the fate of lesser countries—to be caught in the whirlpool of great-power politics. During the War of the American Revolution, the vortex worked to America's advantage as France and Spain helped spin Americans free from Britain's grip. But France and Spain did not desire to help Americans so much as they desired to hurt Britain; and once Americans gained their independence, they lost most of their appeal for Paris and Madrid. If anything, Spain now looked on the United States as a potential rival for predominance in North America, while both France and Spain eyed the United States as a hotbed of republicanism whose radical notions might give seditious ideas to the subjects of the French and Spanish empires.

The end of the war against Britain also revealed another set of problems for the Americans. The war had imposed a measure of unity on the thirteen states, but the peace showed the United States to be a political term best construed as plural. When the imperial crisis began in the wake of the Seven Years' War, little had united the thirteen colonies beyond a common aversion to British policies. James Otis himself had predicted in 1765, "Were these colonies left to themselves tomorrow, America would be a mere shambles of blood and confusion." John Dickinson, a prominent lawyer, foresaw in independence "a multitude of commonwealths, crimes and calamities, centuries of mutual jealousies, hatred, wars of devastation." Otis and Dickinson later changed their minds about independence, largely because of the success of the colonies in pulling together against Britain. Otis and Dickinson and others watched Americans from the different colonies cooperate in committees of correspondence, in the Continental Congress, and in the Continental army, and they became more optimistic about the possibilities of collaboration. Nonetheless, for many Americans, perhaps most, national unity remained a matter of wartime necessity rather than peacetime conviction.

In 1781 the states agreed to the formation of a national government under the Articles of Confederation, but the Confederation government reflected its designers' suspicions of centralized power. Lacking enforcement authority, it was a creature of the states, which could—and often did—ignore its requests for such essentials of operation as tax revenues. The Articles assigned the national government the responsibility to wage war and otherwise conduct foreign affairs but neglected to give the national government the power to meet its responsibilities. It had to request (it could not demand) appropriations from the states to raise and support an army and to send emissaries abroad. It might negotiate treaties with foreign governments, but it relied on the states to honor the terms of the treaties. The states retained authority over commerce, both between states and with foreign countries. The Articles might be amended, but only by the unanimous consent of all the states.

There were good reasons for the hedging in of the power of the central government: the revolutionaries fighting against King George wanted to prevent a similar concentration of power in the hands of an American government. Yet the deconcentration of power made it difficult for the United States to deal with foreign countries. Weak as it was, the American government held no terror for foreign governments. It could not conduct a meaningful foreign economic policy because it could not tax imports or otherwise restrict international trade—the principal tools of foreign economic policy. It could not guarantee compliance with treaties it concluded, so foreign governments had little incentive to negotiate pacts with the United States. Whether it could fight a war against a foreign country depended on how the states felt about such a war: if the war was popular, they might send troops and supplies; if it was not, they would not. And even in popular wars each state would suspect the others of doing less than their full share. The Revolutionary War had been as popular as any war was likely to be, but the bickering in that conflict drove George Washington and other national leaders nearly insane.

Foreign countries took advantage of America's weakness under the Articles of Confederation. The British refused to evacuate forts in the northwestern territories they had nominally ceded to the United States in the Treaty of Paris. London contended, with justice, that the United States had failed to live up to its side of the bargain: that several of the states were blocking claims by British creditors against Americans (they were) and were not restoring property confiscated from the Loyalists (they were not). But creditors' claims and compensation of individuals are comparatively small matters in international affairs; maintaining military forces on someone else's soil is a major affront. Had the United States possessed a strong central government, it would have dispatched American troops to root the British occupiers out. But the American government was weak. It lacked the necessary troops and energy, and the British stayed put.

Spain similarly exploited the Americans' weakness. Angry at not winning back Gibraltar and still distrustful of the Americans' republicanism and possible territorial ambitions, the Spanish attempted to establish a buffer between their own holdings in North America and the lands inhabited by the Americans. To discourage settlement in the Mississippi Valley, Madrid in 1784 closed the lower Mississippi River (which lay between Spanish Florida on the east bank and Spanish Louisiana on the west) to American traffic. The move threatened to strangle the American settlements all the way up the Mississippi and Ohio rivers, for these settlements relied on the lower Mississippi as an avenue for shipping their goods to market. The Confederation Congress directed John Jay to attempt to persuade the Spanish to rescind their new policy, but possessing few enticements and wielding few credible threats, Jay got nowhere.

Beyond the paralysis produced in foreign affairs, the deficiencies of the Articles of Confederation contributed to domestic disturbances. Congress could not cope with the new nation's acute fiscal problems, including a devaluation of the currency that gave American culture a phrase for utter valuelessness: "not worth a Continental." Nor could Congress prevent insurrections among disaffected (and armed) veterans of the Revolutionary War, such as that led by Daniel Shays of western Massachusetts in 1786.

Together the internal and external shortcomings of the Articles catalyzed a movement for a fundamental restructuring of the national government. The restructurers, headed by James Madison and Alexander Hamilton, worked stealthily; they knew that the central government was weak because many Americans liked it that way, and they knew that its lack of vigor in foreign affairs reflected a belief on the part of many Americans that foreign affairs were something best left to the intriguing courts of Europe. As early as the 1780s an influential school of thought was developing that argued that the Atlantic Ocean was and should be America's most effective foreign policy: a moat in war, a reminder against meddling in Europe's affairs in peace. To avoid provoking the adherents of this school, Madison and Hamilton suggested a conference merely to amend the Articles of Confederation. Such a conference seemed innocuous enough: any state could block unwelcome changes by casting its veto.

But when the delegates, after one false start, met at Philadelphia in 1787, they proceeded to ignore the Articles and start afresh. The result of their labors, the Constitution of 1787, specified a government fundamentally different from the government of the Articles. Where the old government was a *confederation,* with sovereign power residing in the separate states, the new government was a *federation,* possessing itself sovereignty over the states. (In practice it would require eighty years and a civil war to vindicate this principle, but in theory—federalist theory anyway—the principle was there from the beginning.)

Regarding foreign affairs, the new government enjoyed the powers normally associated with sovereign governments. It could make war and conclude peace treaties; it could raise armies and establish diplomatic missions abroad; it could regulate commerce with foreign countries; it could levy taxes to support these and other activities. But where most governments of the time vested these powers in a single person or legislative body, the American Constitution split them among competing branches, in particular the executive branch (the president) and the legislative branch (Congress). (The judicial branch, headed by the Supreme Court, was essentially excluded from foreign affairs.) Thus the Constitution named the president commander in chief of the armed forces but reserved to Congress the power to declare war. The president's appointees negotiated treaties, but Congress (specifically the Senate) had to approve them. The president selected ambassadors, but the Senate had to accept his selections. The president could initiate foreign policy, but Congress had to provide the money to fund the initiatives.

The Constitution of 1787 was very much a document of its day. In its attempt to create a government out of the thin air of human reason, it clearly showed its Enlightenment roots. Other governments evolved over centuries, often irrationally; America's was created at one blow, along rational lines laid out by the country's best minds. In its division of authority among three branches, it reflected the teachings of Montesquieu ("the immortal Montesquieu," according to one proclamation by the Continental Congress) as well as Americans' continuing distrust of centralized power. Each branch would check any exaggerated ambitions in the others. Regarding foreign affairs, the splitting of power between the president and Congress reflected a desire to ensure care and deliberation in the making of foreign policy. During an era when communication between America and other countries required months, care and deliberation came cheap. International crises tended to build slowly; little would be lost and much gained if the president and Congress had to hammer out a policy both could agree on. Besides, almost no one in the 1780s expected the United States to play a major continuing role in world politics. Europe was far away, Asia was much farther still, and Americans wanted mostly to be left to their own business.

Another Kind of Revolution: France

On April 30, 1789, George Washington took the oath of office as the first American president under the new Constitution. Washington was an aristocrat if ever America produced one. During a break in the Philadelphia Constitutional Convention during the summer of 1787, Gouverneur Morris had accepted a challenge from Alexander Hamilton to go up to Washington, slap him on the back, and call him George. "Never have I paid so dearly for a wager," Morris said afterward; Washington's icy gaze had almost frozen Morris to the spot. Washington disliked the pushing and shoving of politics even more than he disliked the familiar touch of his associates, and he hoped to remain above such sordid things. A series of events that began a week after his inauguration guaranteed his disappointment.

On May 5 the French States General convened for the first time in more than a century and a half. Louis XVI called the members of the national assembly to Versailles, not out of any love of representative government, but for the same reason the kings of England had initially summoned parliaments to Westminster: to shake money out of their pockets. The English kings had discovered the hard way that once the members of Parliament got together, they started comparing complaints and became difficult to manage. One thing led to another—stalemate to civil war to regicide and so forth—and before anyone could say William of Orange, Parliament came out on top.

Something similar happened, or started to, when the States General gathered at Versailles in May 1789. Louis badly needed money: after the long struggle with Britain, including the War of the American Revolution, the French treasury was near bankruptcy. The extravagant habits of Louis's court had not helped matters, nor had Americans' tardiness (largely the result of the weaknesses of the Confederation government) in repaying loans from France during the recent war. A tax increase appeared inevitable. But those who spoke for the business classes in the States General, the probable targets of any tax hike, demanded that Louis straighten out his affairs before they gave him any more money. During the next several weeks, their demands escalated; in June they called for a constitution like that the Americans had just adopted. When Louis fired one of his ministers, a popular reformer, the momentum for change spilled into the streets. A Paris mob stormed the Bastille, and the French Revolution began.

Most Americans applauded the early stages of the French Revolution. The French people seemed to be following the trail the Americans had blazed during the previous decade, rejecting a king, overthrowing his corrupt regime, and replacing it with a form of government responsive to popular demands. Conservatives in America got a bit queasy reading about the riots in Paris, but at first these were hardly worse than the riots that had followed passage of the Stamp Act in 1765.

Before long, however, it became apparent that the French Revolution was something different from what the American Revolution had been. The American revolutionaries had tossed King George's officials out of the colonies and given their positions to people committed to American rights and American self-government; but aside from some effervescence in the states and the ill-treatment of some Loyalists, the American Revolution had not gone much further than that. It had produced no wholesale rejection of the American social order, and the new leaders of the country, men like Washington and John Adams, were hardly flaming radicals. Even Jefferson, judged a wild-eyed anarchist by some of his critics, proved a pillar of respectability when his turn in office came.

The French Revolution, by contrast, simply grew more radical as the months and then years passed. Moderates gave way to extremists in French politics; the king was arrested, humiliated, tried, and executed; thousands of aristocrats and other alleged enemies of the revolution were guillotined. The revolution devoured one set of leaders after another, with the head-loppers of today becoming the head-losers of tomorrow. At the height of the turmoil, France's erstwhile government declared war on Austria, partly to preempt counter-revolutionary intervention from Austria or its allies and partly to distract the French people from the deficiencies of the rulers in Paris. The ensuing wars of the French Revolution eventually involved most of the countries of Europe— and the United States.

Both revolutions, the American and the French, were products of the Enlightenment. Both sought to apply the principles of human reason and natural law to relations among people and between people and government. Both rejected monarchy and supplanted it with republican institutions: with governments answerable to the people.

But where the American Revolution was primarily political, the French Revolution was as much social and ideological as political. Americans changed their government without significantly changing their society. Although the attacks on the Loyalists had some effect in reshuffling the social deck in certain states, no large group of people demanded wholesale changes in the class structure of American society. Chiefly a fight for political home rule, the American Revolution left American society essentially intact.

The French Revolution, in contrast, aimed at tearing apart and then reweaving the very fabric of French social life. Where American revolutionaries focused their attacks chiefly on foreigners (George III and the British government) and only secondarily on Americans (the Loyalists), the French revolutionaries focused primarily on other French. Eventually they included foreigners in their animus, but the fundamental thrust of the French Revolution was always domestic. It quickly became a class conflict, with the lower and middle classes waging a war on the aristocracy.

Some American observers of the French Revolution initially had difficulty distinguishing that revolution from their own. The rhetoric of the two was similar: the French slogan "Liberty, equality, fraternity" sounded much like the "Life, liberty, and the pursuit of happiness" of the American Declaration of Independence. Some participants in the two revolutions were the same: the marquis de Lafayette, who had served with Washington in the American Revolutionary War, commanded the French national guard after 1789; Thomas Paine propagandized for French radicalism and was named to the French National Convention. But the common points masked the fundamental difference between the pragmatic American fight for home rule and the ideological French quest for social leveling.

This confusion about revolutions would vex American international relations for two centuries. Americans liked to think of themselves as a revolutionary people, inhabitants of a nation born of revolution. And when revolutions broke out in other countries against monarchical or otherwise oppressive rule, Americans' first reaction was usually to profess support. But frequently the other revolutions followed the ideological and social model of the French revolution rather than the more narrowly political model of the American revolution; when this happened, Americans commonly felt betrayed and disillusioned.

The feelings of betrayal and disillusionment set in soon after the outbreak of the French Revolution. During the 1790s the turbulence in France disrupted the celebratory atmosphere in America that had accompanied the launching of the new federal government, and it helped trigger the formation of the first system of American political parties. George Washington flattered himself that he was above politics, that as president he served the national interest and not the interests of some narrow political faction, and he expected the same of the people he appointed to his administration. While Washington's self-estimate was reasonably accurate, his subordinates fell short of his expectations. Two personalities dominated Washington's cabinet: Alexander Hamilton, the treasury secretary, and Thomas Jefferson, the secretary of state. In later times American secretaries of state would deal exclusively with matters relating to foreign policy; in the early days of limited American involvement in world affairs, however, they also handled a variety of domestic chores, such as running the post office.

So it was not especially odd that the secretary of the treasury and the secretary of state should lock horns. And hornlocking was nearly unavoidable when the two individuals who occupied those posts held diametrically opposed views about the proper role of government. Hamilton advocated an active and powerful central administration, one with the energy to impose good government on the American people even when they were not sure they wanted it. Jefferson, at least until he became president himself, held that power was best left with the people, that the best governments were those that governed least.

Hamilton and other American conservatives viewed the French Revolution with alarm. The confusion and violence in France seemed to the conservatives to be the natural consequence of letting too much power slip into the hands of people unqualified to wield it. French revolutionaries preached liberty, equality, and fraternity, but what they needed was a good dose of law and order. France was cutting its own throat—literally—by attacking its educated and talented classes. If Americans wanted to do France and themselves any favors, they would take steps to prevent the revolution from spreading to other countries and would try to restore power in France to those who knew what to do with it.

Jefferson and his supporters, by contrast, considered the French Revolution an extension of the same fight for human freedom Jefferson had spearheaded in writing the American Declaration of Independence. The Jeffersonians forgave the French revolutionaries their perhaps excessive violence. Everyone made mistakes, the Jeffersonians reasoned, and a mistake in the name of freedom weighed less in the scales of eternal justice than a mistake in the defense of tyranny. If America wished to be true to itself and to its historical mission, it ought to support the French Revolution against its domestic and foreign foes.

Initially the debate in America over the French Revolution consisted chiefly of dinner-table skirmishing. During the early phases of the revolution, Americans had plenty to do putting their new Constitution into effect, passing a bill of rights, and otherwise getting their own affairs in order. But the outbreak and spread of war in Europe in 1792 and 1793 forced the Washington administration to take a stand. The French, citing the alliance that still bound the Americans to them, demanded American assistance against France's enemies, which by now included Britain. Jefferson and such associates as James Madison argued in France's favor. Madison contended that the "cause of liberty" required American aid to the French. Jefferson avowed that the "liberty of the whole earth" depended on the outcome of the European contest, and he predicted that if France's European enemies succeeded in crushing France and its experiment in republicanism, the United States might be next. "It is far from being certain they might not choose to finish their job completely, by obliging us to a change in the form of our government at least," Jefferson said. France had helped the United States in America's hour of need, the Jeffersonians reminded their compatriots; the United States should return the favor in France's time of trial. Besides, the European war was pushing the French Revolution to extremes; thousands of people were being branded traitors and executed.

Should France regain a sense of security, as by means of American assistance, the revolution might return to a more moderate course. Finally, though the American war with Britain had ended, the British were no friends of the United States. They continued to occupy forts along the northwest frontier and to encourage the Indians there to violence; more threateningly in the long run, they dominated American foreign commerce. The United States might have won political independence from Britain, but with three-quarters of American overseas trade being with Britain, and with most of that trade consisting of British imports to the United States, America remained something of an economic colony of Britain. To break this economic dependence, as well as for the other reasons, the United States ought to back France. Perhaps a declaration of war against Britain would be too much, but at least the United States ought to offer friendly aid to France short of war.

The Hamiltonians believed the Jeffersonians had the whole argument wrong. The United States owed nothing to France: the French had entered the 1778 alliance out of concern for French interests, not American. Circumstances, including the nature of the French government, had changed completely since then, and it would be the height of foolishness for the United States to get involved in a European war from some misty-eyed gratitude to a government that no longer existed. "I am glad to believe," Hamilton said, "there is no real resemblance between what was the cause of America and what is the cause of France—that the difference is no less great than that between liberty and licentiousness." The United States had to avoid excessive attachment to foreign governments and entanglement in foreign affairs. "The former will generally be found hollow and delusive," Hamilton declared. "The latter will have a tendency to lead us aside from our own true interest and to make us the dupes of foreign influence." The French Revolution was beyond retrieval. The revolutionaries had beheaded their king and taken to murdering each other. For their foreign troubles the French had only themselves to blame. True, American commerce tilted heavily in Britain's direction, but this simply reflected the complementary nature of the economies of the two countries. No one was putting a gun to the heads of American consumers who purchased items produced in England; they bought English goods because they were the best available at a price Americans wanted to pay. American interests in the long term paralleled those of Britain more closely than those of France. This was partly the result of complementary commerce, but more fundamentally of a common culture. As Hamilton explained to a British envoy, "I have always preferred a connexion with you, to that of any other country. We think in English, and have a similarity of prejudices and of predilections." If the European wars forced the United States to choose sides, Hamilton and his supporters contended, it ought to side with the British.

President Washington did not desire to choose either side, and he did not. In April 1793 he declared American neutrality. In this as in many other ways—retiring after two terms, for instance—Washington set an example for his presidential successors. The example in this case was both procedural and substantive. Procedurally, Washington's decision to proclaim neutrality without asking Congress for approval seemed to some Americans a violation of at least the spirit of the American Constitution, which reserved declarations of war—and presumably declarations of nonwar—to the legislature. Washington ignored these complaints, and the precedent stood. Substantively, the decision for neutrality foreshadowed a lasting American desire to avoid formal involvement in Europe's quarrels.

Two considerations motivated Washington's neutral policy. First, the issues the Europeans were fighting about had little intrinsic importance for the United States, certainly not enough to fight a war over. Second, a neutral America trading with both sides in the European war appeared likely to profit handsomely.

Had Americans stayed entirely out of Europe's war, they would not have run into the kind of difficulties they eventually did. Most of the countries of the world were neutral in the European war, and most encountered no troubles whatsoever on that account. But Americans did not want to stay out of the war; they wanted to participate selectively. In particular, they wanted to do business with the European belligerents. Since even noncontraband American trade enhanced the warmaking capacity of America's trading partners—American food fed soldiers, American naval stores outfitted ships—it was unrealistic of Americans to think that trade with belligerents would not lead to deeper involvement. Yet, unrealistic or not, the American government took the view that trade *should not* lead to deeper involvement.

Throughout the 1790s the war in Europe formed the background to American international relations. The war went badly for France at first, what with enemies all around and French conservatives conspiring with foreign governments to overthrow the revolutionary regime. But the very danger to the revolution inspired its supporters to great efforts. The revolutionary leaders proclaimed a *levée en masse,* a mobilization of all the nation's human and material resources, thereby transforming the war into a struggle of the French people, rather than the French monarchy, against France's foes. In this respect France set the pattern for most modern wars, which have been characterized by the complete marshaling of resources for conflict. The revolutionary leaders also attempted to export their revolution, declaring a "war of all peoples against all kings" and calling on the nations of the world to throw out their monarchs and replace them with democratically chosen representatives. In this regard as well, the French strategy anticipated later developments: ideological warfare would become a staple of international life, practiced by regimes of both the left and the right.

In one notorious case the French tried this method of appealing to foreign peoples over the heads of their governments against the United States. In the spring of 1793 the new French minister to America arrived in South Carolina. Edmond Genêt (called "Citizen" Genêt after the revolutionary fashion) was enthusiastic but not very prudent. Interpreting the warm welcome he received as evidence of popular American support for France against Britain, he began issuing licenses to American ship captains to privateer against British vessels. Privateering, or authorized piracy, was common practice in those days, but it did not accord with the Washington administration's neutralist policy.

The administration warned would-be privateers to ignore Genêt, and it told him to halt his recruiting activities at once. Genêt responded by threatening to ignore the administration and take his case directly to the American people. Even Jefferson, Francophile that the secretary of state was, found Genêt's attitude intolerable. With Washington's approval Jefferson demanded that the French government recall Genêt and replace him with someone more diplomatic. The French government happily obliged, not because it agreed with the Washington administration, but because it now included some of Genêt's enemies, who had booked him a date with the guillotine. Genêt relinquished his post and promised to be discreet; he then requested asylum in the United States. Washington, ascribing Genêt's errors to youthful folly, granted the request. Genêt settled down in New York, where he lived unobtrusively for the remaining forty years of his life.

Federalists Abroad

By the beginning of Washington's second term in 1793, the split between the Hamiltonians and the Jeffersonians was taking institutional form. Hamilton's backers, advocating a strong central government, cooperation between the business classes and the government, and good relations with Britain, organized themselves into the Federalist party. Jefferson's followers, stressing individual liberties and states' rights, the importance of farmers and common people as against merchants and the well-to-do, and friendship with France, created the Republican party (later renamed the Democratic party).

Washington continued to eschew party politics, but his actions placed him closer to the Federalist camp than to the Republican. Jefferson, for one, found the president's preference for Hamilton's policies unacceptable, and late in 1793 he resigned as secretary of state. Jefferson nominally retired from politics to manage Monticello, his Virginia plantation; but he stole time from his farming chores to direct the activities of America's first opposition party.

Not long after Jefferson left Philadelphia (then the seat of government), the Republicans found something serious to oppose. The troubles with Britain left over from the Revolutionary War remained unsettled, and the current war in Europe added fresh difficulties. Shortly after entering the fray, the British began seizing American ships bound to and from French ports, including ports in the French West Indies. The seizures grew more frequent as the months passed, and by the end of 1793 several hundred American vessels had been captured. American merchants howled in protest, not least because the British had not given advance notice of the seizure policy. More important, if the British blockade was allowed to persist, it would destroy a trade that was making Americans good money. Related to the problem of British seizures of American ships was the matter of impressment: Britain's habit of boarding American ships searching for deserters from the British navy and hauling away those determined—by the British—to fall into the deserter category.

The problem of the British presence in the Northwest aggravated Anglo-American tensions. Not only were the British still in occupation of forts they had promised to evacuate, but they were also actively engaged in support of Indians who were resisting the establishment of American control of the region. In certain respects the Paris treaty of 1783 had nearly guaranteed trouble between the Americans and the Indians, for it granted the United States title to a great deal of territory that the Americans did not effectively control. During the Revolutionary War, George Rogers Clark and his soldiers had won several victories in the West over the British and their Indian allies—the Indians by this time having decided that the Americans were a more dangerous threat to their homes and way of life than the British—but American control remained spotty and intermittent. This fact was not lost on the British, who hoped to block American expansion by encouraging Indian resistance. During the late 1780s and early 1790s, Indian resistance became a serious problem for the American government. In 1790 an Indian force under the Miami chief Little Turtle smashed an American contingent on the Maumee River; a short while later another American unit met an even more crushing defeat on the banks of the Wabash. The turbulent conditions on the frontier led to repeated demands by westerners for the American government to take action to subdue the Indians and open the territory to safe settlement. A good way to start would be to drive the British from the area.

Washington responded to the complaints of the merchants and the westerners by selecting John Jay, currently chief justice of the Supreme Court, to go to London and try to resolve the assorted difficulties. Thomas Jefferson and the Republicans hoped Jay would give the British a piece of America's mind: that he would declare their arrogance intolerable and threaten retaliation. To stiffen Jay's spine, Congress, led by a strong Republican faction in the House of Representatives, voted a temporary embargo of American goods destined for British (as well as other foreign) ports.

But Jay had no such intentions; and even if he had, they would have been undercut by Alexander Hamilton's reassurance to the British minister in America that the Washington administration desired no rupture with London. Notwithstanding the American alliance with France, Hamilton said, London need not worry that the United States would take action hostile to Britain.

Privy to this information, the British government unsurprisingly did not concede much in the talks with Jay. The British agreed to evacuate the forts in the Northwest, and they allowed American ships to trade with the British East Indies (meaning, essentially, India). Neither concession appeased the Republicans. In promising to evacuate the forts, the British were simply saying they would do what they had said before they would do—and had not done. Trading privileges with India would benefit only a small group of American merchants—a group, moreover, that was far more Federalist than Republican. On other issues Jay got nothing. London refused to suspend its policy of impressment. Likewise it denied American claims of neutral shipping rights. The blockade would remain in effect, and American ships trying to run the blockade would be seized.

The Republicans expressed outrage that Jay would even bring home a treaty as devoid of positive content as this. In fact, getting the treaty home was the hardest part of the whole treaty process, and the contemporary state of transportation technology nearly derailed the agreement. In those pre-telegraph, pre-radio days, for the terms of the treaty to be known in the United States a copy of the treaty had to be physically brought to America. To ensure its arrival, Jay actually sent three copies, two by one ship and a third by another. The ship carrying the two copies across the north Atlantic encountered a French privateer. Knowing that the French had every reason and desire to torpedo a settlement of Anglo-American differences, and not wanting the treaty to fall into French hands, the courier threw the copies of the treaty to the waves. They went to the bottom and were never recovered. The third copy traveled on a ship that ran into stiff headwinds, making its westward progress painfully slow. This ship, too, was approached by a French vessel, whose captain ordered the ship stopped and searched. Fortunately for the fate of the treaty, the French searchers failed to discover it. When the ship arrived at Norfolk after a voyage of three months, the messenger carrying the treaty hired a horse for what he hoped would be a speedy trip to Washington, where Congress was about to adjourn. The horse broke down after thirty-six hours of hard riding, and the messenger had to transfer to a stage. The stage fought the mud and cold of the Virginia winter until the messenger, frantic at its slow pace, found another horse to hire. He finally reached Washington on March 7, 1795, nearly frozen and entirely exhausted—four months after the treaty had left England. To the messenger's dismay, Congress, disgusted at the long delay, had adjourned three days before. Washington was forced to call a special session to meet the following summer.

The delay gave the Republicans time to organize opposition. At first Washington tried to blunt the opposition by keeping the terms of the treaty secret, but opponents leaked a copy to the press. Southerners excoriated a provision barring the export of cotton and sugar to the British West Indies; they also complained of Jay's failure to gain compensation for slaves taken by British troops evacuating the southern states at the end of the Revolutionary War. Westerners decried a provision assuring the British of equal navigation rights on the Mississippi, fearing that this would afford an opening that British vessels would use to control the great river. Farmers objected to Jay's acquiescence in a British definition of foodstuffs as being, under certain circumstances, contraband and therefore subject to seizure.

The opposition grew intense. Crowds in several cities and towns hanged Jay in effigy. One group of Republicans, while declining to waste their efforts on a dummy made up to look like Jay, suggested they might change their minds "if the original were here." Rioters threw rocks at the residence of the British minister in Philadelphia and at Alexander Hamilton in person.

Critics of the Federalists express their opinion of Jay's treaty. *The Bettmann Archives*

The Republican opposition, however, failed to prevent Senate approval of a mildly modified version of the treaty. The pact passed by the slimmest possible margin: 20–10. Supporters of the treaty pointed out that whatever its deficiencies, it possessed the admirable quality of preserving the peace between the United States and Britain. Opponents of the pact might grumble, but what did they offer in place of it? Did they prefer war?

James Madison did not think rejection of the treaty would lead to war; but even if it did, Americans had to stand up for their rights. He thought the Washington administration was conceding far too much to Hamilton's British friends; America deserved better. Madison recognized that his side had lost in the Senate, but he hoped to win in the House of Representatives. Although the Constitution gave the House no explicit role in concluding treaties, Madison claimed an implicit role for the lower chamber by virtue of the requirement that the House concur in (indeed originate) appropriations bills. Madison threatened to block legislation necessary to fund the treaty's provisions.

Washington, however, invoked his tremendous prestige on behalf of the treaty. It helped the president's cause that General Anthony Wayne had recently succeeded in suppressing most Indian resistance in the Northwest. The high point of Wayne's campaign was the battle of Fallen Timbers during the late summer of 1794, at which Wayne's force defeated a coalition of warriors from several tribes. A mopping-up operation during the following twelve months led to the Treaty of Greenville of August 1795, by which the Indians consented to withdraw from most of what became the state of Ohio. (See map p. 50) Although Wayne's actions did not entirely end conflict between Indians and whites in the Northwest, it did ease some of the political pressure on the Washington administration. Washington's stature and the recent developments sufficed to push the bill implementing the treaty through the House of Representatives. In April 1796 the House approved the bill by a vote of 51 to 48.

Yet the opponents of the treaty made an important statement by their opposition. They demonstrated the deep distrust many Americans felt toward the British and toward the idea of diplomacy in general. For more than a century Britain would remain a potent issue in American politics. "Twisting the lion's tail" would be a favorite pastime of politicians lacking answers to domestic difficulties; aspiring candidates for office would campaign against George III for decades after that unlucky monarch went to his grave. As for diplomacy in general, Americans were already showing their reflexive suspicion of the whole business. Most Americans liked to think their relations with other countries were motivated by principles: ethical standards not subject to compromise. But compromising was precisely what diplomats were paid to do. Moreover, diplomacy smacked of European court intrigues. Americans, with the exception of the native Indians, who were already here, and African slaves, who had no choice in the matter, were Americans by conscious decision—either their own or their forebears'. That decision typically represented a rejection of Europe. Americans defined themselves by opposition to Europe, and to the extent that they saw themselves acting like Europeans, they got uncomfortable. The Jay treaty seemed to many Americans to be just the sort of deal a European government would cut, and they did not like it.

They liked another treaty of about the same time—one with Spain—better. They should have; it was a better bargain. And it was a better bargain because the United States had more usable leverage in negotiating it. The basic problem America encountered with Britain was that if push came to shove, Britain could shove harder than America could. The bottom line of diplomacy is always military power. Diplomats get paid to keep relations between countries above the bottom line, but astute diplomats always know how that line will read should they slip. Although Republicans and Federalists might differ regarding how far the United States could push Britain, the fact was that John Jay had to accept an unsatisfactory settlement of outstanding issues with Britain because the alternative to a peaceful settlement was a war the United States was not ready to fight.

Spain was a different case. During the 1780s Madrid had exploited the Americans' weakness and confusion under the Articles of Confederation: the Spanish closed the Mississippi River to American navigation, calculating that the Americans would not be able to agree among themselves on measures to reopen it. The Spanish calculated correctly. But the adoption of the new federal Constitution and the creation of a strong central government altered the picture drastically. Rather than dealing with thirteen small states only loosely tied together, the Spanish now found themselves confronted by one large country joined under a single government—and led by a famous general to boot.

The Spanish had another reason for wanting to conciliate Americans. Spain's monarchy had instinctively joined the counterrevolutionary anti-French coalition of 1793, but before long the Spanish government began reconsidering. By the time it finished reconsidering it had decided that it preferred the company of France, its traditional ally, to that of Britain, its traditional enemy. But antagonizing Britain left Spain—and especially Spain's New World possessions—open to British retaliation. Florida was particularly vulnerable; so, to a lesser degree, was Louisiana. With a pro-British administration in power in the United States, Spain's northernmost American territories were doubly at risk.

As a consequence, when the American envoy Thomas Pinckney arrived in Madrid in 1795 to discuss means of resolving differences between the United States and Spain, the Spanish government was in a mood to listen. Pinckney dropped occasional reminders that the Washington administration had just neogtiated a treaty with Britain (the terms of Jay's treaty were as yet undisclosed) and that Spanish uncooperativeness would tend to cement American ties with Britain. He stressed the importance Americans placed on free navigation of the Mississippi and added that it would be helpful if Americans were allowed to store their goods at New Orleans awaiting space on departing ocean-going ships.

The Spanish agreed to reopen the Mississippi to American navigation and to grant Americans the right of deposit at New Orleans. At the same time, they accepted the American position on the disputed northern boundary of Florida, setting it at the thirty-first parallel.

Pinckney's treaty (sometimes called the Treaty of San Lorenzo) appealed to exactly those groups—southerners, westerners, farmers—that had most vehemently opposed Jay's treaty. Coming up for Senate consideration in 1796, just months after all the uproar over the treaty with Britain, Pinckney's treaty bled much of the steam from the Republicans' anger. The Washington administration, recently charged with being a tool of the eastern merchant class, now could argue plausibly that it looked after the interests of southern and western farmers as well. The Senate accepted the argument and unanimously approved the Pinckney treaty.

Neither Peace nor War: The Quasi-War with France

The good feelings the treaty with Spain induced helped Washington leave office with his illustrious reputation intact. He enhanced his reputation the more with one of the most memorable bits of advice ever given to Americans. As Washington prepared to retire to Mount Vernon for a well-earned rest after a long career in public service, he delivered a farewell address to his compatriots. Washington warned against the designs of scheming politicians and other individuals who placed personal ambition above the welfare of the country as a whole. Of more lasting importance, he cautioned against tying America to any foreign country. "Observe good faith and justice towards all nations; cultivate peace and harmony with all," he said. But do not get too close to any or, for that matter, too far from any. "The nation which indulges toward another an habitual hatred or an habitual fondness is in some degree a slave." In particular, the United States must avoid embroilment in Europe's vexations. "Europe has a set of primary interests which to us have none, or a very remote, relation. Hence she must be engaged in frequent controversies, the causes of which are essentially foreign to our concerns." Washington did not rule out temporary alliances for dealing with emergencies; the winner of the battle of Yorktown, where French forces had made the difference between defeat and victory, could hardly have done so. But he did rule out permanent alliances. "'Tis our true policy to steer clear of permanent alliances with any portion of the foreign world," he concluded.

The Federalists would have been happy to follow Washington's advice, at least as it related to France. But the United States remained fastened to France by the treaty of 1778, and there seemed no easy way out of the pact. John Adams succeeded Washington as president after the 1796 election by the narrowest of margins: 71 electoral college votes to 68 for Thomas Jefferson. For one of the few times in American history, foreign affairs figured centrally in the presidential election. If not for the timely conclusion of the Pinckney treaty, the outcry over the Jay treaty probably would have doomed Adams's candidacy. But Adams squeaked by, albeit burdened with the vice presidency of Jefferson, who as runner-up assumed the number two spot under the original rules for choosing presidents and vice presidents.

The French were already upset at the United States on account of Jay's treaty. Although producing considerably less than an Anglo-American alliance, this treaty between France's ally and its primary enemy hardly conformed to the spirit of the 1778 treaty between America and France. The French government, fighting for its life against Britain and other European foes, thought the Americans owed France more than this.

Adams's accession to the presidency did not improve the French attitude. Adams was not as pro-British as Alexander Hamilton, whom he personally despised and distrusted, but he hardly counted revolutionary France as a cause worthy of American support. Although Adams had been at the forefront of the American revolt against Britain, he was too much enamored of order and good government to tolerate France's recent excesses.

Partly because France's leaders sensed they had nothing left to lose with the United States, they launched a naval campaign designed to deny American trade to the British. French agents in the West Indies enlisted privateers to prey on American vessels; by the summer of 1797 these legalized pirates had seized more than three hundred American ships.

The French offensive infuriated Adams, who pushed for reinforcements to the American navy to smite the offenders. Shipyards in Philadelphia and Boston hastened to construct new vessels; meanwhile Adams appointed a commission to travel to Paris to register America's protest at France's high-handedness.

French foreign policy at this juncture was directed by Charles Maurice de Talleyrand, a slippery opportunist who had been a bishop under the prerevolutionary monarchy, then a supporter of the revolution, then an exile (for a while in the United States—which he did not like, calling it "a country of thirty-two religions and only one sauce"), and now foreign minister of the government of the French Directory. France needed money to keep its war effort going; Talleyrand informed the American commissioners that if they wished to discuss serious matters, they would first have to come up with a token of their earnestness. A $10 million loan would suffice for the French government; for himself, he required only $250,000.

Perhaps Talleyrand overestimated the diplomatic worldliness of the Americans; perhaps he underestimated their political shrewdness. They treated his request for a bribe as an affront to their principles, and they wrote home detailing his attempt to put the arm on the United States. The reports played straight into Adams's hands. The president still faced considerable opposition from the Republicans, many of whom acted as though France could do no wrong and Adams no right. Adams informed Congress of Talleyrand's maneuver, denoting the French foreign minister's agents by code names: X, Y, and Z.

The XYZ affair knocked the wind out of the Republicans. The most vocal critics of Adams fell silent, at least for a time. Congress created a navy department and funded the construction of more ships, and the battle cry of the day—"Millions for defense but not one penny for tribute"—rang throughout the land.

Adams stopped short of asking Congress for a declaration of war against France. The president was no warmonger, and the Republicans could probably muster enough opposition in Congress to make a request for a war declaration chancy. Adams opted instead for an undeclared war fought on the high seas. As commander in chief, the president ordered American warships to patrol the Atlantic and Caribbean lanes and prevent French vessels and privateers from molesting American ships. Unarmed French merchantmen should be left alone, but any French vessel carrying arms was subject to capture or destruction.

Had Adams confined himself to these actions, responsible persons could not much have faulted him. But American politics in those days was a bruising business, and the Federalists, seeing the Republicans down for the moment, moved in for the kill. During the summer of 1798, the Federalists in Congress rammed through a series of measures designed to muzzle the Adams administration's critics. The Alien Act targeted the large number of political refugees of liberal to radical views who had fled the upheavals in Europe during the preceding decade. This act authorized the president to deport foreigners whose activities he did not like. The Sedition Act narrowed the definition of lawful criticism of the government, allowing criminal prosecution for speech or writing that tended to bring the president or Congress into "contempt or disrepute."

The Alien and Sedition acts, along with the Naturalization Act of 1798, which made it more difficult for recently arrived foreigners to become citizens (and Republican voters, the Federalists feared), were a clear case of a majority party using its power to try to stay in power. The Sedition Act particularly placed the Republicans in jeopardy. If they objected, as many did, they were liable to prosecution in federal courts whose judges were largely Federalists. When the Adams administration's prosecutors quickly brought more than a dozen cases to trial, the Republicans knew that their opponents were serious.

While the Republicans fumed, and Americans as a whole pondered the issue of when legitimate opposition shaded into illegitimate sedition, a new turn of events in Europe altered the circumstances that had occasioned the offensive laws. In 1799 France's latest government, the Directory, fell to a military coup engineered by Napoleon Bonaparte. Napoleon had gained a name for himself fighting the Austrians in northern Italy, which he brought into France's sphere of political control. A subsequent campaign against the British in Egypt had gone less well but had done little to tarnish the image of the general from Corsica. By 1799 most of France was sorely tired of the revolution, and many found the idea of a strong man who would restore order appealing.

Napoleon at this time had little interest in fighting the Americans. An empire builder, but one who built his empire a step at a time, he concentrated his formidable energies on consolidating his own position in France and France's position in Europe. (So awesome were Napoleon's energies that admirers considered him almost a force of nature. "God made Bonaparte and then rested," one remarked—inspiring an individual less favorably disposed toward the Corsican to reply, "God should have rested a little earlier.") Napoleon had ideas for reviving France's fortunes in the Western Hemisphere, but he believed that these required American cooperation or at least American acquiescence. The naval war, started by the people Napoleon had thrown out of power, seemed a losing proposition to him.

By this time, too, John Adams was looking for a peaceful resolution of the "quasi-war" with France. Adams was never the mindless partisan some other members of the Federalist party were, and he had grown increasingly suspicious of the excesses of the party's Hamiltonian wing—excesses that included a scheme by Hamilton to lead an American army against the North American possessions of France's ally Spain, starting with Florida and heading toward New Orleans and Mexico. To spoil such schemes and end the hostilities with France, Adams appointed a peace commission to talk things over with the French government.

Napoleon let the American commissioners cool their heels for several months while he marched about central Europe, but eventually he and they agreed to the Convention of 1800. By this accord the United States bought its way out of the treaty of 1778 by dropping claims against France for ships and cargoes seized in the previous several years. (More precisely, the American government assumed responsibility for claims by Americans against the French government. This sort of assumption was, and still is, fairly standard practice in such matters.)

The Convention of 1800 was by no means a victory for the United States—at the cost of millions of dollars America freed itself from an alliance many Americans thought it should have quit long before—but the Quasi-War had some positive effects. It demonstrated to both the world and Americans themselves that the United States would fight in defense of what Americans conceived to be their neutral rights. It also demonstrated that when Americans got serious about fighting, they could bring serious military power to bear. In less than three years the United States expanded its navy from a dozen ships to more than fifty, and this navy captured or destroyed nearly one hundred armed French ships. The United States was still in the minor leagues of world power in 1800, but on present trends it would make at least the second division of the majors before long.

*   *   *

Napoleon's rise to power in France ended the French Revolution and in doing so marked the end of the era of revolution that had begun in the 1770s with the American Revolution. But though the era was over, the ideas the two revolutions set in motion far outlived the revolutions themselves. Between them, the American and French revolutions established the agenda for much of the international politics of the next two centuries. The American Revolution, with its demand for national self-determination, formed the pattern for the anti-imperialist revolutions of the nineteenth and twentieth centuries, leading to the demise of the European empires and the creation of scores of new states from their wreckage. The French Revolution, with its emphasis on ideology and its insistence on social equality, laid the foundation for the socialist revolutions of the succeeding eight generations and the rise of the ideological states of the twentieth century.

For the Americans, the close of the eighteenth century brought a feeling of enormous accomplishment. They had reason to be proud of themselves. Geographically, they controlled a territory larger than that of any European country except Russia. Militarily, they had shown they could look after their nation's interests. By the end of the 1790s, they had fought two wars against the two most powerful states of Europe—probably of the world, though extra-European comparisons were difficult. During the Revolutionary War, they had bested Britain, with help; during the recent undeclared naval war, they had fought France to a draw. Diplomatically, they had negotiated treaties with the major powers of Europe—learning the hard way, in the case of France, that treaties can be harder to get out of than get into. Politically, they had solved, or at least gone far toward solving, the problems of establishing an effective national government (not to mention the governments of the separate states). Intellectually, their ideas were catching on, modified to fit local circumstances: witness the French Revolution. Or perhaps it would have been more accurate to say that the ideas they had appropriated from the Enlightenment were being appropriated by others as well. But either way of putting the matter spoke well of America's judgment. Economically, Americans were playing a large role in the commerce of the Atlantic world: witness the efforts by both Britain and France to deny American trade to the other.

George Washington died at Mount Vernon in December 1799. He was uniformly respected and often revered by his compatriots; other nations honored him as well. On news of his death, ships of the British navy fired their guns to commemorate the great man. Washington remained alert until the last days of his life. Much of what he saw in his country—the partisan feuding between Federalists and Republicans, the tendency of politicians to place personal ambition above the public interest—he did not like. He still fretted about the alliance with France; the Convention of 1800 was months away. And he continued to warn against permanent entanglements in the affairs of foreigners. But on the whole he had to be pleased. The country had come far since the end of the Seven Years' War. If it had far to go, getting there was for a younger generation to accomplish.

Sources and Suggestions for Further Reading

Robert W. Tucker and David C. Hendrickson, *The Fall of the First British Empire: Origins of the War of American Independence* (1982), examines the crisis in the British empire that led to the American Revolution. Older but still valuable is Charles M. Andrews, *The Colonial Background of the American Revolution* (1961).

The best concise account of the diplomacy of the American Revolution is Jonathan Dull, *A Diplomatic History of the American Revolution* (1985), although Richard W. Van Alstyne, *Empire and Independence: The International History of the American Revolution* (1965) is also good. Samuel Flagg Bemis, *The Diplomacy of the American Revolution* (1957 ed.) is more thorough and slower going. Richard B. Morris, *The Peacemakers: The Great Powers and American Independence* (1965), traces the road to Paris.

Biographies of some of the founding fathers who doubled as diplomats contain considerable material on their activities as agents of American foreign policy; among those devoted especially to foreign affairs are James H. Hutson, *John Adams and the Diplomacy of the American Revolution* (1980), and Gerald Stourzh, *Benjamin Franklin and American Foreign Policy* (1954). William Stinchcombe, *The American Revolution and the French Alliance* (1969), describes the liaison with France, while Jonathan Dull, *The French Navy and American Independence* (1975) concentrates on what French sailors brought to the relationship.

For the early national period in American international affairs, Lawrence S. Kaplan, *Colonies into Nation: American Diplomacy 1763–1801* (1972), and Reginald Horsman, *The Diplomacy of the New Republic 1776–1815* (1985), afford brief introductions, as well as treating the events of the American Revolution. Frederick W. Marks III, *Independence on Trial: Foreign Affairs and the Making of the Constitution* (1986), and Abraham D. Sofaer, *War, Foreign Affairs and Constitutional Power: The Origins* (1976), discuss the influence of international affairs on the writing of the Constitution of 1787. Paul A. Varg, *Foreign Policies of the Founding Fathers* (1963), covers much of the same ground. Alexander DeConde, *Entangling Alliance: Politics and Diplomacy under George Washington* (1958); Felix Gilbert, *To the Farewell Address: Ideas of Early American Foreign Policy* (1961); and Frank T. Reuter, *George Washington's Foreign Policy* (1982), examine the Washington administration's foreign policies.

Charles R. Ritcheson, *Aftermath of Revolution: British Policy toward the United States 1783–1795* (1969), deals with the ambivalent relations between the new republic and its former master, as does Bradford Perkins, *The First Rapprochement: England and the United States 1795–1805* (1955).

Relations with France form the basis for Albert H. Bowman, *The Struggle for Neutrality: Franco-American Diplomacy during the Federalist Era* (1974), and Alexander DeConde, *The Quasi-War: Politics and Diplomacy of the Undeclared War with France 1797–1801* (1966).

Treaties of the period are dealt with in Samuel Bemis, *Jay's Treaty: A Study in Commerce and Diplomacy* (1962 ed.), and *Pinckney's Treaty: America's Advantage from Europe's Distress 1783–1800* (1960 ed.); and Jerald A. Combs, *The Jay Treaty: Political Battleground of the Founding Fathers* (1970). Daniel C. Lang, *Foreign Policy in the Early Republic: The Law of Nations and the Balance of Power* (1986); and Peggy K. Liss, *Atlantic Empires: The Network of Trade and Revolution 1713–1826* (1983), provide international context.

Chapter 3

'Twixt the Devil and the Deep Blue Sea, 1800–1823

After an exhausting third of a century, from 1763 until 1800, Americans might have hoped for a bit of rest at the beginning of the nineteenth century. Things did slow down a little between the United States and the rest of the world, but plenty happened even so. The new century had not aged three years before Jefferson doubled the size of the American domain, swallowing his small-government scruples in the process. A couple more years brought a renewal of the British-French squeeze play on American shipping. A few years beyond that the United States was in a war—a real, declared one—with Britain. The war ended as the undeclared war with France had ended: inconclusively. It left some hard feelings between the United States and Britain, but not enough to prevent the working out of an unspoken, yet understood alliance between the two English-speaking nations that was designed to keep other countries from muscling in on the Western Hemisphere. Meanwhile the United States had done some muscling itself—of Spain out of Florida.

Three features marked American foreign relations during the first quarter of the nineteenth century. One was a familiar story: the continuing struggle to defend American interests in a world of greater powers. Britain and France took a short break from fighting at the century's start, but for most of the time until 1815 the British and Napoleon were locked up in a death clinch. American merchants and shippers, trying to earn a profit as neutrals, got battered in the fighting. Thomas Jefferson tried suspending trade with the belligerents but could not make the suspension stick. James Madison took America to war, with only slightly better results.

The second feature, the expansion of American territory, was also familiar. Twenty years after the Treaty of Paris, by which Britain had used a gift of the eastern half of the Mississippi Valley to draw the United States away from France, France used a cut-rate deal on the other half of the Mississippi Valley to raise American funds to fight Britain. The Louisiana transaction proved once again that the contest between the European superpowers could be a blessing as well as a curse: it hammered American commercial activities abroad but also dropped big chunks of real estate into America's lap. In acquiring

Florida, the United States was the one that played the big power, persuading the Spanish to leave peacefully before they were thrown out.

The third feature of American foreign relations in the early part of the nineteenth century, the consolidation of presidential power, would become familiar with passing time. It was ironic, yet more meaningful for the irony, that Thomas Jefferson should discover the virtues of a strong presidency in conducting international affairs. Like many out-of-office advocates of limited central government, Jefferson found the possibilities of power, once they lay within his grasp, too tempting to resist. Building on Washington's example of presidential decisiveness in declaring American neutrality in 1793, Jefferson stretched presidential authority much further in buying Louisiana from Napoleon. His successful 1807 demand of Congress for an embargo, which summarily shut down a sizable portion of the American economy, signaled a sweeping assertion of presidential power. The War of 1812, called by its critics "Mr. Madison's war," likewise extended the president's power, as wars always do. The Monroe Doctrine, which became a pillar of American international relations, was enunciated by James Monroe simply on his authority as chief executive. Later observers would express concern, sometimes alarm, at the gathering of power in the hands of the president. Regarding international affairs, the gathering started early.

Priced to Sell: Louisiana

Modern Quebeckers, the descendants of the original French inhabitants of Canada, hold to their French culture passionately. They have long resisted assimilation into the English-speaking Canadian majority; many have agitated to separate Quebec from the rest of the country. As evidence of what would happen to them should they fail to resist the advances of Anglophonia, some have pointed to the Cajun culture of Louisiana. The Acadians—later corrupted to "Cajuns"—arrived in Louisiana after Britain captured Acadia (Nova Scotia and environs) from France at the beginning of the eighteenth century and later expelled them. Once part of the culturally dominant class in a small country, they became merely a distinctive subculture in a much larger country.

Crawfish connoisseurs will contend that worse could have happened; and those who take history with their red sauce know that the Cajun experience might have been entirely different had Napoleon not been so hard pressed for cash in 1803. France might have held on to Louisiana, the way Britain held on to Canada, until that territory was strong enough to stand on its own, the way Canada eventually was. Then the Quebecois would have had lots of Francophone cousins south of the forty-ninth parallel, and New Orleans's Mardi Gras would be even more French than it is.

But Napoleon did not care for crawfish, preferring caviar. Maybe the First Consul for Life (soon to become emperor) had not explicitly worked out his

Chronology

1800	Convention of 1800 ends hostilities with France; Louisiana returned to France by Spain
1801	American naval expedition against Tripoli
1802	Peace of Amiens between France and Britain; France suppresses revolt in Santo Domingo; U.S. Military Academy at West Point founded
1803	France sells Louisiana to United States; renewed war between France and Britain
1805	British navy defeats France at Trafalgar; Napoleon defeats Austria and Russia at Austerlitz
1806	Britain blockades France; Napoleon institutes "continental system" with Berlin decree; American Non-Importation Act
1807	*Chesapeake* affair; British orders in council; French Milan decree; American Embargo Act; Fulton's *Clermont* ascends Hudson River
1808	Congress outlaws African slave trade
1809	Non-Intercourse Act; Erskine fiasco
1810	Macon's Bill Number 2; rise of Simón Bolívar in South America leads to independence for several Spanish colonies
1811	Battle of Tippecanoe
1812	Beginning of war with Britain; Napoleon invades Russia
1813	Battle of Thames River
1814	Napoleon defeated and banished to Elba; Congress of Vienna convenes; British burn Washington; Treaty of Ghent
1815	Battle of New Orleans; American expedition against Algiers; Napoleon's Hundred Days and defeat at Waterloo
1817	Rush-Bagot agreement
1818	Convention of 1818 between U.S. and Britain; Jackson in Florida against Seminoles
1819	Adams-Onís treaty
1820	Missouri Compromise
1821	Moses Austin receives charter to colonize Texas
1823	Monroe Doctrine

Napoleon was too busy conquering Europe and seizing American ships to sit still for the rest of this portrait. *The Granger Collection*

plans for invading Russia, but he clearly had his eyes on the conquest of Europe, which sooner or later would require dealing with the czar.

For a time Napoleon had had a sweet tooth, particularly a taste for West Indian sugar. France's Caribbean colonies continued to provide France with the kind of revenues Napoleon needed to keep his armies in the field. But in the 1790s a revolt broke out in the French colony of Santo Domingo (Hispaniola: later Haiti plus the Dominican Republic). The rebels, led by François Dominique Toussaint L'Ouverture, declared independence and proceeded to treat French rule as terminated. The United States, in the middle of its Quasi-War with France, secretly sent aid to the rebels in exchange for favorable trading rights.

The revolt in Santo Domingo did more than threaten Napoleon's treasury. Ever since 1763 French expansionists had been mourning the loss of most of France's American empire to Britain and Spain. Canada was probably gone for good; if the British could not hold it, the Americans would probably seize it. Recognizing this fact, the French government in its 1778 treaty with the United States had renounced any desire to recapture Canada. But Louisiana, ceded to Spain in 1763, might be retrievable—as indicated by France's 1778 refusal to include it in the renunciation. Spain was a much less formidable foe (in fact often an ally, which proved the point) than Britain, and the United States was still far away. Yet the Americans were growing stronger, and governed as they were during the 1790s by a group hostile to France, they posed an increasing threat to French interests. If the French could regain Louisiana, they could both recapture their lost glory and hedge in the Americans. At the same time, French reacquisition of Louisiana would help even the balance with Britain.

During the late 1790s France pressured Spain to hand Louisiana back. Paris argued that the Spanish would never be able to resist American encroachment, so sparsely settled was the region with Spain's subjects and so insufficient were Spain's military forces in the area. Moreover, once the Americans moved into Louisiana, there would be nothing to prevent their moving into Mexico. Meanwhile, the British government, never satisfied with the size of British holdings, was intriguing to expand its American assets at Spain's expense as well as at the Americans'. If Spain could not defend Louisiana, France could, to the benefit of both Spain and France.

In 1800 Spain allowed itself to be persuaded by French reasoning, and in a secret treaty finalized at almost the same moment American and French negotiators concluded the Convention of 1800, Spain returned title to Louisiana to France.

France had reason to keep the treaty a secret. The Americans were acutely sensitive on the subject of Louisiana and the Mississippi River, as they had demonstrated in the negotiations leading to Pinckney's treaty, and despite the termination of the undeclared naval war, they were not particularly well disposed toward France. American border jumpers already composed a majority in certain regions of lower Louisiana. They did not particularly like Spanish rule, but since that rule in Louisiana did not amount to much, they were not ready to fight to throw it off. French rule would be a different matter. If they caught wind that France was going to take over running the territory, they would probably appeal to their compatriots back on the east side of the Mississippi and seize the place by force of arms. The American flag would be waving over New Orleans before the French could do anything about it.

In fact, rumors did surface almost at once of a secret deal between Spain and France giving Louisiana back to the French. Napoleon denied the rumors. Many Americans did not believe the denials, though a delay in the actual transfer of authority made the denials plausible. The Spanish-French treaty regarding Louisiana contained a clause saying that Spain could keep Louisiana until Napoleon handed over some territory in Italy. Unexpected difficulties prevented the French leader from following through right away, so for the time being Spanish officials continued to collect customs duties and otherwise exercise the powers of government in Louisiana.

The revolt in Santo Domingo also occasioned delay. Napoleon did not have enough troops available to put down the rebellion there and occupy Louisiana simultaneously. Common sense dictated reestablishing control in Santo Domingo before embarking on new ventures. Besides, Napoleon saw Santo Domingo, together with the other French West Indian islands, and Louisiana as complementary parts of France's western empire. Louisiana would provide the food that allowed the islands to concentrate on growing sugar. Until now most

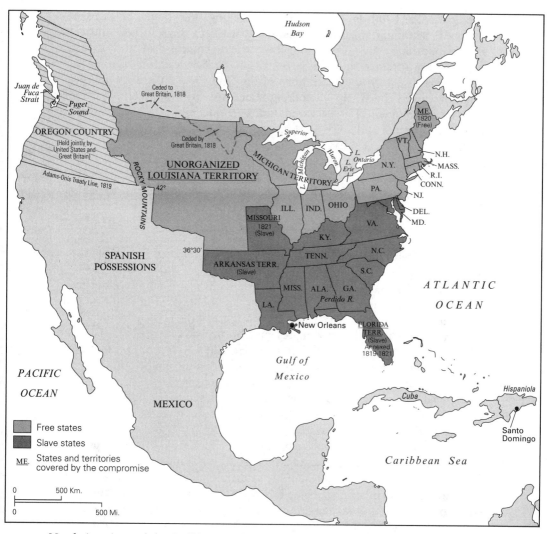

North America and the Caribbean in the 1790s

of that food had come from the United States, making the sugar islands too dependent on the Americans. Without Santo Domingo, Louisiana would lose much of its value.

Lest the revolt ruin his designs for a western empire, Napoleon dispatched a force of thirty thousand troops to the Caribbean under the command of one of his best generals, who happened to be his brother-in-law. To assist in the suppression of the Santo Domingan rebels, Napoleon tried to enlist the help of the United States.

Jefferson had mixed feelings about the French project in the Caribbean. On one side of the issue, Jefferson retained some warm sentiments toward France.

The Quasi-War had been a Federalist undertaking, and though he had said in his fence-mending inaugural address that Americans were all Federalists and all Republicans, he did not intend to carry the togetherness so far as to accept responsibility for everything his predecessors had done. Moreover, while he felt sympathy toward the aspirations of the Santo Domingans for self-determination, he could not help shuddering at the brutality that accompanied their insurrection. Besides, the rebels were mostly former slaves, and Jefferson was a white southerner and slave-holder; nothing struck terror into the hearts of white southern slave-holders more than the thought of a slave revolt.

On the other hand, Jefferson distrusted Napoleon. The French leader clearly had megalomaniacal tendencies, and he seemed bent on undoing all the good work of the French Revolution. To make matters worse, much of his megalomania appeared to be directed at the Western Hemisphere. Jefferson had strong reason to believe that the reports of the Spanish cession of Louisiana to France were true and hence that the effort to quash the rebellion in Santo Domingo might be merely the first step on the road to a revived French empire in America.

Pulled both ways, Jefferson vacillated. The president initially indicated to the French government that the United States would assist in restoring order to Santo Domingo. But once he learned of the size of the French invading force, he became convinced that this represented an invasion of the Western Hemisphere and not merely of Santo Domingo. He asked Napoleon to explain why France needed so many troops simply to deal with a local rebellion. Napoleon mumbled unpersuasively in reply, confirming American fears. When the French proclaimed a blockade of the island, Jefferson refused to honor it. He went so far in the opposite direction as to encourage the shipment of American guns and other supplies to the rebels.

Despite some early successes, including the capture of Toussaint (who was packed off to France, where he died in prison), the campaign went poorly for the French. Napoleon did not help his soldiers by ordering the reinstatement in Santo Domingo of slavery, which had been abolished throughout the French empire by the revolutionary government in Paris several years before. Knowing that the best they could hope for was a return to chains, the rebels fought harder than ever.

They gained assistance from yellow fever, one of the tropics' deadliest weapons against European imperialism (until the late nineteenth century, when medical advances largely neutralized it). The disease filled French coffins by the thousands. Between the fever and the fighting, the French lost some twenty-four thousand soldiers by the autumn of 1802.

With his army in the Caribbean melting away, Napoleon reconsidered his plans. A separate development also encouraged reconsideration. In March 1802 France had signed the Treaty of Amiens with Britain, thereby ending the most recent phase of war between the two perennial rivals. Napoleon had hoped the treaty would afford him a respite in Europe, during which he could concentrate on the affairs of the Western Hemisphere. But within a matter of months the peace started disintegrating. The British suspected Napoleon of what the French leader was in fact plotting—including France's reaggrandizement in America—as well some sins he had not contemplated. George III, still king of Britain, warned Parliament to prepare for a resumption of hostilities, which it did. Napoleon did not want to be caught off guard, and he did likewise. His American project began to seem a distraction, then a burden.

By the spring of 1803 Napoleon was ready to drop the whole thing. It had cost him tens of thousands of soldiers, a medium-sized fortune, and trouble with the United States at a moment when he was expecting worse trouble with Britain. He decided to abandon Santo Domingo to the Santo Domingans and asked the Americans whether they wished to purchase Louisiana.

The Americans liked the idea immensely, although they had not expected to be offered the whole territory. The essential part of Louisiana was the Mississippi River, and essential to the Mississippi was New Orleans. The port city of the delta had long been the key to the commerce of the Mississippi Valley, including the eastern part that already belonged to the United States. Owning New Orleans would have been nice, but as long as Americans had the right to use its docks, they did not press the issue. The central accomplishment of Pinckney's treaty had been to secure this right, and for several years after the signing of that treaty all was well. Technically, the right of deposit granted under the treaty had lapsed in 1798, but the Spanish authorities continued to let American shippers leave their cargoes on the docks unmolested. By the treaty, if the Spanish decided to terminate deposit rights at New Orleans, they had to provide equivalent rights elsewhere on the lower Mississippi.

In October 1802, however, the Spanish intendant (governor) of Louisiana summarily suspended the right of deposit at New Orleans without providing such equivalent rights. As justification, he charged the Americans with abusing the right by smuggling merchandise of various sorts into the region.

The smuggling charge was accurate, but the Americans claimed that the punishment was far out of proportion to the crime. They contended that Spanish tariffs on imports into Louisiana were stranglingly high; an honest merchant had to turn dishonest to make a living. If Spain would set the rates realistically, Americans would pay up.

But Americans were complaining too much. The Spanish action did *not* close the Mississippi to American traffic, although western shippers often spoke as if it had. Americans could still load their cargoes directly from the flatboats that brought the goods downstream onto ocean-going vessels in New Orleans harbor. They simply could not demand the use of the city's dock and warehouse facilities. Moreover, regarding certain staple items such as flour, the Spanish intendant allowed Americans to sell their products in New Orleans just as before, at a modest duty of 6 percent.

Regardless of the merits or demerits of the American complaints, the Spanish pinching of American trade on the Mississippi produced cries of pain in the United States that Jefferson could not ignore. Westerners demanded that Washington (not George, now deceased, but the new American capital) come to their rescue by forcing the Spanish to back down or preferably by seizing New Orleans. Federalists, sore from their losses in the 1800 election, always ready to strike a blow against a friend of France or an enemy of Britain, and desiring dearly to embarrass Jefferson, shouted for war against Spain.

Jefferson refused to be stampeded, despite knowing that a war against weak Spain probably would have bolstered his popularity significantly. Like the people of most nations, Americans have long been suckers for military victory, almost regardless of the caliber of the opponent. Instead, he sent representatives to Europe to find a peaceful solution to the Louisiana problem.

By now no one was bothering to disguise the fact that France held title to Louisiana. Accordingly, Jefferson instructed his envoy James Monroe to go to Paris. The president told Monroe and the American minister in Paris, Robert Livingston, to make an initial offer to buy Florida (thought perhaps to have been included in the Spanish cession to France) and New Orleans. This would have solved the Mississippi problem by giving the United States control of the east bank of the Mississippi clear to the Gulf of Mexico and thereby, under international custom, the right of navigation on the river.

If France would not or could not sell Florida, Monroe should try to buy New Orleans alone. Then at least the right of deposit would be secure. If France was not in a selling mood at all, Monroe and Livingston should try to get Napoleon to guarantee free passage of the river to American ships. Finally, if Napoleon was completely cantankerous and rejected every offer, the envoys ought to go to London. The British would surely be happy to cooperate in a scheme to knock Napoleon down a few pegs. Such a scheme might include a solution of one sort or another to America's Mississippi problem.

Monroe's and Livingston's instructions provided no guidance in the event Napoleon wanted to sell *more* of Louisiana than New Orleans, which, in fact, he did. French foreign minister Talleyrand asked the Americans to make an offer for the whole territory. He suggested 100 million francs and American assumption of new claims against France for recent seizures of American trading ships at sea. The Americans understood that the French were offering them the property deal of the century, but like good hagglers they pointed out the territory's deficiencies—including uncertainties regarding where its boundaries lay—and said the price was too high.

After more dickering the two sides cut a deal. The United States would pay 60 million francs to the French government and would assume American claims against France up to 20 million francs. At the going rate of exchange, the total of 80 million francs amounted to $15 million. In return the United States would receive Louisiana, with boundaries described only vaguely—at the insistence of the Americans, who intended to claim as much as they could against the Spanish.

Because of the deficiencies of communications at the time, the negotiations in Paris were beyond the reach of the American government in Washington. Monroe and Livingston might have asked for a few months to consult with Jefferson, but they sensed that Napoleon was in a hurry, and they feared he might change his mind unless they hurried, too. Britain and France once more were on the verge of war, which might well disrupt the talks over Louisiana. And should Britain or Spain catch on to what the Americans and French were doing, either country might try to sabotage the transfer. So Monroe and Livingston did their dealing and told Jefferson about it later.

The president was thrilled, albeit a bit concerned, too. Believing that the strength and virtue of the American republic rested on individual farmers and their families, Jefferson could not help but cheer the acquisition of enough territory to support American farmers down to the sixth or eighth generation. And the purchase of Louisiana solved the problem of navigation on the Mississippi once and for all. No longer would a foreign government be able to cut the economic lifeline that linked the interior of America to the world.

Jefferson's concerns involved the legality of the Louisiana deal. He searched his copy of the Constitution for authority to purchase land from foreign governments and attach it to the Union and found nothing that would survive a challenge. He then considered proposing a constitutional amendment granting the necessary authority, but his advisers told him to think again. Amending the Constitution, they noted, was a slow process. The expected war between Britain and France had already begun, and failure to capitalize on this wonderful opportunity might result in its slipping away.

Jefferson let himself be persuaded. Setting aside his strict-constructionist scruples, he simply presented the treaty containing the terms of the Louisiana Purchase to the Senate as though negotiating and approving such a treaty were entirely within his and the Senate's rights.

A few diehard Federalists opposed the purchase. Some cited the constitutional question—an ironic objection coming from them since the Federalists, as loose constructionists, had usually been willing to give the central government the benefit of doubts regarding authority for strong action. The Federalists' real complaints were two: that the Louisiana Purchase would be a stunning political victory for Jefferson and Republicans and that the acquisition of such an immense territory would tilt the future of America toward Jefferson's beloved farmers and away from the merchant class that formed the backbone of Federalist strength.

The Federalist critics were less correct on the second count than on the first. Although the Louisiana Purchase did improve farmers' prospects, America's business classes also gained from the opening of the interior of the continent, if somewhat more slowly than the farmers. As for the politics of the purchase, it did indeed turn out to be overwhelmingly popular; even some Federalists defected and supported it. The Senate approved the Louisiana pact by substantially more than the necessary two-thirds, and the House of Representatives quickly approved funding.

In November 1803 the Spanish finally got around to handing Louisiana over to France; the following month France delivered possession to the United States.

Republican Principles: The War of 1812

For three weeks in December 1803, the residents of Louisiana lived under the Code Napoléon, the system of laws that eventually became the French leader's most lasting contribution to world culture. The Napoleonic code represented the climax of Enlightenment thought regarding the relationship of individuals to government. In contrast to the English common-law tradition, which operated inductively, starting with specific cases and abstracting general principles from them, the Napoleonic code, like the civil-law tradition from which it sprang, operated deductively, starting with general principles and devising specific statutes from them. Common-law judgments are based on precedents, on the belief that wisdom accumulates through the efforts of generation after generation to deal with issues of justice and equity. Trial by jury of one's peers is a cardinal tenet of the common law. Civil-law judgments are based on codes like that of Napoleon and on the belief that a single group of people acting at one time is wise enough to devise a blueprint for resolving present and future conflicts. Judges, rather than juries, render the majority of decisions in the civil law. The common law serves as the basis for the legal systems of most countries that once were British colonies, including the United States; the civil law serves as the basis for the legal systems of most of continental Europe and Latin America (and the state of Louisiana). In later years, a shared attachment to the common law would help make it comparatively easy for the United States and Britain to cooperate in international affairs, especially on matters relating to international law. Americans never had such good fortune working with countries of the civil-law tradition.

Another Napoleonic innovation was less successful than his law code, and it was even more difficult for Americans to appreciate. When the peace patched together at Amiens in 1802 broke down several months later, the second hundred years' war between Britain and France moved into its final decade. The British recognized Napoleon to be by far the most threatening champion the French had ever put forward; his vaulting ambition, combined with his intuitive grasp of the principles of modern warfare and his organizational genius, dictated that he must be destroyed. (Napoleon himself was often overwhelmed by his own greatness. He once remarked to his secretary that the secretary would become immortal. The man asked why. "Are you not my secretary?" replied Napoleon. To which the candidate for immortality responded wryly, "Name Alexander the Great's secretary.")

To destroy Napoleon, Britain resorted to its tested method: the blockade. But blockading Napoleon's France was a huge undertaking, far beyond the ability of even Britain's fleet if the British abided by the blockading principles laid down by the League of Armed Neutrality during the American Revolutionary War. Aside from questions of what constituted contraband, the sticky issue regarding blockades was how close the blockading ships had to be to the harbors they were blockading. Catherine of Russia and the other armed neutrals had insisted that the blockaders be right at the harbors; that way neutral vessels could approach a harbor, assess the situation, and turn around if it was closed, without losing their ships or cargoes.

Not surprisingly, the British never accepted this interpretation, which worked in favor of land powers such as Catherine's Russia (and Napoleon's France) and against maritime powers such as Britain. Blockaders would have to deploy enough ships to close every enemy harbor; in the fight against Napoleon this meant almost every port in continental Europe. During the half decade after the renewal of hostilities, the French emperor (he had himself crowned in 1804) won a succession of brilliant battlefield victories that extended his control to most of the continent. The campaign at sea went less well: at Trafalgar in 1805 the British navy blasted the combined fleets of France and Spain. The consequence was an asymmetrical contest in which France was supreme on land, Britain at sea. For the next several years, the two rivals maneuvered to utilize their distinctive advantages against each other.

Britain's naval advantage implied the use of the blockade, but because of the great length of coastline under Napoleon's rule, this had to be a blockade at a distance rather than the close-in kind specified by Catherine's rules. By a series of executive edicts called orders in council, the British proclaimed the closing of the entire coast of Napoleon-controlled Europe (leaving open inconsequential Portugal and inaccessible Sweden and Russia). Ships that violated these orders would be considered prizes of war, subject to search and seizure. London later amended the orders to allow neutral ships to trade with Napoleon's realm but only after landing at a British port, registering their cargoes, and paying a tax.

Napoleon retaliated with some trade-tightening proclamations of his own. By decrees issued from Berlin in 1806 and Milan in 1807, the French emperor established what was called the continental system. This included a blockade of Britain and, more significant—because he had a better chance of enforcing it—a ban on visits to the Continent by ships that submitted to the British rules about stopping in Britain or allowing a search by the British navy. Violators would be subject to French seizure.

Between them, the French continental system and the British orders in council fairly well outlawed American trade with Europe. The point of neutrality during wartime is to avoid having to choose between belligerents; Napoleon and the British, engaged in a fight to the finish, were trying to force the Americans to choose.

If Jefferson and the Republicans did have to choose, they seemed likely to choose France. Their choice would reflect not so much an affinity for the French, which Napoleon was fast weakening, as an aversion to the British, who added personal injury to the pecuniary insult of the blockade. Strapped more than ever for able-bodied seamen—not least because of horrendous conditions of service ("Rum, buggery and the lash," in Winston Churchill's later summary)—the British navy searched high and low for sailors. British boarding parties found many on American ships. Some of these had deserted from the British navy; others had never seen the inside of a British man-of-war. It

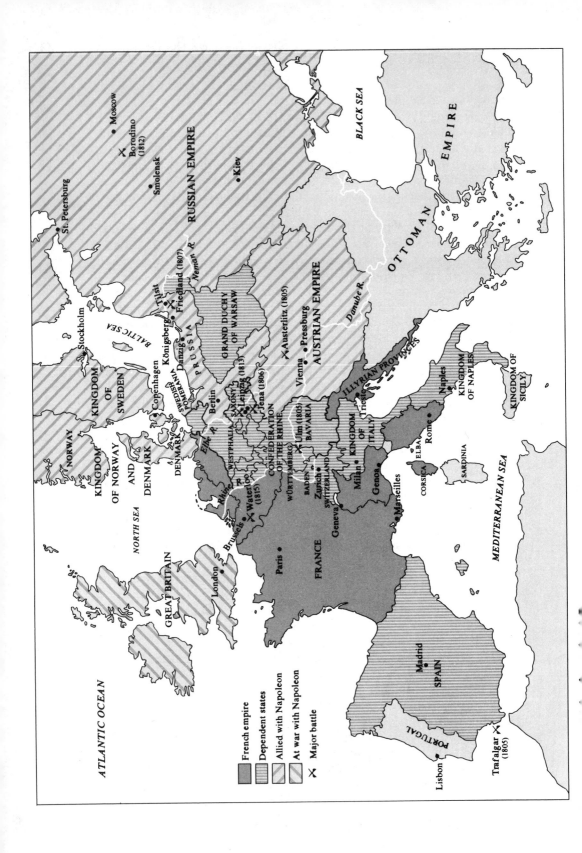

ATLANTIC OCEAN

BLACK SEA

OTTOMAN EMPIRE

RUSSIAN EMPIRE

• Moscow
✗ Borodino (1812)
• Smolensk
• Kiev

• St. Petersburg

BALTIC SEA

Stockholm •

NORWAY

KINGDOM OF SWEDEN

KINGDOM OF NORWAY AND DENMARK

Copenhagen •

DENMARK

SWEDISH POMERANIA

NORTH SEA

Tilsit •
✗ Friedland (1807)
Königsberg •
Danzig • Neman R.

PRUSSIA

GRAND DUCHY OF WARSAW

Berlin •
Elbe R.
WESTPHALIA
SAXONY
✗ Leipzig (1813)
✗ Jena (1806)

AUSTRIAN EMPIRE

Vienna •
✗ Austerlitz (1805)
• Pressburg
Danube R.

GREAT BRITAIN

London •

Brussels •
✗ Waterloo (1815)

Rhine R.
CONFEDERATION OF THE RHINE
WÜRTTEMBERG
BADEN
SWITZERLAND
Zurich •
Geneva •

✗ Ulm (1805)
BAVARIA

ILLYRIAN PROVINCES
Trieste •

FRANCE

Paris •

Marseilles •

KINGDOM OF ITALY

Milan •
Genoa •

ELBA
CORSICA
Rome •
SARDINIA

Naples •
KINGDOM OF NAPLES

KINGDOM OF SICILY

MEDITERRANEAN SEA

PORTUGAL

SPAIN

Madrid •

Lisbon •

✗ Trafalgar (1805)

French empire
Dependent states
Allied with Napoleon
At war with Napoleon
✗ Major battle

was all the same to the British captains who had been commanded to fill out their crews by whatever means necessary. In this case, the cultural similarities between America and Britain worked to America's detriment. Fifty years later, when the evolution of speaking styles and other cultural markers more clearly distinguished American nationals from British, the British would have had a harder time convincing themselves that American citizens were British fugitives; but in the first generation after American independence, American citizens and British subjects sounded, looked, and acted much alike. Moreover, the British government did not acknowledge the right of expatriation: once a British subject, always a British subject, in London's interpretation.

To most Americans of Jefferson's day, British impressment was hardly more than organized kidnapping. The British had no business stopping American vessels on the high seas; they had still less business bodily removing people from those vessels. If the removed people really were British deserters, the British actions were a travesty of legal procedure. If the removed were American citizens, the actions were a travesty of justice. (The impressed men could be both British deserters and American citizens, which complicated things.) The United States had no choice but to protest in the most vigorous language. War might not be too extreme a measure to deal with such provocation.

Jefferson himself did not want war. The United States, he feared, was not ready to take on the British. During the Revolutionary War, the United States had beaten Britain only with the help of France. Now France had other worries, and the French government was not favorably disposed toward the United States.

Initially Jefferson tried diplomatic argumentation against Britain's orders in council and the impressment of seamen from American ships. The Republican administration contended that British practice violated international law regarding blockades; Britain's long-distance blockade was not a proper blockade at all but rather was an excuse for waylaying ships doing legitimate business with European customers. Impressment was a gross violation of American sovereignty, which properly extended to American ships at sea.

Jefferson got nowhere with his protests. Britain, wielding the world's strongest navy, had no interest in a broad definition of neutral rights. The blockade was Britain's traditional weapon of choice, and British leaders had no desire to restrict its usefulness. Even if they had been willing to entertain the general idea of restrictions, they considered Napoleon dangerous enough to warrant exceptions.

The British gave no ground on the impressment issue either. They charged Americans with sheltering fugitives from British justice—a charge that was sometimes accurate. But occasional accuracy counted for less than Britain's dire need for bodies to operate its ships. With an empire at stake, British leaders did what they thought they had to; if they overstepped the niceties of legal procedure or if they picked off a few of the wrong people, that was too bad.

Jefferson's frustration grew as British violations grew more egregious. In June 1807 a British ship, the *Leopard*, drew alongside the American frigate *Chesapeake* not far out of Hampton Roads, Virginia, and demanded the right to search for deserters. The commander of the American vessel refused, where-upon the British ship fired several cannon volleys into the *Chesapeake*. The ship was disabled, three Americans were killed, and more than a dozen were wounded. The British then boarded the *Chesapeake* and carried off four sailors.

The *Chesapeake* affair shocked most Americans. Until now British assaults on American rights had been largely nonviolent and confined to private American commercial ships. In this case, however, the British attacked a ship of the American navy representing the American government and people as a whole; and they had shed American blood in the attack. The war had already started, some said; the Jefferson administration needed to admit it and fire back. If the British got away with their crime, Americans would never be able to hold their heads up again.

Jefferson still did not want a shooting war, knowing that the country was ill-prepared for it. So he opted for an economic war. At his behest the Republican-controlled Congress passed the Embargo Act of December 1807, which forbade American exports to foreign countries and barred American ships from overseas trade.

There was some logic to Jefferson's decision. The president calculated that Britain needed American goods to keep its war against Napoleon going. Once deprived of these goods, the British would soon come to their senses and straighten up. In the meantime, keeping American goods and American ships out of harm's way would diminish the chances for further affronts to American honor. It would also give the administration time to strengthen American defenses in case the British required more forceful chastening in the future. To this last purpose, Jefferson persuaded Congress to fund the building of 188 new gunboats and the renovation of some older, larger ships.

The Embargo Act generated widespread dissatisfaction. Westerners who did not care much for the profit margins of eastern merchants and shippers and who might otherwise have supported the president saw the embargo as a surrender to Britain. The merchants and shippers themselves denounced Jefferson for meddling where he had no business. It was their own money they were risking in trading with Europe, they said; if they wanted to take the risk, they ought to be able to do so. They did not have to add that they were making money hand over fist since cargoes that got through the blockade brought top dollar; presumably this part of the argument would not have moved Jefferson very far. They conceded that impressment was a problem and that the government ought to protest British actions in the matter. But cutting off all trade was like trying to cure a cold with a dose of pneumonia.

Jefferson's embargo soon proved a disaster. The export and shipping ban idled tens of thousands of sailors, dockworkers, ship-riggers, and others whose livelihoods depended on overseas commerce. "How much longer are you going to keep this damned Embargo on to starve us poor people?" a Boston man wrote to Jefferson, under the salutation "You Infernal Villain." Entire coastal communities suffered from terminal depression; some once-thriving northeastern ports such as New Haven never recovered. New Englanders talked darkly of secession. This self-induced stagnation spread to the interior as farmers who had exported cotton and wheat now watched it rot on the ground or pile up in warehouses. Although Republican almost to a man (women could not vote), the southerners and westerners found their patience with Jefferson wearing thin as their unsold surpluses grew fat.

Not only did the embargo alienate almost everyone; it did not even work. Americans had not lost their pre-independence flair for evading government regulations; some merchants slipped their cargoes out of American ports by the dark of the moon, while others sent their goods overland to Canada and thence across the Atlantic. John Jacob Astor, who was gaining a name and a start in the China trade, smuggled a ship and cargo out of port by means of an elaborate charade. One of his clerks, representing himself as "the Honorable Punqu Wingchong, a Chinese mandarin," applied for special permission to charter a ship from New York to Guangzhou (Canton), so that, he said, he could pay filial respects to his recently deceased grandfather. Jefferson, recalling a British trade and diplomatic mission to China of several years earlier that had proved a spectacular fiasco, granted the request in hopes of stealing a march on the British. In addition to chartering the ship, the purported Punqu was allowed to take with him a cargo of trade goods. The ship was long gone before Jefferson realized that he had been fooled; Astor made a killing by the ruse, which contributed materially to his emergence as the wealthiest person in America.

Finally, to the incomplete extent that the embargo did work, it was highly debatable whether it hurt the British more than it helped them. British textile manufacturers suffered from the cutoff of American cotton, and the British West Indies suffered from the loss of American food supplies; but because the British controlled the seas, they could probably find alternative suppliers if the embargo lasted very long. Blockaded France, in contrast, had far fewer prospects in this regard; French losses from the American embargo could not be made up so easily. Under the dire circumstances confronting Britain in its fight against Napoleon, London considered beneficial almost anything that hurt France.

Like most proud people, Jefferson did not enjoy admitting his mistakes. And his hold over the Republican party was such that he would not let Congress admit his mistake for him. For fourteen long months, the embargo remained in effect. Only in the last days of Jefferson's second administration did Congress repeal the act, replacing it with the impressive-sounding but largely toothless Nonintercourse Act of 1809. (Some Americans and doubtless more than a few British perceived a parallel with the replacement of the Stamp Act by the Declaratory Act in 1766.) The Nonintercourse Act continued the American embargo against both Britain and France and their colonies but opened American trade with other countries. In practice the latter part of the act gave American shippers a ready opportunity to trade with Britain and France: they could leave American ports saying they were bound for St. Petersburg or Buenos

Aires and then change their minds at sea and head for Britain or France. They still had to deal with the British blockade and the French restrictions, but they had been willing to risk dealing with those all along.

The Nonintercourse Act was not entirely a face-saving gesture. It included a clause empowering the president to rescind the measure as it applied to Britain if the British decided to respect American shipping or as it applied to France if the French did.

There was a problem with this part of the act, however. The president would have to settle for a mere declaration of Britain's or France's intent to repent since no American vessels were supposed to be currently trading with either country. (The French in fact used this specious supposition against the Americans. They seized American ships with impunity, saying the ships must really be British vessels because American law forbade American ships from trading with Britain.)

The law invited confusion, which soon arose. James Madison, early in his first term as president, negotiated a deal with the British minister in Washington according to which Britain would repeal its orders in council in exchange for a continuation of the American embargo against France. This satisfied the terms of the Nonintercourse Act, and it satisfied Madison. Unfortunately, it did not satisfy the British minister's boss. British foreign secretary George Canning wanted the Americans to agree to a rule the British had invented during the Seven Years' War, to the effect that neutrals should not expand trade during wartime to countries they had not traded with beforehand. British merchants were behind the measure: it employed the British navy to protect their market shares against encroaching neutrals. Canning also demanded the right to enforce America's own Nonintercourse Act—against France, obviously.

The British minister failed to inform Madison of Canning's conditions, and the president agreed to lift the embargo against Britain without consenting to them. In the spring and early summer of 1810, hundreds of American ships filled with merchandise for Britain weighed anchor and set off east. The British government let the ships land their welcome cargoes in British ports and then closed the trade once again. Canning declared that until the Americans accepted his conditions, the orders in council would stand.

Madison came away from the affair embarrassed and angry. When the Nonintercourse Act expired, he arranged its replacement by something called Macon's Bill Number Two. This law opened American trade with Britain and France but allowed the president to reimpose the export ban against either country should the other begin acting more honorably toward the United States. The test for Britain was to lift the orders in council; for France, to withdraw the Berlin and Milan decrees.

This time Napoleon embarrassed Madison. The French government announced that it would withdraw the decrees and stop seizing American ships provided that the Americans forced the British to respect American neutral rights. There was some confusion, however, regarding whether the repeal of the decrees would precede Britain's respecting of American rights or follow it. Madison, frustrated at Britain, chose to ignore the confusion, and in the autumn of 1810 he declared that nonintercourse would resume against Britain if the British did not drop their orders in council within three months. Madison's deadline came and went, and the British did not comply. Napoleon, citing the failure of the Americans to force the British to respect American rights, considered himself relieved of his commitment. French seizures of American vessels continued, albeit at a reduced rate. Madison wound up red in the face again. Somewhat surprisingly, however, he overlooked the French depredations and persisted with the ban on exports to Britain.

American troubles regarding trade and impressment persisted, and they appeared likely to persist as long as the war between Britain and France did. Whether they would have sufficed to provoke American entry into that war on one side or the other is an open question. In fact, other irritations and other interests contributed to the American decision to go to war in 1812—against Britain, if not exactly on the side of France.

Westerners still had complaints against Britain on the subject of relations with the Indians on the frontier. After a time of relative quiet following the 1795 Treaty of Greenville, friction had resumed as whites pushed ever deeper into territory occupied by the Indians. During the first part of the nineteenth century, the friction grew most intense in the aptly named territory of Indiana. Two Shawnee leaders (and brothers), Tecumseh and the Prophet, embarked on an ambitious plan for uniting Indians to resist the pressure of white expansion. British traders and officials across the border in Canada did not play a major

Tecumseh and Prophet, two charismatic Shawnee politicians, forged an unlikely alliance of Indian tribes against encroachment by white settlers. Outgunned, the alliance collapsed after the battle of Tippecanoe. *The Granger Collection (Prophet)*

part in the Indian effort, but neither did they see any reason to oppose something that might slow American expansion, which, not incidentally, threatened Britain's hold on Canada. The Indian resistance evoked greater pressure by the white Americans, and in 1811 the two sides fought a major battle on the banks of Tippecanoe Creek. The whites, led by Indiana governor William Henry Harrison, defeated the Indians while suffering many casualties themselves. (Americans remembered the victory more than the casualties and later rewarded Harrison with the presidency.) Afterward Tecumseh, hoping to revive his fortunes, applied more directly for help to the British, who did not turn him away.

In the view of many Americans, the British were the principal villains in this performance: the Indians were just savages who could be expected to act like savages until forced to do otherwise, while the British were civilized whites who ought to know better. Recommendations for dealing with British crimes on the Indian question ranged from punitive raids against British forts in Canada to the conquest of Canada.

Calls for the conquest of Canada fit in with a growing sense that America's destiny was to overspread the entire North American continent. Before the Revolutionary War, such thoughts had occurred to only the most deluded; but the 1783 acquisition of the territory between the Appalachians and the Mississippi put the idea of a continental future into many American heads. Contributing to the plausibility of this idea was the fact that the eastern Mississippi Valley more or less fell into American hands without great effort on Americans' part. God (acting through London in this case) seemed to have something big in mind for the new republic. The Louisiana Purchase reinforced both the notion of American continentalism and the belief that it was divinely ordained. Out of the blue the American domain doubled in size; could anyone doubt that further growth was in store?

Canada appeared a likely next addition to the United States. The population there was thin and the resources immense—a perfect combination for an American takeover. One Republican representative from New Hampshire predicted that under American control Canada could easily support 4 million inhabitants. "This great outlet of the northern world should be at our command, for our convenience and future security," he declared. Another Republican, a Tennessean, urged the conquest of Canada as a blow simultaneously against the British and the Indians. "We shall drive the British from our continent," he said. "They will no longer have an opportunity of intriguing with our Indian neighbors, and setting on the ruthless savage to tomahawk our women and children." Some of the expansionists thought the Canadians would cooperate in the transfer of title from Britain to the United States; who in their right minds would want to live under British colonial rule? But if the Canadians did not cooperate, the transfer might be effected by American arms.

American expansionists also had their sights on Florida. Broad constructionists of the hazy boundary clauses of the Louisiana Purchase agreement contended that the United States already owned at least the western part of Florida. Because of the secrecy that had surrounded French and Spanish dealings regarding Louisiana, hard facts about who had owned what were hard to come by.

More than an itch for land inspired American interest in Florida. Southerners living near the border with Florida had complaints similar to those of westerners about the British in Canada: that they were abetting Indian attacks on American settlements or at the minimum were doing nothing to prevent such attacks. Americans might and in some cases did chase Indians across the border for purposes of chastisement, but the American frontier with Florida would never be secure, the southern expansionists said, until it was erased—until Florida became part of the United States.

Other considerations colored the desire for Florida. From a strategic perspective control of Florida would add immensely to American security. So long as Florida remained in foreign hands, it remained in potentially hostile hands. Whatever foreign country held Florida, particularly the splendid harbor of Pensacola, could jeopardize the approaches to the Mississippi and thereby the safety and prosperity of what by now had become the majority of American territory. At the moment, Spain claimed Florida. But if war broke out between the United States and Britain, as seemed increasingly likely, the British would probably occupy Florida and use it for operations against the United States. The threat was intolerable.

Furthermore, the addition of Florida to the United States would help maintain the balance of political power between the slave South and the by now nonslave North. On present trends the territory above the Ohio River would never have slaves; nor would most of the Louisiana territory. Sooner or later those regions would become states and would send senators and representatives to Congress. Slave-holders had more or less reconciled themselves to the loss of the House of Representatives because its membership was based on population and because the population of the North was growing much faster than the population of the South. But the South might hold its own in the Senate, where representation was by states, and in that chamber might block unfriendly legislation. Florida, a likely place for slaves, would help in the holding.

A final element added to the momentum for war. Everybody gets tired of being pushed around; Americans, after being caught in the quarrels of Britain and France for 20 years (120 years, if one counted the colonial period), were no exceptions. But Americans had an extra reason for not wanting to be bullied. After the collapse of the French republic into Napoleonic despotism, the United States was a lonely republic in an unfriendly world. By the time Napoleon showed his true colors, attempting the conquest of all of Europe, the Enlightenment had essentially run out of steam; the view that people could manage their own affairs by the light of reason was getting increasingly hard to justify. Perhaps people could handle their domestic affairs, though the French experience made one wonder. But in the predatory world of international relations, only the strong survived, and the strongest countries seemed to be the countries with the strongest rulers. Napoleon was gobbling up

Europe; the only significant state on the Continent he had not subdued was Russia, with a czar who was every bit as despotic as the French emperor. In this bleak context, the ability of America to defend itself assumed extra significance. If America failed, faith in human rationality and self-responsibility would probably fail, too. The monarchists, the religious zealots, and all the other cynical preachers of human fallibility and original sin would claim victory. The principle of republicanism—after which the Republican party of Jefferson and Madison took its name—might disappear from the earth forever.

Motivated by this mixture of covetousness and altruism, Americans moved steadily toward war during 1811 and 1812. Had neutral rights been the only issue, the United States might have gone to war against France as well as Britain: both countries stood stubbornly by their policies of trying to deny American trade to the other. But Britain's list of crimes also included impressment, incitement of Indians, ownership of Canada, and a greater capacity for making trouble from Florida. It would have required sheer stupidity for the American government to take on Britain and France simultaneously; as during the Revolutionary War, the only hope for victory lay in the fact that whichever country the United States declared war on would be fighting its historic rival at the same time.

Strong though the momentum for war was by the beginning of 1812, it could have been turned aside had the technology of long-distance communication been more advanced. After nearly ten years of unsuccessfully trying to put Napoleon down, the British were reconsidering their strategy. Even more than the Americans, the British were a people who lived by trade. The orders in council had hit British businesses and British consumers harder than they had hit the Americans: British manufacturers were complaining of lost export markets and sources of supply, British workers were complaining of lost jobs, and British homemakers were complaining of high prices and empty shelves. The British government finally succumbed to the pressure of these complaints. On June 16, 1812, the government announced that it was lifting the orders in council.

It was too late—or it would be by the time the news of the lifting reached America. Congress was already debating the necessity for war against Britain; on the second day after the British announcement, the legislature voted in favor of a war declaration.

The favorable vote was hardly overwhelming: 19 to 13 in the Senate, 79 to 49 in the House of Representatives. It split sharply along party lines: every Federalist voted against the war, while the great majority of Republicans voted for it. The decision was also ominously sectional: 49 of the 62 negative votes came from the northeastern states, while only 13 came from the West or South.

These partisan and sectional differences regarding the war threatened to tear the country apart. Many northeasterners believed that the Madison administration was sacrificing their interests to appease southern and western warhawks—young hotheads such as John Calhoun of South Carolina and Henry Clay of Kentucky. New England merchants and shippers refused to back the war effort and went so far as to trade with the British. The British, recognizing

Andrew Jackson (seated heroically on the white charger) directs the defense of New Orleans. Off canvas, a ship is racing from Europe with the news that the war is over and the battle is unnecessary. *The Granger Collection*

the division in America, tried to exacerbate it; during the first two years of the war, while British warships blockaded most of the American coastline, the British navy let the New Englanders carry on their illegal commerce. Needless to say, people in other parts of the United States were incensed, and when British troops landed in Maine, the Madison administration made little effort to throw them out. The divisiveness escalated to the point where important voices in the New England states started talking about secession, complaining that the government in Washington no longer represented them. Representatives to an 1814 convention of regional political leaders at Hartford did not quite recommend leaving the Union, but they did advocate making sweeping changes to the federal Constitution that would give their section a veto over commercial legislation and declarations of war. To those people in other parts of the country who were actively supporting the war effort, the Hartford convention smelled of sour grapes at best, sedition or treason at worst.

Wars that go well and quickly rarely get controversial, in America or elsewhere. One of the reasons the War of 1812 grew so controversial was that it went neither well nor quickly. The war faction in Congress spoke as though taking Canada would be a job for a couple of companies of Kentucky riflemen; when three major invasion attempts fell short, in fact resulting in the loss of territory on the *American* side of the border, much of the hot air hissed out of American ambitions, and finger pointing began. Although American naval forces on the Great Lakes gave a good account of themselves, American vessels in the Atlantic and the Caribbean were greatly overmatched. During the summer of 1814, a British force sailed up Chesapeake Bay and took Washington from behind. The British troops burned the Capitol building and the White House; the Madisons escaped from the latter just hours before the invaders arrived.

For all the drama of the sack of Washington, the War of 1812 was strangely lackadaisical. The British had never been excited about fighting the Americans; they were still preoccupied with France. In 1812 Napoleon invaded Russia, gambling to win Europe on the czar's home field. He captured Moscow in good time; but then winter set in. The icy weather ravaged his troops and compelled him to retreat. The Grand Army, as it was called, melted away—or rather froze—as it traveled west, succumbing to cold, hunger, and harassment by czarist troops. Seeing Napoleon's weakness, his allies deserted him, and his enemies took heart. By March 1814 it was all over. An anti-French coalition captured Paris and required Napoleon to abdicate.

(Actually it was not quite over. In 1815 the ex-emperor escaped Elba, his place of exile, and returned to France. For a glorious few months—the Hundred Days—he played an encore. But his enemies remobilized and in June 1815 defeated him at Waterloo in Belgium.)

Once the British defeated Napoleon—the first time, in the spring of 1814—they lost most of their reason for doing the obnoxious things they had been doing to the Americans. The blockade had been a weapon in the war against France; impressment had been a device to keep British ships operating during that war.

On the American side, once the expansionists discovered they could not drive the British out of Canada, they lost much of their enthusiasm for the fight. Some victories over Britain's Indian allies, including one near Lake Erie that resulted in the death of Tecumseh (whom the British had made a brigadier general), shattered the Indian confederacy and helped satisfy the frontier folks' need to feel secure.

Americans lost still more enthusiasm in the spring of 1814 when they learned that Britain and its European allies had defeated Napoleon. Until this time the British had not been able to put their best soldiers in the field against the Americans; now they could. There was even talk of sending the duke of Wellington, the hero of the Peninsular War against France in Spain, to America to take charge of the campaign against the Americans.

Fortunately for the Americans, Wellington turned down the government's offer. The Iron Duke replied that what Britain was missing in the war against the Americans was not a general or sufficient troops but naval superiority on the Great Lakes. "The question is whether we can acquire this," he said. "If we cannot, I shall do you but little good in America." When it became evident that the government could not or would not achieve superiority on the lakes, Wellington recommended peace negotiations. He added for good measure, "I think you have no right from the state of the war to demand any concession of territory from America."

Informal discussions between American and British diplomats regarding an end to the war had been going on almost since the first battle; after Wellington's recommendation the tempo of the discussions picked up. They never exactly raced, since the British were far more interested in concurrent negotiations at Vienna regarding the creation of a post-Napoleonic structure of European international relations. But eventually the two sides reached an agreement. The Treaty of Ghent, signed on December 24, 1814, at a small town in Belgium, ended the war on terms of *status quo ante bellum*—the way things were before the war. The British agreed to relinquish the territorial gains they had made during the fighting; the Americans dropped claims regarding seized shipping and demands for a renunciation of impressment. The American dream of annexing Canada was so far gone as not to merit even mention.

It was a tepid end to a war begun with great heat. The one thing that made the treaty at all palatable had nothing to do with the treaty but much to do with the still slow nature of communications. Early in January 1815, while news of the treaty's signing made its painstaking way across the winter Atlantic, American forces under General Andrew Jackson met and routed a British force approaching New Orleans. In a war that had not produced much for Americans to cheer about, Jackson's victory at New Orleans, which made him a national hero, cast a bright glow across an otherwise gloomy landscape. The reports from New Orleans reached Washington and the rest of the American east coast before the news from Ghent, tempting the Madison administration to put a better face on the treaty than the treaty deserved. The president and his advisers succumbed to the temptation; the administration and its supporters claimed Jackson's victory as their own and asserted that the Ghent treaty represented a proud vindication of the principles of both republicanism and Republicanism. The Senate, happy to have the war over, approved the treaty unanimously.

Florida and Other Loose Ends

Although the War of 1812 cooled American ardor for Canada—not least by demonstrating that the vast majority of Canadians did not want to join the United States, incomprehensible as such a position might be to Americans—it only inflamed the American desire for Florida. After the purchase of Louisiana in 1803, the Jefferson administration had begun arguing its interpretation of Louisiana's boundaries as including Florida. Spain did not buy the American argument, and Jefferson did not press the issue. But American settlers did. Illegally they moved across the border into Spanish territory and staked out claims. By 1810 they had grown restive of Spanish authority, little attention though they paid to it, and in that year they staged a revolt. They seized Baton Rouge (then part of Florida) and proclaimed a republic. The republic, which comprised—to the extent it comprised anything at all—only the western half of Florida, from the Perdido River to the Mississippi, soon declared itself part of the United States. The Madison administration did not complain about the transfer, but Spain did. Yet because Spain was currently being fought over and in by the British and the French, Madrid did nothing to put substance into its complaint. Once more Europe's troubles helped add territory to the United States: by 1812 West Florida was effectively American.

Seizing East Florida took a bit longer. During the War of 1812, certain Indian tribes in Alabama, most notably the Creeks, sided with the British, just as Tecumseh's confederacy did in the Northwest. The Anglo-Creek alliance gave the Americans what minor excuse they felt they needed to launch a military campaign against the Creeks. Andrew Jackson, who usually needed no excuse whatsoever to do what he wanted, led a band of Tennessee volunteers, in league with some of the Creeks' Indian enemies, against the Creeks in the autumn of 1813. The campaign succeeded in breaking the back of Creek military power and, equally to the point of the expedition, opening up most of Alabama to white settlement.

Jackson did not catch quite all the Creeks in Alabama; some jumped the line into East Florida. When these linked up with a British commando group that had landed in Pensacola, Jackson decided to kill two birds with one stone. He crossed the border with his troops—without asking permission from either Spanish or American officials—and thrashed the Anglo-Creek force, which also included a number of blacks who had escaped from slavery in the United States. (Make that three birds with one stone.) He proceeded to take Pensacola.

Jackson subsequently went on to New Orleans and fame, but he did not forget Florida. After the war, when the American government began negotiations with Spain over the future of East Florida, a principal argument in the American diplomatic arsenal was that the Spanish had shown themselves unable to keep order in their territory, to the detriment of American interests and the hazard of American lives. Lately members of the Seminole tribe had tangled with Americans tracking runaway slaves near the border; one thing led to another and a group of Seminoles raided communities on the American side. Jackson again enlisted for service. This time with the permission (he claimed) of the American government, he crossed over into Florida to punish the Seminoles. He captured some Seminole leaders and for emphasis arrested two British traders working the Florida territory.

Had Jackson gone no further, most of the ensuing ruckus would not have occurred. But he decided to teach the British, the Spanish, and anyone else who might be paying attention a lesson in Indian relations. He hanged one of the British merchants and shot the other after charging the pair with inciting the Indians to attack Americans. He also hanged two Seminole leaders. (Jackson was not prejudiced against foreigners or Indians in his summary treatment of troublemakers. When he had taken command of the Tennessee militia in the War of 1812, desertion was a chronic problem. Jackson quickly cured the malady by executing a few who tried to de-enlist without permission.) Jackson then marched to Pensacola. He captured the town again and threw out the

Spanish governor. Mightily pleased with himself, Jackson went home to Tennessee and another hero's welcome.

The Spanish were incensed at Jackson's violation of their territory; the execution of the traders provoked the British as well. The Seminoles presumably were upset, too, but they were easier to ignore. Yet though the London newspapers called for a stern response to this latest American outrage, the British foreign secretary, Lord Castlereagh, was not about to let British policy be deflected by the fate of two British subjects engaged in dubious activities on Spanish soil in America's backyard. He let the Americans off with a warning.

The administration of James Monroe hardly needed the warning, being irritated itself at Jackson's highhanded actions. Secretary of War John Calhoun contended that the general had exceeded orders and called for a court-martial. Speaker of the House Henry Clay reminded the president that Julius Caesar had also got his start chasing bandits in the provinces.

Of Monroe's close advisers, only John Quincy Adams supported Jackson's deeds. Adams detested Jackson personally, but the secretary of state correctly judged that the British would not take any serious action against the United States, and he argued that the Spanish would learn something useful from the affair.

What the Spanish learned, as if they did not already know, was that they had already lost Florida to the United States. Defending Florida by sea against an America that could send troops there by land was an impossible task. Keeping out the thousands of Americans who hungered after Florida's land would be equally hard. There were too many of them and not enough Spanish soldiers. In any event, those Spanish soldiers were needed elsewhere; half of Latin America was in revolt against Spain.

For some time Adams had been negotiating with the Spanish minister in Washington, Luis de Onís, regarding the future of Spain. Jackson's escapade provided Adams with the clincher to the argument he had been making: that Spain could not hold Florida and would be better off turning it over to the United States. The recent events left Onís with no choice but to agree. Yet he could not take home a treaty that simply gave Florida away; he would lose his job, and the Spanish government would refuse to accept the treaty. He proposed that the United States compensate Spain for Florida by assuming claims of American citizens against Spain totaling around $5 million, by renouncing whatever rights to Texas the United States might have acquired by the Louisiana Purchase, and by refusing to recognize the independence of the Latin American republics that were in revolt against Spain.

Adams said he would accept all but the last part of the deal—How could a country born of an anticolonial revolt refuse to recognize countries trying to follow the American example?—if Spain threw in its claims to the Oregon country. Onís agreed, Oregon being at the back of beyond as far as Spain was concerned and Spain not holding a very good claim to it anyway.

The two men signed the Adams-Onís Treaty (sometimes called the Transcontinental Treaty) in February 1819. (See map p. 77.) Onís had nearly underestimated the amount of sweetening the Florida bargain would take for the Spanish government to swallow it; Madrid required two years to choke it down. But in 1821 it closed the deal, thereby closing a chapter of American troubles with Spain (only a chapter: the book had another eighty years to go) and, not incidentally, improving America's claim to Pacific frontage property.

America's First Hostage Crisis: The Barbary Pirates

The end of the War of 1812 allowed the solution of another problem that had beset American leaders even longer than Florida had. For centuries the Arab-ruled states along the north coast of Africa—the Barbary states—had practiced piracy. From Algiers, Tunis, Tripoli, and other ports, small but fast ships set forth into the Mediterranean and Atlantic and waylaid merchant vessels of the European countries. The pirates seized cargoes and ships and sold them for profit; they captured crews and held them for hostage. It was a lucrative business that kept inhabitants of the Barbary states employed and the rulers of those states supplied with revenues.

Occasionally the navies of the victimized European powers launched punitive raids against the pirates and their bases of operation, but usually the governments of Britain, France, and the other countries found it cheaper to pay off the pirates. In exchange for a regular stipend, the ruler of a particular state would keep the pirates of his country away from the ships of the stipend-paying power. The situation would satisfy everyone for a time until the pirates pushed their price beyond what the market would bear. The Europeans would balk, piracy would recommence, the Europeans would stage reprisals, the two sides would make a new bargain, and peace would return. As an additional consideration, the profitability of piracy waxed and waned according to the state of relations among the European great powers. When the Europeans were fighting each other and were unwilling to cooperate against the pirates, prices and profits rose; when the Europeans were at peace, prices and profits fell.

As long as the American colonies were part of the British empire, they benefited from the protection London bought from the pirates; but once the United States declared independence, the benefits ceased. During the 1780s buccaneers working the Barbary coast hijacked American vessels and threw American sailors into dungeons or lashed them to the oars of the local governors' galleys. In 1787 the Confederation government worked out a deal with Morocco, buying protection from the pirates operating out of that country. In 1792 Congress appropriated funds to ransom American sailors held captive in Algiers and to purchase the cooperation of the Algerian pirates, but the deal fell through before being consummated. The depredations in that area continued until 1796, when the Washington administration arranged an agreement with the ruler of Algiers. For somewhat less than $1 million, the United States got back more than one hundred hostages and received a promise of free passage for American ships.

But the problem would not go away. Other pirates interpreted this pact as evidence that the American government had a soft heart and deep pockets and therefore that taking Americans hostage was a profitable line of work. The governor of Tripoli authorized attacks on American vessels, hoping to raise the stakes with the Americans and improve his profit margins. At the beginning of the nineteenth century, he went so far as to declare war on the United States.

For a while the war did not amount to much, mostly because America's ability to fight a war clear across the Atlantic did not amount to much; but in 1804 Jefferson sent a naval squadron against Tripoli. Jefferson did not dignify the action by asking Congress for a declaration of war; as in the case of the Louisiana Purchase, he was willing as president to loosen his construction of the constitutional powers of the office of chief executive. The American squadron pulled into Tripoli's harbor and bombarded the city. The raid was noisy, yet less than completely successful; one American frigate was captured and its crew imprisoned. A subsequent commando operation succeeded in torching the captured ship, which the pirates were outfitting for their own use, but left the Americans rotting in Tripoli's dungeons.

A third try got better results. From Alexandria in neighboring Egypt, a group of American soldiers and some friendly Egyptians marched overland to Derna, a town on the Tripolitan coast. In cooperation with American naval vessels attacking from the sea, the contingent captured the town. The ruler of Tripoli, evidently deciding that the Americans meant business, decided to negotiate a peace treaty—for a price. He returned the American prisoners and agreed to

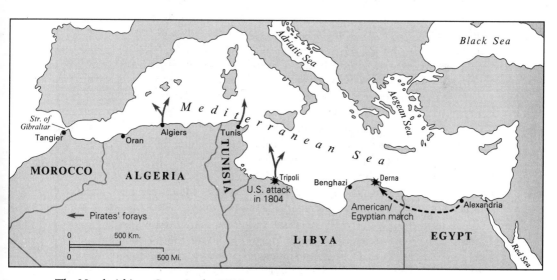

The North African Coast in the 1800s

leave American shipping alone; in exchange the United States paid him sixty thousand dollars.

This solution, however, proved no more definitive than earlier ones. Troubles continued sporadically during the next several years. But until 1815 American merchants and the American government had other things to worry about than the pirate-princes of Barbary—Napoleon and the British fleet, for example.

After the signing of the Treaty of Ghent, the Madison administration made solving the Barbary problem a priority. The solution came easier than before, primarily because the navy the United States had built to fight the British was available for thrashing the pirates. The pirates recognized what they would be up against and chose to make peace. A task force of ten American warships visited the Barbary coast, showed its cannons, and extracted promises of good behavior.

This time the promises stuck, partly because the pirates feared that the cannons would go off if the Americans returned, but mostly because the end of the Napoleonic wars put the powers of Europe in a mood to cooperate in cleaning up the Mediterranean. The business of piracy had thrived on the long hostilities between Britain and France. With peace, the piracy business entered a period of sharp decline.

Parallel But Not the Same: The Monroe Doctrine

The end of the Napoleonic wars made all manner of settlements possible. Beyond the agreements with Spain and the Barbary states, the American government soon resolved several additional, relatively minor disputes with Britain. One involved naval armaments on the Great Lakes. Some of the bitterest fighting of the War of 1812 had occurred on the Great Lakes; most of this fighting had gone well for the United States, chiefly because the British could not bring their big ships up the rapids of the St. Lawrence and over the falls of the Niagara. In the aftermath of the war, the British were in another of their cost-cutting moods. The fleet on the Great Lakes seemed a good place to start.

Americans have generally held the view that military forces are useful in time of war but an unnecessary expense in time of peace; like the British, they were in no frame of mind after 1815 to maintain a big navy on the Great Lakes. This coincidence of thriftiness allowed the signing of America's first arms control agreement: the Rush-Bagot pact of 1817. Under the terms of this executive agreement (an agreement concluded on the authority of the president alone; not as important as a treaty and not requiring Senate consent), the United States and Britain essentially demilitarized the Great Lakes. Each side got to keep a few patrol boats to catch smugglers and pirates, but serious warships went to the scrapyard. (The Senate liked the arrangement so well that it went ahead and approved it anyway.)

A second pact, the Convention of 1818, chiefly concerned the location of the border between the western portion of the United States and the western part of Canada. By the Louisiana Purchase, the United States presumably acquired title to all the land in the western half of the Mississippi drainage. This was a neat theoretical description, but in 1803 no one had anything but the foggiest notion of what it included. The Lewis and Clark expedition of 1804–1806, which ascended the Missouri River, the major tributary of the Mississippi, to its headwaters in the Rocky Mountains and then descended the Snake and Columbia rivers to the Pacific, cleared up much of the mystery. Yet considerable scope for creative cartography remained, especially regarding the region between the Lake of the Woods (a couple hundred miles west of Lake Superior) and the crest of the Rockies.

Where geography spoke ambiguously, the diplomats entered. It aided their efforts that almost no one (no white people, that is) lived in the area in question. They got out their maps and their straightedges and drew a line along the forty-ninth parallel. This they pronounced the boundary. Some of the cartographer-diplomats desired to extend their line clear to the Pacific, but such an extension would have divided the Oregon country, which both Britain and the United States wanted entire. Each side hoped its position in Oregon would improve with time, and the two parties agreed to postpone a decision on Oregon for ten years. During that period both Americans and British could trade, settle, and do whatever else they chose to do there.

The Convention of 1818 included a few other items in addition to the U.S.-Canadian boundary and Oregon. The one that lived the longest in Anglo-American diplomacy involved fishing rights in the Atlantic. Although fishing was not as central to the American economy as it had been at the time of the 1783 treaty with Britain, it remained a big item in the economy of the New England states. Monroe desired to reunite the country after the divisiveness of the War of 1812, and with the Federalists weaker than ever after their flirtation with secession, he hoped to pick up some votes in the Northeast. Adams, a Massachusetts man, had never lost sight of the importance of the codfish. The 1818 agreement assured Americans perpetual access to the fishing banks off Newfoundland and Labrador. It also granted Americans certain rights regarding the collection of firewood and the drying of fish along the shore. Because the diplomats knew even less about fishing than about geography, they neglected certain other issues, such as bait-purchasing privileges, that should have been dealt with. Maybe that was just the diplomats' way of making sure they would have work for the next hundred years—which, on the cod question, they did.

Between them, the Rush-Bagot accord of 1817 and the Convention of 1818 revealed a remarkable degree of cooperativeness between the United States and Britain. This cooperativeness was all the more remarkable given that just a few years earlier the two nations had been fighting a bitter war. To some extent, this change of attitude derived from a change of personnel. Never in the history of Anglo-American relations have the foreign affairs of the two countries simultaneously been in better hands. The United States has never had a more adept secretary of state than John Quincy Adams, a cold fish of a man (some observers suggested that his personality gave him special insight into the cod question) who never let emotion cloud his view of where American interests lay. Lord Castlereagh, the British foreign secretary (and a man after Adams's cold heart who was known for having few friends), likewise adopted a pragmatic, passionless, but perceptive approach to foreign affairs.

Yet regardless of their personal gifts (and limitations), what made Adams and Castlereagh so effective as diplomats was their ability to see clearly what the interests of their respective countries required. And what made for the smooth relations between the United States and Britain during the two men's terms in office was their grasp of the parallelism of American and British interests.

The parallelism was not obvious. Americans were especially touchy about anything that smacked of bowing to their former colonial master, and the American political system, nearing the end of its transition from the proper republicanism of George Washington's day to the raucous democracy of Andrew Jackson's, rewarded candidates who waved the bloody shirt against perfidious Albion. Many people in Britain were still sore at having lost the American colonies and thought the rambunctious Yanks ought to be reminded of their proper place.

But Adams and Castlereagh, being unemotional types, saw beneath the surface froth. Castlereagh looked at Britain's partners at the Congress of Vienna, the peace conference convened to draw the map of post-Napoleonic Europe, and realized what a reactionary lot they were. The strongest personality at the congress, Prince Metternich of Austria, was the most reactionary. Metternich believed that the restoration of monarchy was the precondition for lasting peace in Europe, and he advocated that the right-thinking monarchies combine to crush revolution and other challenges to the status quo wherever they occurred. Czar Alexander I of Russia, another dominant figure at Vienna, agreed with Metternich. Alexander sponsored the creation of the Holy Alliance, a club that eventually included nearly all the monarchs of Europe and took as its goal the suppression of nationalism and other destabilizing dissent.

Castlereagh was no radical—far from it—but the British foreign secretary recognized that Britain's constitutional monarchy did not pass muster in the eyes of Metternich and Alexander and the other Holy Allies. (Britain also failed to pass muster with Metternich in matters of culture. The Austrian prince complained that even the most educated English spoke French, the language of culture and diplomacy, abominably. "The common people of Vienna speak French better than the educated men of London," Metternich complained to a British diplomat. To which the British diplomat replied, "That may be so, but Your Highness will recall that Bonaparte has not been twice in London to teach them.") The Holy Allies could not help seeing Britain as an ideological threat, an example to the other peoples of Europe of what they might aspire to. For his part, Castlereagh similarly saw the Holy Alliance as a danger. Britain wished to ensure a balance of power on the European conti-

John Quincy Adams was America's greatest secretary of state and one of its least successful presidents. He spent his final years in the House of Representatives, stubbornly fighting slavery. *Brown Brothers*

nent, with no single country or group of countries gaining too much influence. Napoleon had disrupted the balance, which was why Britain opposed him; now the Holy Alliance might do the same thing.

The Holy Alliance also threatened to undo recent developments in the Western Hemisphere that had worked to Britain's favor. The Enlightenment had been slower to arrive in Latin America than in British North America, largely because it had been slower to arrive in Spain and Portugal than in Britain. But the revolutions in the United States and France had opened the eyes of many, especially in the Spanish colonies, to the possibilities of self-government and constitutionalism. The French Revolution had an additional impact: it produced Napoleon, who invaded Spain in 1808 and placed his brother, Joseph Bonaparte, on the throne. Beyond triggering the Peninsular War, in which Britain aided Spanish rebels against the French, Napoleon's manhandling of the Spanish government gave aspiring nationalists in Spanish America the signal they needed to raise the banner of revolt.

Revolution was a painstaking business in Latin America. News traveled even more slowly in that geographically difficult region than it had in the thirteen British colonies to the north, and the populations of the countries involved were more diverse and stratified. Native Indians occupied the mudsill of society; mestizos were slightly higher up; European-descended but American-born Creoles came higher still; European-born peninsulars held the best jobs and the most favored social positions. (In the colonies with sizable populations of African slaves, notably the Caribbean plantation colonies, those unfortunates shared the mudsill.) In some colonies—Argentina, for example—the revolutions principally pitted Creoles against peninsulars. Elsewhere—such as Mexico—Indians and mestizos contested against Creoles and peninsulars.

By the end of the Napoleonic wars, when the deposed Ferdinand of Spain had been restored to his throne, the revolutions in Spanish America were well begun but far from finished. Ferdinand, not surprisingly, hoped to quash the uprisings and regain his American empire. His monarch colleagues of the Holy Alliance wished him the best; there was even talk of assisting him in the endeavor. But Ferdinand's position in Spain was none too secure, and until he shored it up, the talk remained only talk.

Talk was enough to worry the British, however. For several decades British merchants had gradually worked their way into the markets of Spanish America. During the Napoleonic wars, when Spain was unable to enforce its colonial restrictions, when the revolutionaries in Spanish America wanted to broaden their commercial connections, and when the British navy ruled the Atlantic, Britain's market share expanded enormously. Any reimposition of Spanish rule in the Americas threatened to negate Britain's commercial gains. The British business classes did not like this idea one bit, and neither did the British government.

Nor did the American government. To a lesser extent, American merchants had similarly benefited from the revolution-induced opening of Spanish America to foreign trade. They, too, desired to see these markets stay open, and they made their wishes felt in Washington. Strategic considerations also entered the calculations of the Monroe administration. Countries almost always feel more secure when surrounded by small, weak neighbors than they do when the neighborhood contains big countries, which tend to be bullies. For the United States, the crackup of Spain's American empire promised to produce a dozen or more inconsequential states, none of which would be able to cause the United States much trouble. Some rebel-visionaries, like Simón Bolívar, dreamed of a United States of South America, but the project appeared geographically, ethnically, and culturally improbable.

Bolívar did not lack for American cheerleaders. The revolutions in Spanish America predictably touched a chord in Americans who saw the rebels as following in American footsteps. For many in the United States, the Latin American revolutions represented a great improvement over the French Revolution. Unlike the French Revolution but like the American Revolution, they were mostly moderate revolutions; they replaced foreign-based governments and elites with local ones but did not strike at the foundations of existing class structures. And again, whereas revolutionary France was a powerful state capable of threatening others, including the United States, the revolutionary republics of Spanish America, if they succeeded in securing their independence, would threaten no one except maybe each other.

Many people in American thought the United States government ought to give active assistance to the revolutionaries. Henry Clay called on the Monroe administration to provide all aid short of war. A few hotter heads neglected to add Clay's qualifier. A large group, perhaps a majority, thought the least the administration could do was recognize the independence of the aspiring republics.

John Quincy Adams disagreed. Adams was no apologist for autocracy, nor did he take second place to anyone in his devotion to human freedom. Following four difficult years as president during the 1820s, he would serve in the House of Representatives as a representative from Massachusetts, and until the end of his life (he died from a stroke that laid him low on the House floor) he protested vigorously and often against slavery.

But Adams believed that Americans could best serve the cause of human liberty by following the advice of Voltaire and cultivating their own garden. America should be an example to the world, not the savior of the world. Speaking of America's mission, Adams declared, "Wherever the standard of freedom and independence has been or shall be unfurled, there will her heart, her benedictions, and her prayers be. But she goes not abroad in search of monsters to destroy. She is the well-wisher to the freedom and independence of all. She is the champion and vindicator only of her own." The problem with world saving, Adams explained, was that it would enmesh America in problems too large for Americans to handle and would undermine the very institutions that made America worthy of emulation. Instead of liberty, the American watchword would become force. America might become the ruler of the world but would lose its spirit.

Adams had other, less philosophical reasons for not wanting to recognize the Latin American republics. Until 1819 he did not want to disrupt his negotiations with Onís over Florida and the boundary between Spanish (for now) Mexico and the United States. Afterward he hesitated to extend recognition until it became clear just what and whom the United States would be recognizing.

Yet even though Adams opposed immediate recognition, he shared Lord Castlereagh's desire to prevent Madrid from reconquering Spain's lost colonies. This was the most obvious of the parallel interests between the United States and Britain, and it grew more pronounced early in 1823 when France invaded Spain to rescue Ferdinand from his liberal foes. France, now under Louis XVII, had joined the Holy Alliance, and Europe was rife with rumors that after guaranteeing monarchy in Spain, the French would send an expedition to America to help the Spanish regain their colonies.

Another parallel interest between Britain and the United States involved Russia and the Oregon country. In the 1780s Russian fur traders had planted the czar's flag in the far northwest corner of North America, in what would become Alaska. During the next three decades, Russians had expanded their operations in Alaska and established auxiliary settlements down the coast nearly to San Francisco Bay. During the same period, British and American explorers and traders had visited and set up posts in Oregon, to the south of Alaska.

In 1821 Czar Alexander, believing that the Anglo-Americans were encroaching on his territory, proclaimed the closing of the northwest coast. From the

Bering Strait south to the fifty-first parallel (about the northern tip of Vancouver Island), non-Russians would have to keep out.

Alexander's action annoyed Americans and British both. The merchants of both countries had done a regular business with the towns of Russian America, and they did not like being cut off from this trade. Moreover, the fifty-first parallel ran right through the Oregon country, which the British and Americans wished to quarrel over themselves. The czar's ukase appeared an attempt at a significant extension of Russian territory in America at the expense of Britain and the United States.

Recognizing their mutuality of interests, the American and British governments discussed how best to promote them. The British foreign secretary, George Canning—back in office after Castlereagh's sudden death—suggested to the American minister in London, Richard Rush, a joint statement of purpose. Britain and the United States would go on record as opposing interference by European powers in the independence of the Latin American republics and opposing new colonization in the Americas as well. As an expression of their own good will, Britain and the United States would forswear any territorial aggrandizement for themselves.

Canning's proposal possessed substantial appeal. As a joint declaration by the greatest power in Europe and the greatest power in the Americas, it would carry great weight. It probably would not cost much: the mere threat of Anglo-American opposition likely would keep the French, the Spanish, and the Russians on the straight and narrow. Those countries were not being asked to *do* anything, only to *refrain* from doing and to refrain from doing something they were not deadly determined to do anyway. Retaking the Latin American republics would be a big job for Spain and France, even without British and American disapproval. The Russians were not making much, or any, money out of their American operations, and they did not seem to have any genuinely overwhelming compulsion to expand them. A joint statement such as Canning suggested might well be the little nudge the French, Spanish, and Russians needed to decide against intervention or expansion in the Western Hemisphere.

There was another kind of appeal to Canning's offer. Ever since 1776 Americans had labored under the knowledge that theirs was a second-class country. Britain and France had pushed them around while fighting each other, paying attention to them only when it served British or French purposes. To a large degree, the War of 1812 had been an attempt by Americans to force the British to respect American rights. Canning's offer included implicit recognition that the United States had arrived as a major power. The United States and Britain would be speaking as equals. Foreign powers could no longer dismiss the United States as unimportant. This factor alone made Canning's offer worth considering.

President Monroe considered it and was ready to accept; but Adams was not. While the secretary of state conceded that sharing the stage with Britain might seem an honor for the United States, he contended that taking the stage alone would be even more of an honor. Indeed, why were the British proposing this statement? Out of any love for the United States? Of course not. They were proposing it because the policy the statement outlined suited British interests. This policy would still suit British interests regardless of whether the United States joined in the statement. And because it would suit British interests, the British government would take the measures necessary to enforce such a policy. Moreover, a joint statement with Britain might be awkward for the United States to interpret as the United States saw fit. American expansion was almost certainly not at an end; would Washington have to ask British permission to acquire Cuba or Texas?

Political calculations entered the picture as well. Adams was already campaigning to succeed Monroe as president, and though Monroe had been unopposed in 1820, his secretary of state expected a tough fight. Two opponents were Andrew Jackson and Henry Clay, both of them Britain-bashers from the days of the War of 1812. (A fourth candidate, John Calhoun, also a warhawk from 1812, dropped out of the race but cleverly attached himself as vice presidential candidate to both Adams and Jackson, thereby essentially assuring himself of election to the backup position.) Regardless of the international ramifications of a joint statement with Britain, Jackson and Clay would make political mincemeat out of anyone who even suggested such collaboration with America's recent enemy.

Adams concluded that the United States should put forward the proposed statement alone. Though American military forces were not sufficient to prevent European meddling in America, British forces—particularly the British navy—were. Thus, the United States could announce the no-interference policy and leave it to the British to enforce. The British might be miffed at this sharp dealing by the Americans, but they would not be miffed enough to ignore their own interests.

Although Adams had to work hard to win over the president, he ultimately did. At the end of 1823, in his annual message to Congress, Monroe delineated what came to be called the Monroe Doctrine. Declaring the political system of the Americas to be "fundamentally different" from that of the powers of Europe, the president warned that the United States would interpret any effort by the Europeans to extend their system across the Atlantic as "dangerous" to the peace and safety of the United States. In keeping with this view, he added that the American continents should not be considered subject to future colonization by European powers. Monroe went on to pledge that the United States would not interfere with any existing colonies in the Americas. Nor would the United States interfere in the affairs of Europe.

The last point, about American noninterference in European affairs, was almost a throwaway line, but not quite. In 1821 nationalists in Greece had revolted against Ottoman Turkey, which had ruled Greece since the fifteenth century. Even more than the Latin American revolutions, the Greek war for independence elicited sympathy in the United States. Educated Americans knew their Greek authors; they recognized Greece as the birthplace of democracy and the fountainhead of Western civilization. References to Greece had abounded during the era of the American Revolution, and citations of the Greek classics were still common in American oratory and literature. The

John Quincy Adams (far left) explains to James Monroe (standing) why the president should issue his famous statement on European noninterference in the Americas as a unilateral declaration rather than in conjunction with Britain. *The Bettmann Archives*

Greek rebels had almost everything going for them in terms of gaining American support: they were the underdogs fighting a great power; they were Europeans fighting Asians (in the age of slavery and for a long time after, most Americans were unapologetic racists—as were most people in most other countries); they were Christians fighting infidels (Muslims, to be precise); they were enlightened constitutionalists fighting a medieval despotism. They also had a highly effective propaganda organization that spread the word of the Greeks' heroic struggle throughout Europe and America.

Many of the same people who had pushed for American aid to the Latin American republics pressed the Monroe administration to assist the Greek rebels. On his own, Monroe might have. But Adams rejected the idea even more forcefully than he rejected aid to the Latin Americans. Greece was far away and was confronting formidable enemies—perhaps, according to some reports, soon to include members of the Holy Alliance. (As matters turned out, the Holy Christian Allies decided it would be too incongruous for them to help the Muslim sultan of Turkey suppress his Christian subjects.) If the United States intervened on Greece's behalf, Adams argued, the action would set a pernicious precedent. The previous couple of millennia had shown that the Old

Worlders were always fighting one war or another; the United States should simply let them kill each other in peace.

Monroe's message provided Adams with a convenient way to deflect the Greek issue. In the context of demanding noninterference by Europeans in American affairs, the administration abjured American interference in European affairs. To get something you have to give something. Sorry, Greeks.

Although Adams, like most national leaders, was a bit of an egotist, even he could not have guessed what a long-lasting role the Monroe Doctrine would have in the history of American international relations. Its importance took a while to become apparent; no one bothered to call it a doctrine for more than a generation. Until the 1860s the United States did almost nothing to defend the position the doctrine described, and only in the 1890s did it assume inviolable status to most Americans. But from then on, the Monroe Doctrine became a fixture of American international affairs.

Various foreign countries, including Britain and most of the nations of Latin America, pointed out that the Monroe Doctrine had no standing in international law. Nor, for that matter, did it have any standing in American law. It was simply a statement by one American president of what he conceived American interests to include.

But statements of interests are stronger than international law when the interests involved belong to countries with the power to enforce them. For several decades, the Monroe Doctrine relied on the British navy for enforcement; later the United States became powerful enough to handle enforcement itself.

*   *   *

At the close of the first quarter of the nineteenth century, Americans could feel that one of the problems that had plagued them for most of the period since their country's independence—getting caught in the quarrels of the Europeans—was diminishing. The peace in Europe was holding, and no country with the capacity to disturb it much had serious reason to do so. The one question mark at the Congress of Vienna, defeated France, had been reintegrated into the balance of power with relatively few hard feelings.

The United States had contributed to this favorable trend in two ways. First, by fighting the War of 1812, if only to a draw, the American government demonstrated that trampling on American interests cost something. It did not cost enough to prevent countries that felt their very existence was at stake—Britain in danger from France, France from Britain—from strong-arming Americans; but it made them think twice about pushing the Americans around for lesser reasons. Second, by issuing the Monroe Doctrine, the United States government staked out an unambiguous position regarding the Western Hemisphere. European powers might or might not wish to cross the line John Quincy Adams and James Monroe drew in the ocean, but at least they knew where the line ran. Wars and other conflicts often start from ignorance and the fear ignorance produces; after Monroe proclaimed his doctrine, no one had any excuse for ignorance on the topics it covered.

In the area of territorial expansion, Americans in the mid-1820s were just getting up steam. Most of the central latitudes of North America lay within the boundaries of the United States, acquired by a combination of luck, guile, and force. Efforts to gain Canada had failed, but who could say that future efforts would not be more successful? Texas and Mexico beckoned in the South, Oregon and California in the West. As much as Americans had won, there was still more to win.

If the country as a whole was gaining strength relative to other countries, so the executive branch of the government was gaining strength relative to the other branches in the conduct of international affairs. Jefferson negotiated the purchase of Louisiana on his own authority and presented Congress with a bargain even Jefferson's Federalist opponents had a hard time criticizing. At Jefferson's insistence Republicans in Congress passed the Embargo Act, which embodied a strategy roughly equivalent to cutting off one's feet to prevent shoes from pinching. Without asking Congress for a declaration of war, Jefferson went ahead and fought the Barbary states. Madison led the nation into an anti-British war that a significant minority wanted nothing to do with. Madison, Adams, and Monroe—with the help of future president Andrew Jackson—wrested Florida from Spain. Adams and Monroe devised a doctrine that would bind their successors and the American people down to the seventh generation—and counting.

Most political theorists from the classical Greeks through the Enlightenment rationalists agreed that a country intending an active foreign policy needed a strong central government. Weak governments were usually slow, and although slowness might encourage deliberation and perhaps wisdom, in the tooth-and-claw world of international affairs the race was usually to the swift and strong.

In the early aftermath of the American Revolution, most Americans had not wanted an active foreign policy, and most had not wanted a strong central government. But during the first half century of America's national existence, an increasing number came to appreciate the merits of an active foreign policy designed to defend American commercial interests against predatory Europeans and to expand American territorial frontiers. An appreciation, or at least an acceptance, of strong government followed almost inevitably.

Sources and Suggestions for Further Reading

Jefferson's approach to international affairs is treated in Lawrence S. Kaplan, *Jefferson and France* (1967); Lance Banning, *The Jeffersonian Persuasion* (1978); Dumas Malone, *Jefferson the President* (1970–74); Forrest McDonald, *The Presidency of Thomas Jefferson* (1976); and Merrill Peterson, *Thomas Jefferson and the New Nation* (1970). The Louisiana question is the subject of Alexander DeConde, *This Affair of Louisiana* (1976). Roger Brown, *The Republic in Peril: 1812* (1964), examines the causes of the War of 1812, as do Reginald Horsman, *The Causes of the War of 1812* (1961); Bradford Perkins, *Prologue to War: England and the United States, 1805–1812* (1961); and J. C. A. Stagg, *Mr. Madison's War* (1983). Richard J. Ellings, *Embargoes and World Power* (1985); Burton Spivak, *Jefferson's English Crisis: Commerce, Embargo, and the*

Republican Revolution (1979); Louis Martin Sears, *Jefferson and the Embargo* (1966 ed.); and Clifford L. Egan, *Neither Peace nor War: Franco-American Relations, 1803–1812* (1983), trace specific aspects of the vexatious era. James A. Field, *America and the Mediterranean World, 1776–1886* (1969), describes the battles with the Barbary states, and places the problem in a longer chronological and larger geographical setting.

The aftermath of the War of 1812 shows up in Bradford Perkins, *Castlereagh and Adams: England and the United States, 1812–1823* (1964); Samuel Flagg Bemis, *John Quincy Adams and the Foundations of American Foreign Policy* (1949); and George Dangerfield, *The Awakening of American Nationalism* (1965). The Florida question and the Adams-Onís treaty of 1819 play central roles in Philip C. Brooks, *Diplomacy and the Borderlands* (1936). Robert Rimini, *Andrew Jackson and the Course of American Empire, 1767–1821* (1977), delineates the activities of the hot-tempered Old Hickory.

The Monroe Doctrine has undergone much analysis and interpretation; among the best such are Dexter Perkins, *The Monroe Doctrine* (1927); and Ernest May, *The Making of the Monroe Doctrine* (1975). Contributing factors to the promulgation of this fundamental doctrine are covered in Arthur P. Whitaker, *The United States and the Independence of Latin America* (1964); and Howard I. Kushner, *Conflict on the Northwest Coast: American-Russian Rivalry in the Pacific Northwest, 1790–1867* (1975).

Chapter 4

The New Empire in the West,
1823–1848

Expansion was the watchword of American international relations during the second quarter of the nineteenth century. Expansion had two meanings for Americans. In the traditional sense it meant taking new territory, adding fields and pastures beyond the back fence. Most Americans made their living from farming, and more land promised a better life for present and future generations. Land-hungry from the time of the nation's birth, Americans constantly looked for additional real estate to satisfy their appetite. That appetite only grew with the eating, and no sooner had they swallowed one parcel than they were on the lookout for another. During the 1830s and especially the 1840s, they ate plenty.

Expansion's second meaning for Americans was nearly as old as the first. Americans had been traders as long as they had been farmers, and where the farmers wanted more land, the traders desired new markets. The traders got their markets during the same years the farmers were getting their land. The traders had to be cleverer than the farmers to get what they wanted since the traders lacked the political and cultural appeal of the yeoman tillers of the soil. While the farmers enlisted God on their side, describing a career of continental conquest as America's "manifest destiny," the traders came closer to allying with the devil. At least they did during the 1840s, when American merchants piggy-backed on British drug dealers who shot their way into the Chinese market, demanding the right to sell Indian opium to the inhabitants of the world's most populous country.

Developments occurring outside the realm of international relations per se made both forms of expansion—territorial and commercial—more possible and attractive than they had been before. The Industrial Revolution had been under way in Britain since the latter eighteenth century; it jumped the Atlantic during the early nineteenth. Industrializing countries grew wealthy and therefore powerful, and they gained new means of projecting their power to the far corners of the earth. Innovations such as railroads and steamships helped knit the United States more closely together and helped knit the United States more completely into world affairs. Settlement of new territories became easier and more profitable, giving an impetus to territorial expansion. Foreign markets drew closer, increasing the incentive of American merchants to venture across the seas and enhancing the ability of the American government to smooth their way.

The Real Revolution

One fundamental measure of a revolution is how much it upsets people's lives and for how long. The American Revolution was not especially upsetting to the lives of most Americans; they carried on after 1776 much as they had before. The French Revolution was more upsetting to the French people: the whole idea of the French Revolution was to overturn the status quo. But even the French Revolution, after the great furor and violence it unleashed, eventually ran out of steam, yielding to a post-Napoleon reaction that went far toward erasing all vestiges of revolutionary thought and action.

More radical than either the American or French Revolution, in the sense of changing people's lives, was the Industrial Revolution. Despite the deceptive simplicity of its name, the Industrial Revolution involved far more than developments relating to industry. It comprised sweeping changes in politics, technology, economics, intellectual affairs, and daily life, leaving almost no area of human existence untouched.

Commencing in Britain in the second half of the eighteenth century, the Industrial Revolution was a consequence of the scientific revolution started by Copernicus and Galileo, and more directly of the agricultural revolution of the seventeenth and early eighteenth centuries. As new methods of cultivation became common throughout Britain, fewer workers were required to till the soil and tend the herds. Meanwhile, the new methods filled the pockets of the landowning class. The combination of former farmers looking for jobs and wealthy landlords looking for opportunities to invest their money provided just the right mix for a shift to a factory mode of production. Numerous other ingredients were necessary, too: ingenious tinkerers who devised ways of harnessing the power of falling water and coal to machines, colonial markets to absorb the surpluses the mills churned out, a commercial mindset that honored the ability to make money, a system of courts and laws that protected private property, and a political system responsive to the needs of the new entrepreneurial class.

Britain possessed the needed mix sooner and more completely than did other countries, and for this reason British manufacturers became the vanguard of the Industrial Revolution. Britain's leading position gave it a crucial edge over its competitors, especially France, in the race for predominance in Europe. By most measures of national strength—population, extent of territory, natural resources—France outstripped Britain. But Britain's industrial lead provided the British with mobilizable wealth that the French could not match. Britain's wealth built the best navy in the world and supplied subsidies to Britain's European allies, the countries that furnished most of the soldiers for fighting

Chronology

1825	Erie Canal opened to traffic
1826	Panama Congress of Latin American republics
1828	"Tariff of Abominations"
1830	Revolution in Paris
1831	*Cherokee Nation* v. *Georgia*
1832	*Worcester* v. *Georgia*; Black Hawk's War; nullification crisis commences; British Reform Act
1836	Texas wins independence from Mexico
1837	Victoria becomes queen of Britain
1838	Anti-Corn Law League established in Britain
1839	"Aroostook war" reaches climax; Britain attacks China in Opium War
1840	First regularly scheduled transatlantic steamship service: Liverpool to Boston
1842	Webster-Ashburton treaty; Treaty of Nanjing ends Opium War and transfers Hong Kong to Britain
1843	Major migration to Oregon begins
1844	Treaty of Wangxia with China; Polk elected on expansionist platform
1845	Annexation of Texas; U.S. Naval Academy established
1846	Mexican War begins; Oregon question answered
1847	American forces occupy Mexico City; potato famine in Ireland prompts large emigration to America
1848	Treaty of Guadalupe Hidalgo; revolutions throughout Europe; *Communist Manifesto* published

against France. And wealth begot wealth: in elbowing France out of India, for example, Britain assured itself of markets and supplies that would fuel its economic development for the next two hundred years.

Britain's industrial preeminence helped cause—and was partly caused by—a change in British thinking about economic matters. In 1776 a Scottish professor of moral philosophy named Adam Smith published *An Inquiry into the*

Nature and Causes of the Wealth of Nations. In its own way, Smith's book, the landmark manifesto of the nascent free trade movement, was as damaging an attack on Britain's mercantilist empire as Thomas Jefferson's Declaration of American Independence of the same year. Smith contended that the mercantilist view of international commerce was shortsighted and wrong. Individuals should be able to trade with customers and suppliers in other countries without the hindrance of tariffs and other restrictions on imports and exports. By means of free trade, efficiency would win out over inefficiency, to the long-term profit of all concerned.

Likewise at home, Smith said, government should keep its nose out of the economy. A free market was the best guarantee of prosperity because when government intervened in economic affairs it invariably fouled things up. The "invisible hand" of competition, rather than government supervision, would ensure that consumers received what they wanted at the best prices. Smith placed no particular faith in the benign intentions of merchants or manufacturers; indeed, he wrote, "People of the same trade seldom meet together, even for merriment and diversion, but the conversation ends in a conspiracy against the public or in some contrivance to raise prices." But he did place faith in competition. If a merchant or manufacturer started gouging customers, someone else would enter the market, undercut the gouger, and claim the customers. The driving force of the free enterprise system was the pursuit of individual self-interest, a commodity that historically has never been in short supply. By contrast, a system of government economic supervision required wisdom and unselfishness, which almost always have been.

Smith's argument for a government policy of laissez faire (French for "allow to do") provided just the intellectual ammunition the advocates of the new industrial class were looking for. Desiring the freedom to invest and do business wherever they chose, on terms suitable to themselves and whomever they might be doing business with, they used Smith's theories to augment their attack on government regulations and restrictions in economic matters.

At the same time, the success of industrialization in Britain made Smith's arguments more palatable than they otherwise would have been. Free trade naturally appeals to the country with the most advanced and most efficient economy. On a level international playing field, that country will score more profits than its opponents. British free traders could contend quite credibly that opening international markets to the merchants of all nations would result in a boom in British exports. Britain's balance of trade—the essential figure for mercantilists—would only grow more positive.

During the second quarter of the nineteenth century, at the moment of Britain's greatest industrial predominance, the free traders captured the heights of British public policy. The key battle in the offensive involved Britain's "corn laws." These laws, which restricted imports of foreign grain products, protected British farmers from international competition and kept the price of food artificially high. Industrial workers objected to the corn laws on the obvious ground that they raised the cost of living. Industrial owners objected on the same grounds—not that the mill owners were seized by a sudden solicitude that their workers eat well, but the cost of bread set a floor beneath wages. Starving workers were not very productive. If the cost of living fell, the wage rate might follow, to the larger profit of British industry.

Supporters of the corn laws argued that once Britain opened its markets to foreign food, food dependence would inevitably follow. Britain might have the strongest navy in the world, but the nation would be at the mercy of whatever country supplied Britain grain. Representatives of the farming interests held that repeal of the corn laws would be the ruin of British agriculture. These representatives, speaking chiefly for the landlord class, added that the ruin of British agriculture would mean the end of the system of aristocracy that the agricultural system supported and that had served Britain well for centuries.

The battle raged hard and hot during the 1830s and 1840s. Repealers formed an Anti–Corn Law League, funded by big manufacturers. The league carpeted Britain with pamphlets and posters and thickened the British air with speeches. A parliamentary reform act of 1832, which increased the clout of industrial cities such as Manchester, aided the repealers' cause. Retainers fought back with similar tactics of propaganda and political pressure. The ground slowly shifted toward repeal, with the decisive development coming in the mid-1840s when the Irish potato harvest failed and drove already high prices for grain higher still. In 1846 Parliament repealed.

The repeal of the corn laws, which signified the triumph of the doctrine of free trade and the ascendancy of the new industrial class, had an immediate effect on Britain's relations with the United States. The Tory government of Robert Peel, recognizing the domestic furor repeal would produce, chose not to stir things further by risking war with the United States over the currently troublesome issue of Oregon. For the sake of peace and quiet, Peel's government accepted a settlement with Washington that granted the British less than they might reasonably have demanded. Of equal importance, the opening of British markets allowed the expansion of American exports of grain and other commodities, encouraged America's own agricultural revolution, and fostered a transatlantic community of interest among British and American business leaders.

While the British were debating whether to implement Adam Smith's ideas, the United States was getting aboard the industrial train. Some American inventors had seats in the first car. In the 1790s Eli Whitney put together a device for mechanically separating cotton seeds from fibers. Whitney's cotton gin enormously increased the efficiency of the cotton-cleaning process, thereby lowering the price of cotton cloth and making it competitive with wool cloth. This development encouraged a particularly close connection between the cotton-producing American South and cotton-processing Britain—a connection that would acquire great importance as the sectional division between North and South in the United States deepened. (Although Whitney was a brilliant inventor—he also pioneered a system of manufacturing based on standardized, interchangeable parts—he had little knack for business. He failed to secure adequate patent protection for his cotton gin and as a result made lots of other people, but not himself, rich on royalties.)

Another American, Robert Fulton, led the way in the development of steam travel on water. Bolting an imported English steam engine onto a riverboat, Fulton in 1807 traveled up the Hudson River, for the first time showing the feasibility of regular, low-cost transportation against river currents. Fulton's feat promised the opening of upstate New York to broader economic growth; more important, it foretold the integration of the Mississippi Valley into the American national economy. Before the steamboat, bulk goods could travel only *down* the Ohio and Mississippi valleys, usually on flatboats that drifted with the current. Transportation *up* the valley was generally confined to small, high-value items that could absorb the cost of overland travel. (In practice most such goods traveled across the mountains from the East Coast.) The steamboat changed all this. Transportation up the valleys became almost as cheap as transportation down, and the interior joined the Atlantic seaboard as part of a single national market.

Locals flock to the riverbank to see Robert Fulton's steamboat splash its way up the Hudson River. *Brown Brothers*

By opening up the American heartland, the steamboat helped lay the foundation for America's rise to world power in the late nineteenth and twentieth centuries. Other innovations—canals, railroads, improved methods of producing steel and processing rubber—would further the trend toward the creation of the largest and most powerful economy on the planet. As the American economy grew during the nineteenth century, it made possible the subsequent emergence of the United States as the most powerful nation on earth.

The hitching of steam to water transport also transformed international relations in the shorter term. Twelve years after Fulton chugged from New York City to Albany, an American ship, the *Savannah,* added steam-driven paddle wheels to its sail rigging for a crossing of the Atlantic. By the late 1830s ships were traversing the Atlantic under steam power alone. By the late 1850s, when the more efficient screw propeller supplanted the paddle wheel, steamships were coming to dominate transatlantic traffic.

Once steamships started making regular runs across the ocean, travel between America and other continents became faster and more predictable than before. The immediate effect was to improve communications between countries. Diplomats in foreign capitals found themselves on a shorter leash than before; had Napoleon offered Louisiana for sale in 1853 rather than 1803, James Monroe and Robert Livingston would probably have had time to refer the offer back to Jefferson in Washington, for better or worse. Although Andrew Jackson still might have fought the British at New Orleans, the news of his victory there would have arrived in the American East after the news that the war was over; his reputation would not have gained the luster it did.

Beyond improving communications, the development of maritime steam power also had important strategic and economic implications. Steam-driven warships increased the military advantage of the rich industrializing countries over the poor, nonindustrialized countries. In the days of sail, rich and poor were equal before the wind, or lack of it. When the wind blew, everyone's ships sailed; when it fell still, all stopped. The introduction of steam gave a crucial edge to the rich countries in that their ships could continue operations regardless of the wind. The American task force that bombarded Tripoli in 1805 lost a frigate in an adverse wind that drove the vessel aground. Steam navies had no such worries—which increased the worries of the countries whose navies lacked steam.

Ocean-going steamships effected changes in the world economy similar to those that steam riverboats did in the American economy, though more slowly. Steamships tied distant parts of the world together in a way that had not been possible previously. People and goods traveled the oceans as never before. Immigrants in unprecedented numbers left Europe and Asia for the Americas; American grain competed in Liverpool with grain from Russia and Argentina; wool from Australia undersold wool from Scotland; a failure of the Indian monsoon boosted cotton prices in the American South. Increasingly, successful large businesses had to think globally. As they did, they began to become players in their own right in the game of international relations.

Hard Sell: The China Market

A few businesses had been thinking globally for a long time already. Western merchants had been trading with China for more than a thousand years, through intermediaries at first but directly since the early sixteenth century. The trade had never been easy, for the Chinese had never much liked foreign traders. The mandarins who ruled China disdained commerce as a form of social bloodsucking; merchants produced nothing, they contended, merely buying low from producers, selling high to consumers, and taking the unearned difference as profit. The Chinese as a people looked down on foreigners, who struck them as uncouth and uncivilized. Foreign merchants thus were doubly damned as predatory barbarians. On various occasions in Chinese history, the Chinese government had tried to keep foreign merchants out; at the best of times (for the foreign merchants) the government let them in but narrowly curtailed their activities. The foreigners usually could purchase only a few specified items and could sell still fewer.

The British were the first Westerners to pursue trade with China in a major way, and they found this situation unsatisfactory. In the age of mercantilism, the China trade produced an unfavorable balance: the British bought more from the Chinese than the Chinese bought from the British. Yet only in the late eighteenth century did the deficit grow sufficiently large to cause the British government to undertake to remedy the condition. The British had got thoroughly hooked on tea, generating far greater deficits than before, and the cost of the tea was steadily draining money out of the empire.

In 1792 George III's government and the East India Company dispatched George Macartney to Beijing (Peking) to rectify matters. The Chinese Qianlong emperor (one of the greatest of Chinese emperors and one of the longest-lived: he ruled from 1736 to 1799) received Macartney courteously and examined the latest examples of British technology the British envoy brought with him. But Qianlong refused to grant the British the trade privileges Macartney requested. Qianlong explained that Britain had nothing China could not easily do without. "We have never valued ingenious articles, nor do we have the slightest need of your country's manufactures," the emperor said.

Polite diplomacy failing, the British tried other means of bringing their trade with China into balance. Having become addicted to one of China's principal exports, they sought to discover something addictive China might import. Eventually they found it in opium. Opium fit Britain's needs admirably: it was produced in British India, it was easy to transport, and it generated a highly loyal (to say the least) customer base. To exploit these advantages, British officials pushed opium hard in China. Despite continuing restrictions on foreign activities in China, sales rose splendidly.

Chinese officials, however, frowned on Britain's solution to the problem of the trade imbalance. Opium-drugged Chinese failed to meet their social obligations and neglected families, jobs, and taxes. In addition, heavy imports of opium overcorrected the balance-of-trade problem, draining China of gold and silver. In the 1830s the Chinese government launched a war on drugs. The government proclaimed a death penalty for trafficking in or using opium, and it appointed an antidrug director to clean up Guangzhou, the worst den of the drug dealers. This energetic individual quickly directed a major bust in the southern port, seizing and burning warehouses full of the illegal drug.

The British opium pushers cried foul. The Chinese government, they asserted, was violating their rights as merchants and contravening the fundamental principle of free trade. The British government, not yet converted to free trade at home—the repeal of the corn laws remained several years in the future—nonetheless decided that it ought to apply to China. London sent a fleet of warships to Guangzhou to enforce the principle.

In 1839 the British warships exchanged gunfire with Chinese vessels, touching off the Opium War. Militarily, the fight was no contest. British ships battered the Chinese navy and Chinese shore positions at will. But the Chinese government in Beijing refused to capitulate to the foreign devils until 1842. In that year the Chinese agreed to a peace settlement ceding the island of Hong Kong to Britain, opening five ports to Western trade, lowering tariffs on Western goods, and establishing the principle of extraterritoriality for Westerners in China. (This last concession meant that Westerners in China were subject to their own laws, not Chinese laws.)

For a decade and a half the Chinese government did its best to circumvent the terms of this treaty, provoking British forces to return in the late 1850s and wage another war (with French help) to guarantee the gains of the earlier conflict. Partly because the Chinese government labored under the concurrent difficulty of having to deal with what was probably the largest and bloodiest domestic insurrection in history—the Taiping Rebellion—the second war ended even more disastrously for China than the first. The 1860 treaty terminating the war expressly opened China to foreign opium and allowed Christian missionaries for the first time to proselytize in the interior of the country. (Not surprisingly given the circumstances, many Chinese tended to view Christianity and opium as jointly destructive of Chinese values and culture. This view gained credence from the fact that the leader of the Taiping rebels, who encountered Christianity through the work of American missionaries, proclaimed himself to be the younger brother of Jesus Christ. As matters turned out, it was another American, the Massachusetts soldier of fortune Frederick Ward, who led the mercenary "Ever Victorious Army" that fought on behalf of the Qing dynasty against the Taipings.) The 1860 treaty added several more ports to the list of legal trading sites, it granted Westerners commercial access to the Yangzi valley, and it authorized Western governments to establish diplomatic offices in Beijing.

Although the United States took no part in the fighting of the Opium War, it took solid advantage of the outcome. American traders had been actively engaged in the China trade since the late eighteenth century; they sold a variety of products, including opium, and purchased the usual tea and other Chinese exports. The Chinese liked the Americans about as little as they liked the British, but the Chinese government adopted the strategy, common to weak coun-

China in the Mid-Nineteenth Century

tries confronted by big powers, of playing one big power against the others. Though the Chinese had failed to prevent Britain from forcing its way into China, they hoped to dilute the evil effects of the British presence by inviting other powers in. "Now that the English barbarians have been allowed to trade," the Daoguang emperor declared in 1843, "whatever other countries there are, the United States and others, should naturally be permitted to trade without discrimination, in order to show Our tranquilizing purpose."

By means of the 1844 Treaty of Wangxia, the Chinese government peacefully extended to the United States essentially the same rights Britain had won by war. The United States gained most-favored-nation status, which meant that whatever commercial privileges the Chinese conceded to any country automatically applied to the United States. The Chinese also extended the principle of extraterritoriality to Americans in China. (Other European powers besides Britain gained similar concessions during this period.) When in 1860 the Chinese lengthened the list of their concessions to British (and now French) military power, the United States once more hitched a ride. American merchants began trading out of the new treaty ports, and American missionaries headed for the Chinese interior.

The Lost Tribes: Indian Removal

It stretches the truth only a little to say that the very existence of the United States owed to the China trade: Columbus bumped into what was to him a New World while trying to reach Cathay. He compounded his confusion by calling the natives of the Americas "Indians," as anyone would have who thought he was in the East Indies. The labeling error stuck, partly because the Indians themselves had no collective word for the hundreds of American tribes and partly because Columbus wanted to cover up his seven-thousand-mile error. (He died in 1506 before having to admit the extent of his miscalculation.)

Something else linked the Indians and the Chinese in American history. Both groups—like the black Africans—were treated as racially inferior to the European-descended whites whose culture came to dominate North America. The Indians were worse off than the Chinese since white Americans at least gave the Chinese credit for cultural sophistication—though Americans tended to focus on what seemed bizarre and perverted in Chinese culture, such as footbinding of women and puppies in the stewpot. Indians had almost no redeeming virtues in the eyes of most white Americans. What virtues they did have seemed to disappear on closer inspection: the most violently anti-Indian whites were often those who lived on the frontier.

There was a reason for this—namely, that the frontier settlers were the ones who brought out the worst in the Indians. Competing with Indians for land, they pushed them aside wherever they could. The Indians fought back, often with equal brutality. After a couple rounds of raids and reprisals, it was hard to remember who had started the whole thing.

Treaties usually ended the bloodletting sooner or later; but treaties were difficult to enforce, on both sides. The American government found the frontier types almost as unruly and provocative as the Indians did, and the Indians who signed the treaties often represented no one but themselves and a few likewise paid-off friends.

The intractable problem the Indians faced was a rapidly expanding American population. Few other nations have ever grown as fast in numbers as the United States did during the late eighteenth and early nineteenth centuries. The 1790 United States census showed 3.9 million persons; the 1800 count, 5.3 million; the 1810, 7.2 million; the 1820, 9.6 million; the 1830, 12.9 million; the 1840, 17 million.

Given this great increase, Americans would have had to be far more tender-hearted than most other people historically have been in dealing with less technologically advanced neighboring societies not to have thrown the Indians aside. Americans were not conspicuously tenderhearted, and they did in fact throw the Indians aside. Military operations, from campaigns during the French and Indian War to Andrew Jackson's expeditions against the Creeks and the Seminoles during the 1810s, accomplished part of the task. Disease and dislocation, which especially afflicted old folks and children, accomplished much of the rest.

Those who dodged both the bullets and the microbes usually faced forced removal. This policy was defended by its designers as being in the best interests of both Indians and whites. Thomas Jefferson envisioned part of the Lousiana territory as an Indian reserve; those Indians who converted to white ways of living might remain east of the Mississippi, but those who insisted on retaining their tribal culture would be removed to the west. Although seemingly at odds with the liberalism that had inspired the Declaration of Independence, Jefferson's attitude toward Indians was in reality more humane than that of many people of his day, especially westerners, who wanted all the Indians exterminated.

Indian removal began in earnest—deadly earnest—during the presidential administration of Andrew Jackson. As an old Indian fighter and a politician with particular debts to southerners and westerners, Jackson vowed to rid the parts of the country suitable for white settlement of the red-skinned impediments to progress. By the early 1830s Indian resistance to white encroachment in the region east of the Mississippi and north of the Ohio had just about ended. The Indians' final defeat in the Old Northwest came with the crushing of the Sac and Fox coalition in Black Hawk's War of 1831–1832. In the Southeast, however, considerable resistance remained. The Five Civilized Tribes (Choctaw, Chickasaw, Creek, Seminole, and Cherokee) were so called because of their approximation to such white cultural patterns as farming. Their members hoped this similarity would dispose white government officials to allow them to hold on to their lands.

The officials of the southern states had no such intention. Georgia led the way in asserting state jurisdiction over the Cherokees; other southern states followed suit regarding the tribes within their borders. The Cherokees demonstrated how well they had learned to play by the white man's rules by suing Georgia and taking the case to the federal Supreme Court. The Supreme Court denied the Cherokee complaint. Chief Justice John Marshall and the Court's majority overturned previous custom, by which the Indian tribes had been considered foreign nations in dealings with the American government, and ruled them "domestic dependent nations." The Georgians applauded the decision. In a subsequent case, however, Marshall and the Court determined that the federal government, not the states, had jurisdiction over the Indian tribes. The Georgians jeered the decision.

Andrew Jackson did not like the latter decision any better than the Georgians did. The president, who hated John Marshall anyway—not a particular distinction since Jackson hated lots of people—defied Marshall. "John Marshall has made his decision," Jackson was reported as saying. "Now let him enforce it." Marshall had no troops, of course, whereas Jackson did. The president used the troops to throw the Indians off their lands. The most egregious use of military power occurred in 1838 when federal troops drove the Cherokees out of Georgia to Oklahoma (then called Indian Territory). On this forced march, along what became known as the Trail of Tears, several thousand Indians died of exposure and exhaustion.

Jackson's policy did not solve the Indian problem (the Indians thought of it as the white problem). Troubles between the white majority and the original inhabitants of North America continued for several generations. But the Supreme Court's ruling took most relations with the Indians out of the realm of foreign affairs, as Americans considered them. And by pushing the Indians west, Jackson provided breathing room to deal with other issues he and most Americans of his day considered more important.

God, Malthus, and Jefferson: The Ideology of Manifest Destiny

At the top of Jackson's list was the issue that was at the base of American policy toward Indians: land. To people of agricultural societies, including Americans of the nineteenth century, nothing was more important than land. Land was what made nations strong. Land provided livelihoods for individuals in the present, security in old age, and an inheritance for the next generation. Given the rapid growth of the American population resulting from both immigration and the amazing fecundity of those already resident, no matter how much land the country acquired, more land always seemed better.

Thomas Malthus, a noted English economist of the early nineteenth century, made himself famous by pointing out that populations increase geometrically (1, 2, 4, 8, 16 . . .), while the means of supporting populations increase arithmetically (1, 2, 3, 4, 5 . . .). The means of support increase arithmetically because the basis of the means of support, land, is strictly limited. As real-estate agents like to say, they are not making the stuff any more. In Malthus's formulation, the inevitably faster growth of population inevitably drove standards of living down to the bare minimum necessary for subsistence. David Ricardo, a follower of Adam Smith and Malthus, elaborated Malthus's ideas into an "iron law of wages" that dictated that wages could never rise far above the subsistence level because if they did, workers would have more children, who would then compete for jobs and drive wages back down.

Americans strove mightily to exempt themselves from Malthus's and Ricardo's theories. They strove principally in the area of acquiring land. From the 1780s through the 1820s, their efforts succeeded, with each generation doubling the land available to the next. But because population was also doubling

Despite his dire predictions regarding the future of humanity, Thomas Malthus could look rather dapper. *Brown Brothers*

every twenty-five years, each generation *had* to double the land merely to avoid losing ground.

Americans did not consider themselves greedy in seeking so much land. They looked to the north, to Canada; to the south, to Mexico; to the west, to California and Oregon; and in each direction they saw territories nearly uninhabited or inhabited by populations growing far more slowly than their own. Vast quantities of land were going to waste, they concluded, and would continue to go to waste until populated by industrious souls who would settle and cultivate them. Most Americans believed that land rightly belonged to those who would put it to highest use. The highest use of all was the support of human families and communities. In the predominant American view, the problem with the Indians was not only that they were pagan savages, though that was problem enough, but also that they were hunters and gatherers. Farming, by its nature, supports higher populations than hunting and gathering; therefore the Indians ought to surrender land to white farmers. (Americans consistently and conveniently overlooked the fact that many tribes, including the Cherokees and others in the Southeast, *were* farmers.)

Like the inhabitants of numerous other countries, Americans believed they were uniquely blessed by God. They believed that by expanding the territory of the United States, they would be sharing their blessings, most notably the institutions of political liberty, with other people. John O'Sullivan, one of the principal propagandists of American expansion, proclaimed that it was "our manifest destiny to overspread and to possess the whole of the continent which Providence has given us for the development of the great experiment of liberty and federative self government entrusted to us." When Americans talked of annexing Canada or taking Mexico, they thought they would be doing Canadians and Mexicans a favor. Canadians remained in thrall (until gaining self-government in 1867) to the same British government that had oppressed Americans two generations before; Mexicans, even after their break from Spain in 1821, suffered under a corrupt dictatorship. For either people, attachment to the United States would be a tremendous improvement.

To be sure, behind much of this talk of an American manifest destiny—of America's divinely appointed duty to fill and control the continent—there was the same self-interestedness that usually motivates people. Put another way, concern for others never caused the United States to do something that *contradicted* American national interests. The basic reason Americans seized the land they did was that this land appealed to them and they were strong enough to take it.

Yet the political sermonizing about extending the blessings of liberty to benighted foreigners was not entirely hypocritical; and even that part that *was* hypocritical was significant, for it demonstrated that America had a conscience. Most expansive societies throughout most of human existence have not felt the need to justify their actions with regard to the people whose land they steal. Conquest was supposed to benefit the conquerors, not the conquered. Things changed a little with the introduction of Christianity, which added a new element to conquest: a professed concern for the welfare of the conquered people's eternal well-being. Expansion now had to have the purpose of saving souls, beyond its meaner motives. This requirement did not seriously constrain conquerors, however; there were always souls to save. Nor did the souls have to belong to non-Christians; Christian schismatics would do. In the thirteenth century, the Roman Catholic armies of the Fourth Crusade turned aside from Jerusalem and sacked Eastern Orthodox Constantinople. During and after the Reformation of the sixteenth century, Catholics and Protestants considered each other fair game.

Americans inherited this Christian tradition of supposedly selfless conquest, but they gave it a new twist. The twist was political, largely because Americans could not agree on a national religion. Although Protestant Christianity was the semi-official American religion, there were too many deists, freethinkers, and Catholics around, and the Protestants were too sectarian, to allow any one version to gain the official seal of approval. "In God we trust" was about as far as the consensus went. Under these circumstances, republicanism—government by the people—took the place of a national religion. Though there were plenty of believers in aristocracy and a few outright monarchists in America in the early days of nationhood, these dissenters increasingly felt obliged to disguise their views. Republicanism was what had justified the American Revolution; republicanism supplied the basis for the American Constitution. The 1800 election of Thomas Jefferson enshrined the republican principle. By the time of Andrew Jackson's election in 1828, popular enthusiasm for republicanism had carried the country all the way to the extreme form of republicanism known as democracy.

On its face, republicanism seemed to forbid the conquest of foreign territories. The essence of republicanism is that people should govern themselves, not be governed by others. For Americans to impose their rule on foreigners would seem to fly in the face of republicanism and thereby contradict the basic idea of American history.

Americans never completely figured out how to resolve the conflict between republicanism and territorial conquest. Sometimes they convinced themselves that the inhabitants of the territories they coveted *wanted* to be conquered, regardless of the wishes of the governments of those territories. This was the attitude that prompted the invasions of Canada during the Revolutionary War and the War of 1812. Sometimes they pledged that the conquest would be only temporary and that before long the conquered people would regain control of their own destiny by becoming part of the American republican system. This was what had happened to the French and Spanish inhabitants of Louisiana and Florida, which made the transition from territories to states in relatively short order. Sometimes they contended that the conquered people did not know what was in their own best interest or were so uncivilized as not to merit consideration. This approach typified American treatment of the Indians.

Yet despite such rationalizations, the conflict between republicanism and territorial expansion deterred Americans from enthusiastically embracing colonial imperialism of the sort other great powers practiced unabashedly. Once Americans really got the message that Canadians did not want to join the United States, agitation to capture Canada largely ceased. Once Mexicans began forcibly resisting American advances, American enthusiasm for territory south of the Rio Grande diminished drastically. Americans might become imperialists, but their guilty consciences prevented them from enjoying the experience.

Lone Star Alone No Longer: Texas

There was another reason for the attempts to rationalize American expansion as being in the best interests of those expanded upon. Never did Americans all agree that a particular piece of territory ought to be added to the federal domain. Those persons advocating the addition had to convince the skeptics. Simple appeals to self-interest did not always work, because different groups defined their self-interests differently. Pleading the welfare of others added an argumentative arrow to the expansionists' quiver.

No addition to the American domain prompted more skepticism and debate than Texas. Europeans had first set foot in Texas by accident: in the 1520s a minor-league Spanish conquistador named Álvar Núñez Cabeza de Vaca got himself shipwrecked on the Texas coast and subsequently was captured and enslaved by local Indians. For most of a decade, his hand-to-mouth captors dragged him around, showing him the sights as they migrated from place to place in ceaseless search of small game and edible plants. Eventually Cabeza made his escape to Mexico, and although he had little good to say about Texas, his accounts of the Pueblo peoples of New Mexico—who lived off the fat of the land compared to the impoverished Tonkawas and Karankawas of Texas—gave rise to the myth of the Seven Cities of Cíbola, which produced some of the great wild goose chases in the history of the Americas.

For a couple of centuries, no one paid much attention to Texas. El Paso was a stop on the road to Santa Fe, but otherwise the region evoked little interest among great powers or small. In the eighteenth century, though, the Spanish government started worrying about the British and French possibly encroaching on Mexico from the north; in response, the Spanish promoted the settlement of Texas from the south. They sent missionaries and a few soldiers across the Rio Grande, establishing a line of settlements that ran nearly to Louisiana.

By the early nineteenth century, Spain's big worry regarding Mexico was the United States. The Americans had grabbed Louisiana and Florida; some Americans were talking about taking over the entire continent. It did not ease Spain's worries that certain readings of the Louisiana bill of sale transferring ownership from France to the United States included part of Texas in the transaction.

In a daring but doomed maneuver, the Spanish authorities in Mexico invited requests by Americans to settle in Texas. Recognizing that Americans would enter Texas anyway, the government hoped to gain some control over the invasion. Unfortunately for Spain, the effort to secure Texas for Mexico did nothing to secure Mexico for Spain, and before arrangements with American empresarios such as Moses Austin could be completed, Mexico broke away from Spain.

Moses Austin died during the delay occasioned by Mexico's breakaway, leaving negotiations with the independent government of Mexico to his son Stephen. The new government and the younger Austin eventually agreed to a deal by which Austin would bring three hundred families to Texas, where all would swear loyalty to Mexico and receive generous grants of land.

Whether the new arrivals really meant their oaths would later provoke dispute, for problems arose almost immediately. The newcomers came primarily from states of the American South, and many brought slaves. When the Mexican government outlawed slavery, the Texans had to choose between divesting themselves of their slaves or evading the law. Partly because the authorities in Mexico City were far away and partly because more than a few of the Texans already had considerable practice dodging the law—many were on the run from American authorities—most chose to keep their slaves.

Religion presented another problem. Under the settlement pact, the new arrivals pledged to convert to Roman Catholicism. Some in fact did convert and even went to mass occasionally. Most did not.

To the difficulties of slavery and religion were added others. The Texans and the Mexican authorities quarreled over tariffs, and they argued about whether Texas should be a separate Mexican state or joined to neighboring Coahuila. The most significant development of the period, and the one beneath most of the difficulties between the Texans and the Mexican government, was the swelling tide of Americans entering the region. By 1834 more than twenty thousand free Americans (and two thousand slaves) assumed residence in Texas. They outnumbered the Mexicans there four to one.

Had Mexico enjoyed a strong and stable government, the problems with Texas might have been solvable. But Mexico fared no better during its first decade of independence than the United States had—in fact worse—and with each rumble in Mexico City, the Texans worried that their status quo would come under attack. They feared, at best, an outbreak of law and order, with the Mexican authorities actually enforcing measures already on the books. At worst, they feared a rewriting of the statute books in ways that hurt their interests.

Beginning in 1834 the worst started to happen. In Mexico City, General Antonio López de Santa Anna seized power and scrapped the Mexican constitution. States' rights went out the window and with them what hopes the Texans had for retaining their de facto position in the Mexican political system.

Whatever the sincerity of their conversion to Mexican citizenship had been before this, Americans in Texas experienced little difficulty seeing similarities between their present predicament and that of the American colonists in the days prior to the American Revolution. As King George had trampled the rights of the colonies, they contended, so Santa Anna was trampling the rights of Texas. Americans in the 1760s had only wanted to live their lives in the manner to which they had grown accustomed; Texans likewise would have been happy to continue under the loose rein they had enjoyed during the 1820s. And as the American colonists had resisted in 1775, so the Texans resisted sixty years later.

The Texas revolution began in the spring of 1835. The Texans grew alarmed at reports that Santa Anna was sending troops to reinforce the Mexican garrisons in Texas, and they determined to move first. A group of volunteers captured a Mexican fort at Anahuac, near Galveston. A few months later Texans met and defeated a Mexican force at Gonzales. In December 1835 Stephen Austin—who earlier had demonstrated his good faith toward Mexico by helping to put down an anti-Mexican uprising by Americans in east Texas—led a successful attack on San Antonio.

But in 1836 Santa Anna struck back. Four days after Texans proclaimed the existence of an independent republic, the Mexican general recaptured San Antonio, wiping out the defenders of the Alamo in the process. Two weeks later a Mexican army surrounded a contingent of Texans near Goliad; after the Texans surrendered, the Mexicans killed most of them.

The captured Santa Anna pays his required respects to the wounded Sam Houston after the battle of San Jacinto. *The Bettmann Archive*

The climax of the fighting occurred in April 1836. Santa Anna had marched east from San Antonio to challenge a Texan force headed by Sam Houston. On the San Jacinto River close to the future site of the city that would bear his name, Houston attacked and defeated Santa Anna. Houston took the Mexican leader prisoner and demanded that he sign a treaty recognizing Texas's independence. Santa Anna, who believed in living to fight another day, signed, only to repudiate the signing as soon as he got free.

Americans back in the United States cheered and supported the Texas rebels, albeit unofficially. Some American volunteers joined the fight against Santa Anna; many of the 187 who died at the Alamo were recent arrivals from east of the Sabine River. American–made weapons armed the rebels, while donated American dollars paid for ammunition and other supplies.

Officially, however, the United States kept clear of the Texas uprising. After John Quincy Adams had dropped American claims to Texas in the 1819 Adams-Onís Treaty, the American government left the problem of Texas to Spain and Mexico. Most of the Texas rebels desired annexation to the United States, and Sam Houston, following election as president of the Texas republic, quickly sent an envoy to Washington to discuss the subject; but Washington made no promises. President Jackson did not even extend diplomatic recognition to Texas until nearly a year after the battle of San Jacinto, even though he and Houston were old drinking and brawling buddies from mutual days in Tennessee.

Two factors accounted for the standoffishness. The first and less important had to do with Mexico. The Mexican government refused to accept the seces-

Texas and Mexico at the Time of the Mexican War

sion of Texas, and Jackson understood that annexation by the United States would probably provoke a war. Jackson was never one to back down from a fight, but a good-sized war—as opposed to skirmishes with Indians—was something even Old Hickory wanted to consider carefully.

The second and more important reason for American hesitation regarding Texas was the deepening split between North and South. It did not take much insight to guess that if Texas entered the Union, it would come in as a slave state—perhaps two or more slave states since it was so big. During the first two decades of the nineteenth century, Congress had maintained the balance between slave states and free by alternating between North and South when admitting new states. Louisiana followed Ohio, Mississippi followed Indiana, Alabama followed Illinois. By 1820, though, the process seemed in jeopardy, especially as Congress attempted to decide the fate of the trans-Mississippi West—essentially, the part of the Louisiana territory above the now-state of Louisiana. Many Northerners had assumed that all or most of upper Louisiana would be free. Northerners could generally accept that slavery might remain where it already existed, but to extend it into virgin territory was something else again. Consequently, they were disconcerted when Missouri applied for admission as a slave state. Congress agonized over the issue before linking the admission of Missouri to the admission of Maine—thereby maintaining the North-South balance—and drawing a line across the Louisiana territory dividing future slave states from future free states.

The North-South balance remained intact at the time of the Texas revolution by virtue of the fact that Congress had not admitted any new states since the Maine-Missouri pair. Michigan was about ready for admission, but it had already lined up a partner, Arkansas. No northern territory was available to balance Texas.

Even if a balancer had been available, the spirit of compromise that so far had kept the slavery issue from tearing the nation apart was losing ground on both sides of the Mason-Dixon line. In the North, abolitionists were heartened by Britain's 1833 decision to end slavery in the British empire, and they intended to accomplish in America what their antislavery colleagues across the Atlantic had done. At a minimum, they aimed to block the growth of the barbarous practice. In the South, defenders of slavery circled their wagons, determined to prevent what they saw as discriminatory treatment of southerners in territories belonging to the entire country. They believed, with some reason, that once they conceded the right of the federal government to regulate or abolish slavery in the territories, the days of slavery in the states would be numbered. Moral issues do not lend themselves to compromise; how can you cut a deal with the devil? Before the 1830s, slavery had commonly been viewed as a political question, amenable to the give-and-take that is the essence of politics; but during the 1830s and 1840s, slavery entered the realm of the uncompromisably moral.

While slavery blocked the admission of Texas to the United States, the Texans began investigating other options. The Texans did not lack self-confidence, but they appreciated that they needed help. Mexico still refused to accept Texas's independence, and more than once it sent armies across the Rio Grande to reaffirm its refusal. Twice the Mexicans reoccupied San Antonio. Throughout the nine years after San Jacinto, they harassed and threatened the new republic.

The Texans looked across the Atlantic for the warm reception they were not getting in Washington. Texas diplomats journeyed to Paris, where they reminded the French of Texas's French heritage from the days when France ruled Louisiana, including eastern Texas. The Texans suggested that close ties between Texas and France might restore some of France's lost influence in North America. France, they said, was a natural mediator between Texas and Mexico, another Latin country. The French government expressed considerable interest.

The British were equally interested. For all their acceptance of certain common interests between the United States and Britain, the British were not above hedging their bets—for example, by hedging the Americans around territorially. At the moment, the United States was just about the right size for British tastes: big enough to give the French, Russians, and Spanish pause regarding the Western Hemisphere, but not big enough to challenge Britain. If the United States continued to expand, however, even Britain would have to start worrying. An independent Texas planted squarely on America's southwestern border would do much to halt American expansion.

There was also the question of cotton. As Britain's Industrial Revolution progressed, British mills hummed ever faster, eating cotton at a rate unimagined just decades before. The majority of this cotton came from the American South. No manufacturer likes to be dependent on a single source of supply; this gives the supplier too much leverage over prices. The British government had to pay attention to the cotton issue not simply because it had to pay attention to the political influence of the cotton manufacturers, but also because problems with cotton imports could throw the entire British economy into a depression. Such a depression would be bad for the country, obviously, and bad for the government.

Texas afforded the British the possibility of an independent source of cotton. The main reason all those southerners had gone to Texas with their slaves was to grow cotton. People were still streaming in, and by 1845 the Texas population topped 140,000. Texas's cotton production grew apace, much of it finding its way to British mills. It was greatly to Britain's interest to keep the Texas cotton coming.

Accordingly, when the Texans made diplomatic overtures to Britain, London responded favorably. The British government recognized the republic's independence and exchanged diplomatic representatives. After an 1842 Mexican invasion of Texas, the British minister arranged a cease-fire between the two sides. When the Texas government suggested an alliance with Britain—partly as a sincere effort to ensure Texas's independence and partly as a ploy to increase Texas's attractiveness to the United States—London carefully weighed the matter.

But one thing stuck in British throats: slavery. The antislavery movement in Britain had a long history. In the eighteenth century, Quakers and other out-of-the-mainstream groups had spearheaded the movement, making it relatively easy for Parliament to ignore; yet gradually the abolitionists' message took hold among respectable types. In 1807, under the leadership of William Wilberforce, abolitionists persuaded Parliament to approve a measure outlawing the slave trade. During the next quarter century, Wilberforce and his allies turned up the political heat, succeeding finally in 1833 in obtaining the ban on slavery itself throughout the British empire. As in other countries, the debate in Britain over slavery agitated the political system more than most professional politicians liked. The uproar was not as great in Britain as in the United States, largely because no large segment of the British population owned slaves. For the British, slavery was chiefly a question touching the colonies, which, as in the days of the American Revolution, could not vote in Parliament. But the uproar was great enough that the politicos did not want to roil things any more than necessary. The abolitionists were demanding that Britain strive to suppress slavery throughout the world. The British government was complying, although not as enthusiastically as the abolitionists thought it should.

Under the circumstances, an alliance with slave-holding Texas seemed more of a political liability for the British government than an economic and diplomatic asset for Britain as a whole. Some visionary types suggested that the British government might square the circle by paying the Texans to free their slaves or by at least lending them money to do so. But this scheme would cost more than London was willing to pay for an alliance with Texas. It might also alienate the United States government, which would probably consider such action unwarranted meddling. And it likely would be unacceptable to the Texans, who showed no desire to give up their slaves.

Yet despite London's unwillingness to link Britain's fate to that of Texas, the Texans' European initiatives accomplished one desired result. The interest Britain and, to a lesser extent, France showed in Texas encouraged the American government to reconsider Texas's application to join the Union. Previous efforts by the South to get Washington to annex Texas had hung up on the constitutional provision requiring a two-thirds Senate vote to accept treaties. The South could probably get a simple majority for letting Texas in; nearly all southern lawmakers would vote in favor, plus an odd Northerner here and there. But two-thirds was too much.

Although the congressional arithmetic did not improve by the mid-1840s, the mood in the country shifted sufficiently to alter the rules of counting. Following the 1844 presidential election campaign, in which both the victorious James Polk and (less enthusiastically) his opponent Henry Clay advocated annexing Texas, lame duck president John Tyler adopted the Texas issue as his own. Tyler had few accomplishments to his name, and he hoped before retiring to his plantation in Virginia to usher Texas into the Union. Noting the continued lack of votes for two-thirds approval in the Senate, Tyler proposed that Texas be admitted by joint resolution of both houses of Congress, a maneuver that required only simple majorities in each.

The United States had never annexed another sovereign nation. Precedent therefore gave no guide as to whether Tyler's ploy was legal. The Constitution likewise was silent on the issue. Yet Tyler plunged ahead, relying on the expansionist mood of the country to see him through. He relied astutely, and Congress passed his Texas resolution during his last week in office.

The Texans still had to accept the offer. There was never a serious possibility they would not, although the era of the Texas republic later would be remem-

Like some other politicians, James Polk spoke more belligerently as a candidate than he acted as president. Having threatened two wars, he settled for one. *AP/Wide World Photos*

bered (mostly inaccurately) as a glorious time in Texas history. In July 1845 a special convention gathered in Austin to consider the offer. The convention approved, as did Texas voters in a subsequent referendum.

To the Pacific via Oregon

Texas was one issue in the presidential campaign of 1844. Oregon was another. Americans were in a bumptious mood during the early 1840s. Since 1837 the American economy had suffered a succession of crises and panics. Banks and other businesses in the East had collapsed by the hundreds. In the South and West, farmers watched commodity prices plunge to record lows. As would happen again (notably in the 1890s), pain and confusion at home disposed Americans to look beyond their borders for relief. Some people buy new clothes when they are feeling depressed; Americans in the 1840s went out and got new territory.

During the 1844 campaign Polk and the Democrats pledged to acquire all of Oregon; in his 1845 inaugural address Polk called the American title to Oregon "clear and unquestionable." It was anything but. In 1792 an American ship's captain, Robert Gray, had been the first white person to spot the mouth of the Columbia River, thereby laying the basis for America's claim to Oregon. (A British explorer, George Vancouver, was in the area at the same time but had sailed past the Columbia's mouth without recognizing it. While the river received the name of Robert Gray's ship, Vancouver was honored with the large island off what would become British Columbia.) Lewis and Clark improved the American claim early in the next century, as did agents of the New York–based American Fur Company who established a trading post at Astoria (named for the company's head man John Jacob Astor) at the Columbia's estuary.

But American activity was confined almost exclusively to the southern part of the Oregon country. The British had a far better claim to the northern part of the territory, which extended to fifty-four degrees forty minutes north latitude. British explorers had mapped much of the region; British fur traders had set up a network of forts and trading posts. In 1824 the British-owned Hudson Bay Company built an important post (also named for George Vancouver) on the north bank of the Columbia just above the mouth of the Willamette River. At the time, there were few American settlers in the vicinity, but during the next decade and a half, as Americans started arriving in appreciable numbers, Hudson Bay Company officials gently steered them to farms and homesteads in the fertile Willamette valley on the south side of the Columbia. By the early 1840s the Columbia was the most reasonable dividing line between American and British claims.

James Polk eventually realized this, but he had campaigned on the aggressive slogan "54-40 or fight," and he could not show his new knowledge too soon. And even if politics had not dictated moving slowly on Oregon, demographics did. In 1842 and 1843 what had been a trickle and then a stream of emigrants from the United States to Oregon became a flood. Years of propaganda by a small core of Oregon-boosters were paying off; more important were the reports sent back to friends and relatives about a land of mild climate and generous soil. By 1845 several thousand Americans had made the trek from Independence, Missouri, and other jumping-off points to Oregon. With each party that arrived, the American claim to the region improved. Polk simply had to bide his time.

He did so, albeit rather belligerently, in negotiations with Britain. On several previous occasions, the British had proposed splitting Oregon at the Columbia River. Polk's predecessors had rejected the proposal, and Polk did, too. He reiterated his campaign demand that all of Oregon be America's. To some extent, he was simply playing politics, giving the British lion's tail a bit of a twist. To some extent, he was responding to the desires of Americans planning a large American trade with Asia who wished to ensure that the deep-water harbors of Puget Sound wind up in American control. In December 1845 Polk served notice on Britain that in one year the United States would consider the joint occupancy terminated.

About this time, however, American troubles with Mexico were increasing. The Mexicans were not taking the annexation of Texas very well, and war along the Rio Grande looked likely. Polk was not a brilliant strategist, but he

Oregon Country after the 1846 Agreement

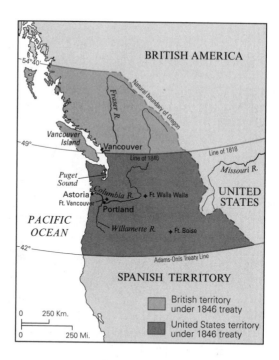

knew enough not to get mixed up in fighting two wars at once. Given the choice, he preferred fighting Mexico to fighting Britain.

Consequently, he quietly backed down from his demand for all of Oregon. He suggested that the United States and Britain simply extend clear to the Pacific the U.S.-Canadian border that ran along the forty-ninth parallel. This still would accomplish the goal of obtaining Puget Sound.

The British also had cause for compromise. The 1840s were a busy period for the British empire. Britain's military forces fought the Opium War in China at the beginning of the decade; they battled Maoris in New Zealand soon after; the Sikh War began in 1845, jeopardizing Britain's hold on India; in Ireland, then a British colony, chronic unrest took a turn for the much worse when the potato crop failed. Most pressingly for the Peel government, the fight for repeal of the corn laws was coming to a head. Repealers were arguing that dropping the import restrictions on grain would mean lower prices for food, a better living standard for workers, and higher profits for manufacturers. Retainers demanded to see proof. Repealers, including the Peel government, realized that a war with the United States would make proof impossible by sending prices soaring regardless of the rules on imports. It would also shred the repealers' contention that Britain need not worry about importing food from such reliable foreign countries as the United States.

Recent precedent likewise argued in favor of compromise. In 1842 American secretary of state Daniel Webster and British envoy Lord Ashburton had concluded a treaty clearing up a number of minor irritants between the United

While American diplomats debated the future of Oregon with British representatives, American emigrants made certain that their side would get the largest part of the territory. *The Bettmann Archive*

States and Britain. The most important of these irritants involved the location of the boundary between the United States and Canada, in particular in the vicinities of Maine and Lake Superior. Webster and Ashburton, eminently reasonable individuals both, deftly gave and took on the various points of friction, reaching accord in the summer of 1842. Though critics on both sides of the Atlantic assailed certain aspects of the Webster-Ashburton treaty, they failed to prevent its ratification.

The critics of the earlier agreement had not fallen entirely silent by the time of the final negotiation of the Oregon question; for this reason the two governments threw their respective critics a few bones in the form of bellicose noises. But this done, the two parties got down to the details of an Oregon compromise. After the requisite dickering, the British accepted the American offer of the forty-ninth parallel as the dividing line, with the exception that Britain should keep that part of Vancouver Island that extended south of the parallel.

Polk never gained a reputation for political bravery, with reason. Refusing to acknowledge that the truncated forty-ninth parallel boundary was the best he could do, he took the unheard of but shrewd step of submitting the proposed pact to the Senate without his recommendation. Some senators grumbled about this buck passing, but a two-thirds majority accepted it for what it was: a fair solution to a dispute that was not worth a fight to either the United States or Britain. His flanks and rear covered, Polk signed the treaty.

The Rio Grande, California, and Other Casi Belli

If politics in Britain worked in favor of accommodation with the United States, politics in Mexico worked in precisely the opposite direction. During the half century after independence, Mexico went through a dizzying succession of governments: two emperors, two regencies, several dictators, and dozens of presidents and provisional chief executives. The various contenders for power had little in common. Some advocated greater central control, on the model of France; others preferred federalism, after the pattern of the United States. Radicals wanted to transfer power to the peasants; conservatives called for leaving power with the wealthy and educated. The institutions of Mexican republicanism were in their infancy, and republicanism's essential characteristic, a willingness to abide by the results of unfavorable elections, had yet to take hold. The result was chronic instability; leaders and would-be leaders rose and fell on a regularly irregular basis.

One thing nearly all Mexicans agreed on, though, was the need to resist pressure from the United States. Like the inhabitants of many new countries, Mexicans found it easier to figure out what they stood *against* than to ascertain what they stood *for.* And for Mexicans, the United States was an easy country to hate. The American rhetoric of manifest destiny was patronizing, at its most benign: Americans often spoke as though civilization would come to Mexico only when Anglo-Saxons arrived. As for the issue of Texas, with hindsight it seemed to most Mexicans to be a clear put-up job: Americans had infiltrated Mexico under false pretenses, when their numbers made them feel strong enough, they revolted against the lawful government, other Americans flocked across the border to ensure the success of the revolt, and after a grace period the United States government annexed Texas. For nearly ten years and through various governments, Mexico steadfastly resisted recognizing Texas's independence. Only at the last minute, after passage of the American joint resolution inviting Texas to enter the Union but before Texas's acceptance, did the Mexican government offer to recognize the Texas republic, and then only on condition that Texas reject the American invitation. The offer came too late, and Texas refused.

Meanwhile, Mexico broke diplomatic relations with the United States for tampering with Texas, in particular by inviting Texas to join the Union. The rupture complicated communications between the American and Mexican governments and thereby exacerbated tensions further. Communication across the Rio Grande was difficult in the best of circumstances; in the supercharged atmosphere of the 1840s it was harder than ever.

In fact, the two sides could not even agree on whether they should be talking across the Rio Grande or across the Nueces River, a hundred miles north of the Rio Grande. In the treaty Sam Houston had extorted out of Santa Anna at San Jacinto, the Mexican president had confirmed the Rio Grande as the southern border of Texas; but the Mexican government never accepted the treaty, and it did not accept the border. When Texas entered the Union, the American government took Texas at Texas's word: that it included the territory all the way to the Rio Grande.

By itself, the dispute over where Mexico ended and Texas began should not have caused a war. Texas was a big state, with or without the strip between the rivers, and Mexico was an even bigger country. But political circumstances in the United States and Mexico convinced leaders in both countries that war was preferable to compromise.

In the United States the Polk administration was trying to make good its expansionist boasts of 1844. The British were showing they could not be bullied on the Oregon question, thereby inclining Polk to deal firmly with Mexico, which probably *could* be bullied. Polk also wanted something from Mexico beyond Texas, namely, California.

For most of the period since the late eighteenth century, California had been a sleepy backwater province at the end of a long and uncertain line of communications from Mexico City. Franciscan padres had established a chain of missions from San Diego to San Francisco and tried with indifferent success to convert the California Indians to Christianity. Settlers from Mexico and Spain, with greater success, had converted much of the region into large cattle ranches.

The cattle were what first attracted Americans to California. Ships en route from Boston and New York to China habitually stopped along the Oregon coast for furs; some of these ships put in at California and discovered that the ranchers there had more cowhides than they knew what to do with. Before long the hide trade developed a life of its own, with American ships bringing manufactured goods from the Atlantic coast and carrying back rawhide for processing into leather products.

Even in those early days California possessed a certain laid-back mystique. The sun always shone. No one asked too many questions about where you had been before or what had brought you to California. Sailors and merchants who visited the California coast longed to return. Some did—to conduct business, to marry local women, to try their hands at ranching. No one expected to get rich, but most expected to enjoy themselves.

The stories the American settlers sent back home caught the attention of Americans in the East; so did the descriptions of California's wonderful harbors at San Diego and San Francisco. Like the harbors of Puget Sound, these promised to be crucially important to future American trade with Asia. Rumors indicated that the British were negotiating with Mexico for the purchase of California. If the rumors proved true and the negotiations succeeded, America might find its Pacific career stunted before it really got started.

This combination of hopes and fears prompted Polk to try to purchase California (and New Mexico for the sake of contiguity). The Democratic president sent a special emissary, John Slidell, to Mexico City to negotiate the purchase; Slidell also had instructions to arrange a settlement of the Texas border dispute.

Slidell was prepared to make a reasonable offer. Polk authorized him to go as high as $40 million, or nearly three times the purchase price of Louisiana. But the Mexicans were in no mood to sell. Slidell's December 1845 arrival in Mexico City coincided with one of Mexico's recurrent political crises. Santa Anna had been tossed out of office and banished several months before, and a coup against his successor was unfolding just as Slidell appeared on the scene. The new strongman, General Mariano Paredes, denounced his predecessor for softness on the American issue, among other sins, and vowed not to relinquish a square foot of Mexican soil without a fight. Paredes rejected not simply the Rio Grande as the border between Mexico and the United States but the Nueces as well. The Sabine River was the true border, he said—meaning that Texas still belonged to Mexico.

Although Polk would have preferred to gain California and the Rio Grande border peacefully, he was not averse to a tangle if the Mexicans insisted. Yet whether by cash or by arms, he was determined to get what he wanted. To increase the pressure on Mexico, the president ordered American troops to occupy the Nueces–Rio Grande strip right down to the north bank of the Rio Grande. In January 1846 General Zachary Taylor moved south from Corpus Christi prepared for a fight. But for three months nothing much happened. Taylor and his Mexican counterpart mostly glared at each other across the Rio Grande. At one point Mexican forces crossed the river and threatened to engage the Americans, but then retired before shooting started.

Polk found the inaction frustrating and was on the verge of going ahead and declaring war anyway, when welcome news arrived. Shortly after the replacement of the Mexican commander opposite Taylor, a large Mexican contingent had crossed the Rio Grande and surrounded a smaller American unit. The Americans chose to shoot their way out. In the exchange of fire, several Americans were killed. The skirmish afforded Polk the incident he needed to justify a war. Asserting that the Mexicans had invaded the United States and shed American blood on "American soil," the president asked Congress to declare war.

Congress complied, although not without dissent. Opposition Whigs doubted that Democrat Polk had exhausted all avenues of diplomacy before resorting to war. Northerners suspected the southern (North Carolinian–Tennessean to be exact) president of being the agent of a conspiracy of slaveholders who aimed to seize Mexico and extend the realm of human bondage. The incident in Texas essentially ensured approval of Polk's war request—not many politicians wished to be portrayed as unpatriotic or uncaring about American lives lost in action—but it did little to calm the suspicions. Northern states contributed volunteers sparingly and with reluctance to what many

Northerners called "Mr. Polk's war." Some northern state legislatures passed resolutions registering their disapproval formally.

The Mexican War

Although after it was over, the Mexican War seemed to many to have been a horrible mismatch, with the victory of the rich, powerful United States over poor, small Mexico a dead certainty, at the time the war happened, the odds appeared closer. The American army comprised less than seven thousand troops, and with the exception of frontier battles against Indians, American soldiers had not marched into combat since the War of 1812. War being a young man's occupation, this meant that the vast majority of the soldiers had never marched into combat at all, Indian fights again excepted. Moreover, the Mexicans could expect greater sympathy from the European powers than the Americans could. By the 1840s the United States was getting too big and boisterous for the restful sleep of British and French officials, and the same power-balancing considerations that had prompted London and Paris to encourage Texas's independence now operated on behalf of Mexico. Mexico lacked Texas's cotton (a minus in the eyes of British and other European textile makers) but it also lacked Texas's slavery (a plus in the eyes of British and other abolitionists). Finally, the war was a defensive one for Mexico but an offensive one for the United States. Defenders have the advantages of internal lines of communication (Mexican reinforcements would travel to the front through friendly territory, while American reinforcements would have to cross hostile soil), familiarity with the terrain (a particular problem in the days before aerial reconnaissance), and the feeling of protecting one's home and family against invasion (while the Americans were left feeling like foreign intruders, which of course they were).

But countries often go to war without fully weighing the costs, and in any event some of Mexico's apparent advantages evaporated in the heat of the war. The Mexican army, which looked good on paper and in the drill square, looked considerably worse on the battlefield. In the campaigns in northern Mexico and California far from the more populated regions of the country, Mexican forces had almost as much trouble with resupply as American forces did. The European powers, while sympathetic to Mexico's plight, did not wish to risk antagonizing the United States.

The war comprised three major campaigns. (See map p. 131.) The first carried American troops across the Rio Grande into northern Mexico during the spring and summer of 1846. General Taylor captured Matamoros in May, then marched west toward Monterrey. American units laid siege to the city and took it at the end of September. In a move that initially seemed militarily appropriate but that soon prompted political controversy, Taylor secured the victory at Monterrey by allowing the Mexican defenders to retreat from the city without surrendering.

Some of the controversy arose from worries in the Polk administration that Taylor was getting too much good publicity. Taylor did nothing to deflate reports that he was looking forward to a political career, which worried Polk and his advisers all the more. Partly on account of an honest difference of opinion regarding military strategy, and partly to pull the spotlight away from the victorious general, Polk placed a large portion of Taylor's force under the command of General Winfield Scott, whom the president ordered to move against Veracruz and Mexico City.

In the meantime, an American contingent under Colonel Stephen Kearny was conducting the second major campaign of the war, in the West. Kearny hoped to capture California after picking off New Mexico on the way. New Mexico fell without a fight, requiring of Kearny and his men only a long walk across the plains and mountains from Kansas and some fearsome grimaces in the direction of the Mexican governor at Santa Fe. California came harder, but not much. For several years California had bubbled with insurrectionary activity. The growing number of Americans in the region did not like living under Mexican authority, which they disrespected as much as they disliked, largely

U.S. soldiers capture Chapultepec castle, laying open the way to Mexico City. *The Granger Collection*

as a result of the ineffectuality caused by the political turbulence in Mexico City.

The Americans' disrespect increased after an accidental invasion of the area by an American naval force in 1842. During the autumn of that year, Commodore Thomas Jones, cruising the Pacific coast, made a mistake that was entirely natural in those days of slow communications. Relations between the United States and Mexico had been strained for some time when Jones received a report that war had broken out. He pondered what to do. Should he wait for confirmation of the report? Should he stop in at a California port and ask the Mexican authorities whether his country and theirs were at war? The latter course would have been the gentlemanly thing to do but might have ruined Jones's career. Jones decided to act first and ask questions later. To the utter astonishment of the Mexicans, the commodore sailed into Monterey Bay and demanded the surrender of the garrison there. The Mexicans, unprepared to fight and wondering what in the world was going on, complied. Jones triumphantly raised the American flag—only to discover to his enormous embarrassment that there was no war. He expressed profuse apologies, struck the flag, and withdrew.

The Jones fiasco reinforced the belief of the Mexican government that the Americans were bent on the conquest of California; at the same time, it convinced residents of California that a Texas-style revolution would be easily accomplished. If they needed any additional convincing, they got it in the spring of 1846 upon the arrival of an American military force under the command of Captain John Fremont. The nominal purpose of the Fremont expedition was to explore and map the western part of the continent; but Fremont, whose political ambitions rivaled those of General Taylor (and doubtless had contributed to his choice of a spouse, the daughter of powerful Missouri senator Thomas Benton), had more in mind than making maps. He wanted to make a revolution.

Fremont reached California a few months before the war with Mexico began. Hewing to protocol, he asked permission of the Mexican authorities to rest his troops and replenish his supplies. Although the Mexicans granted permission, as news of increased tension on the Rio Grande came in, they changed their minds and told Fremont to move along. Fremont grumbled and threatened to stay where he was but eventually packed up and led his men north toward Oregon.

Shortly thereafter, though, an exhausted courier who had chased Fremont halfway across the West caught up with him and delivered a letter stating that war had begun. Fremont was thrilled. He turned his company around and tore south. Fremont's approach, combined with the announcement of the war, encouraged Americans living near Sonoma in northern California to declare independence from Mexico. The rebels hauled down the flag of Mexico and ran up a banner with a picture of a bear on it. Fremont's arrival ensured the success of the "Bear Flag Revolt," which in fact lasted only long enough for the Bear Flag to come down and the Stars and Stripes to go up.

Within weeks an American naval force—whose commander double-checked reports of the commencement of hostilities—took Monterey again. San Francisco capitulated soon afterward. Los Angeles also fell quickly.

But the conquest of California was not to be quite so simple as that. The Mexican Californians did not relish the prospect of being forcibly added to the United States, and during the latter half of 1846 they rebelled against their recent conquerors. They drove the Americans back from positions the Americans had taken easily from the Mexican authorities. Several months and some hot fighting were required to bring the uprising under control. By January 1847, however, California was quiet and in American hands.

While the fighting in the West continued, General Winfield Scott prepared to launch the third and decisive campaign of the war. The assault on central Mexico might have been easier had Polk not fallen for a trick of Santa Anna's. The former Mexican president was amusing himself in Cuba and plotting his return to power in Mexico when the war began. The outbreak of hostilities seemed to him an ideal opportunity: the Americans obviously did not like the party currently in power in Mexico City; perhaps they would help him retrieve his previous position. Through a special messenger, Santa Anna indicated that he would be willing to negotiate a peace treaty the Americans would find acceptable. He could do this, of course, only after he resumed leadership of the country.

Polk may or may not have believed Santa Anna, but in either case the president thought the Mexican exile's scheme deserved a try. Already the Polk administration was encountering a fundamental problem of fighting a weak foe: finding someone with the political stature to effect a surrender. A stronger Mexican government might have evaluated Mexico's position after the American victories in northern Mexico, New Mexico, and California and concluded that continued resistance was futile. The Americans had seized what they had set out to obtain, and there was no reasonable hope Mexico could get Texas, California, or New Mexico back. Continued resistance, in fact, would only further provoke the Americans and perhaps raise their price for peace. But the same forces that had compelled Mexican politicians to hurl defiance at the Americans before the war now required them to refuse anything that smacked of surrender. And, after all, what the Americans were demanding was half of Mexico, if Texas was counted. To sign a treaty relinquishing half of one's patrimony without fighting to the bitter end was unthinkable for any true Mexican patriot.

Yet it was not unthinkable, or at least unpromisable, for Santa Anna. After a secret meeting in Havana with an American naval officer ostensibly hunting privateers, the former dictator received an American promise of safe passage through the American blockade of the Mexican coast. In August 1846, following another turn of the revolving door in Mexico City, which threw Paredes out of office, Santa Anna landed at Veracruz. He journeyed to the capital, where he talked his way back into the presidency and command of Mexico's army.

Somewhere between Veracruz and Mexico City, Santa Anna chose to forget what he had told the Americans about ending the war. Gradually the Polk administration learned that it had been played for the fool and that the result of its scheming was not to shorten the conflict but to lengthen it. By letting Santa Anna back into Mexico, Polk handed control of the Mexican army to Mexico's most capable general. It was a mistake the United States government would not forget (until its next war of conquest, in the Philippines at the end of the century).

Santa Anna regrouped Mexico's armed forces and for a time revived Mexican fortunes. He gathered an army and marched north to confront Taylor. Although he failed in an effort to throw the American general back across the Rio Grande, instead suffering a defeat in the February 1847 battle of Buena Vista, his counteroffensive demonstrated that the Mexicans still had considerable fight left in them.

Winfield Scott in particular found this out in the spring and summer of 1847. After great preparation and much delay, Scott's forces hit the beach near Veracruz in March. They captured that city and ascended west toward Mexico City, following the route traversed by the first conquistador, Hernán Cortés, three centuries before. Scott commanded a much larger force than Cortés, but Cortés had benefited from the defection of many of the local groups the then-dominant Aztecs had suppressed. The Mexicans united against Scott in a way they had not against Cortés—which did not say much for the popularity of the Americans. In fact, there were defections going the opposite way, from the invaders to the invaded: one Mexican battalion included a large number of deserters from the American army.

At the crucial battle of Cerro Gordo, American Captain Robert E. Lee discovered a way around Santa Anna's fortified position; with the help of Lieutenant Ulysses S. Grant and other officers who would go on to glory on both sides of the American Civil War, Lee guided Scott to a brilliant victory. The American forces crossed the pass that led into the valley of Mexico City and shortly afterward arrived before the capital.

The popularity of Santa Anna tended to rise and fall on his success at arms. The general's failure to halt the American advance touched off a wave of opposition in Mexico City. Hoping to call his opponents' bluff, and thinking himself the indispensable man of Mexican politics—an attitude entirely in keeping with his view of himself as the "Napoleon of the West"—Santa Anna offered his resignation. He thoroughly expected the offer to provoke cries of desperation and demands that he remain in power. Instead, it was met by a thunderous silence. He abruptly changed his mind and withdrew the offer.

Scott was aware of the existence of the Mexican dissatisfaction with Santa Anna, if not of its precise details. The American commander chose not to press his military advantage for fear of causing the complete collapse of the Mexican government; should the government crumble, there would be no one with whom to negotiate terms of a peace settlement. Santa Anna cannily magnified Scott's fears by suggesting that his government was closer to dissolution than it really was. When Scott offered an armistice, Santa Anna eagerly accepted.

For two weeks American and Mexican negotiators discussed how to turn the armistice into a peace treaty. The discussions got nowhere, despite the intimidating presence of the American army outside Mexico City. While the diplomats talked, Santa Anna regrouped his forces and prepared for more fighting. That fighting came in September and resulted in an American victory. Scott's troops proceeded to occupy the Mexican capital.

Amazingly, even this definitive defeat did not bring Mexican negotiators to the bargaining table for serious talks. Santa Anna's opponents got the better of him, forcing him from the presidency and arranging his court-martial. No one else much wanted to deal with the Americans, not least because of a law passed by the Mexican congress declaring anyone a traitor who even discussed peace terms with the Americans.

Reality gradually set in, however, and an interim government carefully signaled its interest in ending the war. But American patience was wearing thin by this time, and Polk ordered his chief negotiator, Nicholas Trist, back to Washington. Fortunately for most of those concerned, although infuriatingly for Polk, Trist ignored the president's orders—which took six weeks to reach him from Washington—and proceeded to negotiate a treaty.

The result of his labors was the February 1848 Treaty of Guadalupe Hidalgo. The treaty acknowledged Texas as part of the United States and the Rio Grande as the border with Texas. It transferred California and New Mexico to the United States, compensating Mexico with $15 million in cash and the American government's assumption of a little more than $3 million in American claims against the Mexican government. (The principal purpose of the monetary compensation was to prevent critics from saying that the United States had stolen territory from its neighbor.)

While treaties negotiated by the executive branch of the American government are never sure things until approved by the Senate, this treaty initially did not even have the approval of the president. Polk expressed outrage that a mere state department clerk should defy orders and presume to negotiate on behalf of the president. But the document Trist brought home contained everything Polk deemed necessary, and although he continued to curse Trist for a scoundrel and an ingrate, he accepted the pact. The Senate did, too, in March 1848.

The High Tide of American Expansionism

The remarkable thing about the Mexican War was not how much territory the United States took from Mexico but how little. Since the early part of the nineteenth century, proponents of American expansion had proclaimed that the destiny of the United States was to become coterminous with the North American continent—that the Stars and Stripes should wave from the Isthmus of Panama to the Arctic Ocean. The expansionists' voices grew louder with the acquisition of Louisiana, Florida, Texas, and Oregon. They grew louder still with the outbreak of war with Mexico.

The expansionists adduced various reasons why the United States ought to take all of Mexico. They cited the usual concern for the welfare of poor, ignorant Mexicans and added a claim that the corrupt government of Mexico had brought its overthrow upon itself by its lawless and foolish attack against the United States. The United States government had the right to defend American territory and to insist on an indemnity from Mexico to cover the cost of the defense. The cost turned out to include more than twelve thousand American deaths, and though no indemnity could bring these husbands, fathers, and sons back to life, recompense needed to be made. A suitable recompense might be the territory currently under Mexican misrule. Americans also worried about the future stability of Mexico. The Mexicans, many Americans believed, had shown themselves incapable of managing their own affairs. Chaos across the border would tend to spill over into the United States. By annexing Mexico, the United States would solve the problem at its root and at the same time bring Mexicans the blessings of good government.

Another item relating to American security particularly caught the attention of American expansionists. By the mid-nineteenth century, it had become apparent that there was no easy water route from the Atlantic to the Pacific. The dream of a Northwest Passage had frozen solid in the ice drifts around Baffin Island, while the distant and stormy Strait of Magellan remained the closest Atlantic-to-Pacific channel in the south. Lewis and Clark had exploded the idea of a commercially convenient river road across the North America, and although the Amazon had yet to be fully explored, the tremendous height of the Andes was clearly visible from the west and showed that South America would be even more difficult to traverse than North America.

By the second quarter of nineteenth century, the search for a way across the Americas focused on the narrowest part of the two-continent landmass: Central America. The Industrial Revolution had progressed far enough that engineers could draw not-inconceivable plans for digging a canal across the isthmus that separated the Caribbean from the Pacific. The French engineer Ferdinand de Lesseps was already moving sand in his mind to construct the Suez Canal in Egypt, linking the Mediterranean to the Red Sea, and though a Central American canal would be a more difficult job, the basic idea was the same.

Three locations for a Central American canal recommended themselves. Panama, then a province of New Granada (Colombia), contained the shortest route. Yet the Panama route was the steepest and would require blasting a canyon through a mountain range and constructing locks for raising and lowering ships. A route in Nicaragua was longer but less steep. The Nicaraguan route would incorporate rivers and lakes and would involve considerably less digging than the Panama route. It was also farther north than Panama and hence closer to the United States, the certain source of most of the canal's traffic. The third possible route crossed southern Mexico at the Isthmus of Tehuantepec. The Tehuantepec route was a bit steeper than the one through Nicaragua, but it, too, would use natural watercourses. It was the closest of the three to the United States.

And during the Mexican War the Tehuantepec route possessed the added attraction of being in a country whose capital the United States army was occupying. By annexing Mexico, the United States would automatically gain the right to build and operate an interoceanic canal. Such a canal would facilitate commerce with the markets of Asia and would serve the even more vital purpose of tying Oregon and California (and whatever other Pacific frontage fell into American hands) firmly to the rest of the country. A canal would be built sooner or later, the expansionists pointed out. Better it belong to the United States than to anyone else.

Had the Mexican War occurred a generation earlier or a generation later, the expansionists might have carried the day and attached all of Mexico to the United States. But the war actually occurred during the 1840s, and they did not. One reason for their failure was that the Mexicans indubitably did not want to be taken over. Aside from the fact that many Americans were uncomfortable annexing people who resisted, the Mexican population of 8 million threatened to cause considerable trouble for an American army of occupation. Even if the Mexicans should some day come to appreciate the benefits of American rule, the process would take time. Americans have never been known for their patience.

Moreover, many among the white American majority shuddered at the thought of adding those millions of dark-skinned people to the American population. A Cincinnati newspaper approvingly cited a study of the mixed races of Peru and applied its findings to the mixed races of Mexico. "As a general rule," the paper said, "they unite in themselves all the faults, without any of the virtues, of their progenitors; as men, they are generally inferior to the pure races, and as members of society, they are the worst class of citizens." This view was widely shared in the United States, and it cooled American ardor for taking all of Mexico.

Finally, the northern Whigs in Congress opposed measures that might enhance the power of the slave-holding South. In the 1846 congressional elections, the Whigs recaptured control of the House of Representatives and maintained a strong presence in the Senate. They feared that the annexation of Mexico would lead to the admission of more slave states, and they used their legislative power to block such annexation.

This last source of anti-annexationist sentiment was the most important. If the Mexican War had occurred before the slavery debate in America got so bitter, or if it had occurred after the Civil War ended the debate, the anti-annexationist forces would have been much weaker. Under such circumstances, the American soldiers occupying Mexico might well have stayed, and the whole country might have been added to the American domain (just as the Philippines were added at the end of the century).

*   *   *

As it was, the detachment of California and New Mexico from Mexico and their reattachment to the United States nearly completed the expansion of the United States on the North American continent. Two additions remained: the minor 1853 Gadsden Purchase from Mexico, which bought the best route for a southern railroad, and the major 1867 Alaskan purchase from Russia, which provided a steppingstone, like Oregon and California, to East Asia.

Both territorial and commercial expansionists had reason to be pleased with the developments of the second quarter of the nineteenth century. Americans added huge parcels of territory to the United States: Texas, New Mexico, California, and Oregon. Although New Mexico did not promise ever to be much in the way of farm country, Texas, California, and Oregon included a great deal of land as fertile as any that existed elsewhere in the United States. The commercial expansionists applauded these acquisitions as well, paying particular attention to the harbors of California and Oregon. Equally gratifying to the commercial expansionists was the success of the American government in capitalizing on Britain's efforts in opening the China market to Western traders.

Although the Mexican War produced one of the greatest triumphs of American expansionism, that conflict also marked the beginning of expansionism's eclipse. Slavery had been the dirty little secret of American republicanism from the start, hidden away in the constitution's three-fifths clause (which counted 60 percent of slave numbers in determining how many seats each state received in the House of Representatives). Slavery had remained more or less quiet until the fight over Missouri in 1820, but for a half century after that, slavery colored every aspect of American politics, including American expansionism. The first question people asked about a possible addition to the United States was, Would it be slave or free? Deepening disagreement about the answer diminished the impetus for expansion, slowing acquisition of Texas and preventing the possible acquisition of all of Mexico.

While slavery was responsible for taking the edge off American expansionism, expansionism was largely responsible for bringing the slavery dispute to a climax. If Congress had not had to deal with the question of slavery in the newly acquired territories, a majority of American senators and representatives probably would have been satisfied for many years to let slavery in the southern states alone. Politicians shun controversy: enemies tend to have better memories than friends. But the territories had to be organized, and eventually they had to enter the Union as either slave states or free. In deciding how to treat the territories taken from Mexico, Congress produced sparks that set America aflame.

Sources and Suggestions for Further Reading

Scores of authors have written knowledgeably about the Industrial Revolution. A sampling of introductory volumes includes W. O. Henderson, *The Industrial Revolution in Europe, 1815–1914* (1961); E. L. Jones, *Agriculture and the Industrial Revolution* (1974); Phyllis Deane, *The First Industrial Revolution* (1979 ed.); R. M. Hartwell, ed., *The Causes of the Industrial Revolution in England* (1967); and Allen Thompson, *The Dynamics of the Industrial Revolution* (1973).

Robert Heilbroner, *The Worldly Philosophers,* is the most accessible introduction to the theories of Malthus, Ricardo and Smith. A more sophisticated overview of the development of economic theory is Jurg Niehans, *A History of Economic Theory, 1720–1980* (1990).

On China, the best place to start is Jonathan D. Spence, *The Search for Modern China* (1990), an enthralling account of four centuries of Chinese history that contains a great deal on the impact of the West, including the United States, on China. Various works by John King Fairbank, such as *The United States and China* (1979 ed.), also focus on China but include much on American dealings with that country. Warren I. Cohen, *America's Response to China* (1990 ed.), and Michael H. Hunt, *The Making of a Special Relationship: The United States and China to 1914* (1983), deal more explicitly with the early development of American relations with China. Fairbank, *Trade and Diplomacy on the China Coast* (1953), covers the emergence of the system of treaty ports during the first half of the nineteenth century. Arthur P. Durden, *The American Pacific: From the Old China Trade to the Present* (1992), takes a long view on a large area.

Relations between Euro-Americans and the native American Indian tribes are covered in Bernard W. Sheehan, *The Seeds of Extinction: Jeffersonian Philanthropy and the American Indian* (1973); Michael Paul Rogin, *Fathers and Children: Andrew Jackson and the Subjugation of the American Indian* (1975); and Ronald N. Satz, *American Indian Policy in the Jacksonian Era* (1975).

On the ideology and propaganda of Manifest Destiny, two books are most valuable: Albert K. Weinberg, *Manifest Destiny* (1935); and Frederick Merk, *Manifest Destiny and Mission in American History* (1963). On expansionism generally, Ray A. Billington, *The Far Western Frontier, 1830–1856* (1956), traces the westward movement of America's western border. Norman Graebner, *Empire on the Pacific* (1955), deals with the strategic issues involved in the westward push. William H. Goetzmann, *When the Eagle Screamed: The Romantic Horizon in American Diplomacy, 1800–1860* (1966), explores what empire meant to Americans. David M. Pletcher, *The Diplomacy of Annexation: Texas, Oregon and the Mexican War* (1973) gives a thorough accounting of how those two territories (and New Mexico) came into the possession of the United States. Frederick Merk also deals with Oregon in *The Oregon Question* (1967); and the same author's *The Monroe Doctrine and American Expansion, 1843–1849* (1966), shows how Monroe's statement became a genuine doctrine. Charles G. Sellers, *James K. Polk, Continentalist, 1843–1846* (1966), provides the best account of the election of 1844 and its effects on American expansion.

The issue of Texas is covered in Frederick Merk, *Slavery and the Annexation of Texas* (1972); David J. Weber, *The Mexican Frontier, 1821–1846* (1982); and David Montejano, *Anglos and Mexicans in the Making of Texas* (1988); as well as in the books by Pletcher and Goetzmann.

On the Mexican War, Otis A. Singletary, *The Mexican War* (1960) is direct and to the point. Justin H. Smith, *The War with Mexico* (1919) is exhaustive, while John S. D. Eisenhower, *So Far from God: The U.S. War with Mexico* (1989) is recent and lively. Various additional perspectives on the war and its antecedents show up in Glenn W. Price, *Origins of the War with Mexico: The Polk-Stockton Intrigue* (1967); John H. Schroeder, *Mr. Polk's War: American Opposition and Dissent, 1846–1848* (1973); Ernest M. Lander, Jr., *Reluctant Imperialists: Calhoun, the South Carolinians, and the Mexican War* (1984); and K. Jack Bauer, *The Mexican War* (1974). Rudolfo Acuna, *Occupied America: A History of Chicanos* (1988), looks at the situation from the other side of the border.

Howard Jones has mastered the sources on the Webster-Ashburton treaty and associated matters; his *To the Webster-Ashburton Treaty: A Study in Anglo-American Relations, 1783–1843* (1977) is the best book on the subject. Also dealing with Anglo-American relations are Wilber D. Jones, *The American Problem in British Diplomacy, 1841–1861* (1974); Kenneth Bourne, *Britain and the Balance of Power in North America, 1815–1908* (1967); and Charles S. Campbell, *From Revolution to Rapprochement: The United States and Great Britain, 1783–1900* (1974).

Chapter 5

The Second Age of Revolution, 1848–1865

M aybe it was something in the air, but the period from the late 1840s through the mid-1860s produced a plethora of political and social upheavals around the world. In terms of millions of people killed and dislocated, the Taiping Rebellion, which convulsed China from 1850 through 1864, was the largest; but other revolutions had a greater and more lasting impact on the course of world history. In 1848 fighting broke out in several European countries, pitting advocates of change against defenders of the status quo. The challengers ranged from moderate progressives to root-and-branch revolutionaries. Although the European status quo survived the challenge largely intact, the political and intellectual ferment the period produced lasted far into the future.

The winds of revolution blew west across the Atlantic as well. In Mexico, reformers threw out Santa Anna—for the last time, as it happened—and proceeded to attack existing institutions of property and religion. Conservatives counterattacked, touching off a civil war that eventually provoked foreign military intervention. The presence of the foreigners alarmed the United States government, which strongly considered military intervention of its own.

The winds of change kept blowing west, across the Pacific to Japan. The winds brought Matthew Perry and a fleet of American warships, which forcibly opened Japan to Western trade and, more important, Western ideas. Within a decade the old order was tottering; within a generation it was being remade beyond recognition.

Of all the upheavals of the mid-nineteenth century, however, the most portentous—certainly for America and arguably for the world—was the American Civil War. The dispute over slavery intensified during the 1850s, spilling beyond the borders of the United States and creating turbulence in the Caribbean and Central America. Eventually the dispute led to the most destructive war of the hundred years between the end of the Napoleonic wars and the outbreak of the First World War. Whether the war between North and South constituted a revolution has been a matter of debate among historians ever since; what is hardly debatable is that the conflict had revolutionary results. It settled once and for all the debilitating problem of American slavery, and it propelled the United States on a course leading directly to global preeminence.

Matthew Perry talks business with representatives of the Japanese shogun.
The shadows in the foreground are perhaps those cast by Perry's warships.
The Bettmann Archive

The Specter Haunting Europe

During 1848 a wave of interest in spiritualism swept the English-speaking
world. All across Britain and the United States, people convinced themselves
they could communicate with the dead, foretell the future, and tap into powers
beyond those normally given to mortals. Perhaps it was this contemporary
sensitivity to the supernatural that prompted Karl Marx, a German intellectual
living in London, to pen one of the most memorable lines in the history of
political propaganda. "A specter is haunting Europe," Marx declared: "the
specter of communism."

Marx's interest in the spiritual did not extend beyond its literary suggestive-
ness. On the contrary, his approach to politics and economics—the most important approach to emerge anywhere in the world during the nineteenth
century and one that would transform the nature of international relations,
America's and everyone else's, during the twentieth century—was firmly rooted
in the material world. Marx himself was rooted in the materially comfortable
world of the German middle class. The son of a Prussian lawyer, he received
a good education in philosophy and law. As a young man he never had to
worry much about being able to make a living. Yet middle-class life did not
suit Marx, and by his midtwenties he was already taking part in left-wing
German politics. His editorship of a radical Rhineland newspaper got him in

Chronology

1848	Treaty of Guadalupe Hidalgo; revolutions throughout Europe; *Communist Manifesto* published
1849	Gold rush to California
1850	Clayton-Bulwer treaty; Compromise of 1850; Taiping Rebellion in China commences
1851	Cuba (unsuccessfully) declares independence from Spain
1853	Crimean War begins; Perry arrives in Japan; Gadsden Purchase arranged
1854	Treaty of Kanagawa with Japan; Ostend Manifesto
1855	Walker in Nicaragua
1857	Rebellion in India against British rule
1859	Oil discovered in western Pennsylvania
1860	Lincoln elected, secession starts; Garibaldi proclaims Victor Emmanuel II as Italian king; Anglo-French-Chinese war ends
1861	Civil War begins; *Trent* affair; emancipation of serfs in Russia
1862	Battle of Antietam
1863	Emancipation Proclamation; French troops capture Mexico City
1864	Maximilian installed as Mexican emperor
1865	Civil War ends

trouble with the authorities; he printed the last issue of the paper in red ink before fleeing the country. In Paris he met Friedrich Engels, with whom he began a lifelong collaboration.

The most important product of the Marx-Engels collaboration was the 1848 *Communist Manifesto*. Written in an attempt to place their own mark on the turmoil that was starting to shake Europe, the tract was aimed both at an audience of other leftists and at the broader public. Most of the pamphlet made sense only to persons steeped in ideological hairsplitting, but the opening ("A specter is haunting Europe . . .") and the closing ("Workers of the world, unite! You have nothing to lose but your chains; you have a world to win") gave the manifesto sufficient zing to send its message beyond the narrow circle of the already converted. Marx and Engels decried the system of private-property capitalism beloved of the merchant and manufacturing classes of industrializ-

Karl Marx, busy writing radical tracts and tomes, had little time for shaving. *The Granger Collection*

ing Europe. The problem with capitalism, they asserted, was that it set everyone in society against everyone else. The baker beggared the butcher, if possible, while the grocer gouged the housewife. Worst of all, the most powerful elements in a capitalist system, the factory owners and other industrial barons, ground the least powerful, the unskilled workers, into the mud. The workers received subsistence wages, and these sporadically. As soon as factory orders slumped, workers were thrown out onto the street. Should sickness or injury impair their ability to work, they were tossed aside with less care than a broken spindle (which might at least be sold for scrap). For workers to demand higher wages and better working conditions was hopeless under current conditions, for the police and other institutions of government took the side of the owners, cracking heads as necessary to keep the work force cowed and cooperative. Marx and Engels did not consider capitalists especially evil. The captains of industry, they held, were simply responding to the pressures imposed on them by an economic system that rewarded greed and penalized humanitarianism. Solving the problems of an industrial economy required changing the system.

Although the *Communist Manifesto* touched on the major themes of what later went by the name of Marxism, the full development of those themes kept Marx busy for the rest of his life. The essence of Marxism was a reading of history as economics and of historical development as the consequence of ongoing class struggles. At different times in the past, different groups had controlled the economic systems of different countries; but in all cases one fundamental principle applied: whoever controlled property controlled politics and nearly everything else that mattered in society.

Like many people of his time, Marx was quite impressed by the achievements of scientists, who seemed daily to be unlocking the secrets of the physical world. Partly out of a sincere belief in the scientific method, and partly out of a desire to add to his own credibility, Marx cast his arguments in scientific form. The lion of the scientific world in Marx's time was Charles Darwin, whose 1859 *Origin of Species* described modern animal and plant species as products of evolution based on the survival of the fittest. Marx adapted Darwin's ideas to the study of societies. For Darwin, the appropriate unit of study was the species; for Marx, it was the class. At present the capitalist class, or bourgeoisie, was on top. In earlier days the feudal nobility had held sway. In the future the working class would displace the bourgeoisie. For Darwin, mutations and natural selection accounted for change in the species make-up of the world; for Marx, the contradictions inherent in any mode of economic organization constituted the engine of change. Capitalism, or rule by the bourgeoisie, would give way to communism, rule by the workers, or proletariat. The change would occur after a period during which the bourgeoisie's relentless pursuit of profits utterly impoverished the proletariat, driving the workers to revolution. In keeping with his scientific approach, Marx contended that the future of the class struggle was foreordained. Communism would be the inevitable result of immutable laws of economics and history.

Events of the year the *Communist Manifesto* appeared suggested that the future might be closer than many, even Marx, had recently thought. The excitement of 1848 started in Paris. The restoration of the Bourbon monarchy after the defeat of Napoleon had not extinguished the fires of republicanism in France, which smoldered underground for a decade and a half before flaring up in 1830. The French king at that time, Charles X, overreached himself in asserting royal control, causing the volatile elements in Paris to rise in revolt. Charles, who remembered how a previous generation of revolutionaries had treated his brother Louis XVI, fled in haste to England. But relatively few people in France wanted to relive the first French Revolution, and when moderates proposed Charles's replacement by the duke of Orleans, Louis Philippe, who agreed to govern along constitutional lines, the revolutionary mood dissipated.

Louis Philippe in power proved to be no bargain. During the 1830s and 1840s, he alienated both conservatives and radicals by policies that capriciously careened from political left to right. In February 1848, when Louis tried to suppress dissent with greater vigor than usual, the barricades again went up in Paris. The national guard, called out to disperse the disrespectfuls, refused to attack—until too late, when the troops attacked with massive force and killed dozens of demonstrators. Radicals made instant martyrs out of the deceased, and mobs roamed the city. Within days Louis was on a boat for England, following Charles into exile.

The radicals refused this time to be bought off with promises of a constitutional monarchy. They compressed what had taken three years after 1789 into three months, and by the beginning of the summer of 1848 the red flag of revolution waved defiantly in the breeze off the Seine.

But it did not wave unchallenged. In June the French army struck back. Three days of fighting killed or wounded ten thousand insurgents. The French assembly quickly rewrote the French constitution to provide for a strong—but elected—president and announced elections. The winner in a landslide was a man with all the right names for a French leader: Louis Napoleon Bonaparte, the nephew of the former general-emperor.

While the current Napoleon restored order in France, the virus of revolution spread across Europe. Austria-Hungary followed closely behind France. The Hungarian boat-rocker Louis Kossuth read the reports of rioting in Paris and dared his compatriots to be no less bold in seeking their own liberty. Radicals in Vienna heard Kossuth's voice and took to the streets. The violence there caught Prince Metternich's secret police flat-footed. When the rebels stormed the imperial palace, Metternich, the architect of the Holy Alliance and the symbol of European reaction, resigned in fright, donned a disguise, and hastened off for England.

If Metternich was not safe, it seemed, no conservatives were. Rioting soon broke out in Berlin, forcing the king of Prussia to promise a constitution. The smaller fry of the German principalities caved in to radicals in short order. The citizens of Milan, then a part of the Austro-Hungarian empire, rose against the imperial occupation forces and drove them from the city. Venice declared itself an independent republic, just as in the good old days of the Renaissance. Hungary voted itself almost out of the empire, demanding self-government and merely nodding to the Austrian monarch.

By the beginning of the summer of 1848, while the radicals still called the tune in Paris, most of western Europe was in the throes of a revolution the likes of which almost no one had anticipated. For a brief moment it looked as though the world—or at least a big portion of the European part of it—would be refashioned overnight. Power would pass from monarchs and reactionary assemblies to the people. The shackles of a dead past would fall away, opening the path to a future of self-determination and equality.

But the moment passed before the revolutionaries could consolidate their gains. In central Europe as in France, conservative aristocrats retained their grip on the armies, which were largely composed of traditionally conservative peasants. They counterattacked against the radicals in one city after another. By the end of 1848 the old order was fairly well back in place. A few outbreaks occurred the following year—in Dresden, leftists gave the status quo some solid knocks, while in Rome republicans shot Pope Pius IX's chief minister and forced the pontiff to flee the city—but the reactionaries had recaptured political momentum. At the century's halfway point, all that remained of the revolutions of 1848 were some nightmarish memories for conservatives, and a wandering class of frustrated republicans, many of whom wound up in America.

American Liberalism, American Reaction

Among the latter group was Louis Kossuth, whose 1851 arrival in America sparked an American vogue for European republicanism. Various American political leaders, most notably Daniel Webster, praised Kossuth and the Hungarian revolution, which they described as following in the pattern of the American Revolution. For a time, Kossuth hoped for American aid to revive the forces of change in his homeland.

But the vogue passed, partly because of the shifting concerns of the politicians who feted Kossuth, and partly because Americans as a people could not decide quite where they really stood on the issues Kossuth represented. America in the mid-nineteenth century was a society in which liberalism mixed curiously with reaction. Nineteenth-century liberalism (not to be confused with twentieth-century liberalism) advocated allowing individuals the greatest possible scope for personal liberty. In Europe, liberalism was the ideology of the rising business classes, which for years had had to buck archaic constraints on their economic activities. Like modern American conservatives, classical liberals wanted to get government off the backs of private entrepreneurs. They opposed leftover guild restrictions on business activity, and they tried to limit efforts by trade and industrial unions to create new restrictions. Placing utmost confidence in themselves—and why not?, since they were the creators of the modern industrial society—they distrusted power in the hands of people who had not demonstrated their ability in the rough-and-tumble world of business. They disliked monarchs, except those duly fenced in by constitutions. They frowned on aristocrats, who merely inherited wealth and position. They supported freedom of speech, the press, and religion, not so much from a love of unfettered debate and conscience as from a conviction that such freedom was essential for breaking the last fetters on individual initiative.

In international affairs, the classical liberals favored free trade. Free trade would enrich the countries that encouraged it; it would also enhance the power of the most enlightened class in society: namely, the liberals and their friends. They criticized the maintenance of large armies, regarding military establishments as a drain on national resources. (Navies were a little different; warships might be necessary to safeguard international trade.) The liberals generally disapproved of interventionist foreign policies, for the same reasons they disapproved of interventionist domestic policies and because foreign intervention distracted nations from the more important matter of making themselves rich. Although they opposed revolution—too radical—they rejected the idea of venturing abroad to suppress it.

Of all the countries of the world, the one that most closely met liberal standards during the mid-nineteenth century was Britain. The British had adopted free trade for themselves and were pushing it for other countries. They had closely circumscribed the powers of their monarch. Britain's landed aristocrats were giving way to the industrialists of Manchester and the other manufacturing and commercial centers. People in Britain were fairly free to say and publish what they thought; they could practice the religion they chose, although the Church of England still enjoyed government support. Significantly—and bearing out the liberal belief that the most effective means of preventing revolution was to allow moderate reform, along the lines of Britain's 1832 Reform Act—Britain also avoided the revolutionary upheavals that rent much of continental Europe in 1848.

The United States might have challenged Britain as the liberal paradise but for one glaring anomaly: slavery. Foreign observers of the United States endlessly scratched their heads trying to figure out how Americans reconciled their state-of-the-Enlightenment-art constitution, containing a bill of rights unmatched elsewhere, with the barbarous relic of human servitude. Many America-watchers thought it particularly ironic that such founders of American liberty as George Washington and Thomas Jefferson had owned slaves. Some correctly attributed the discrepancy between American preachment and practice to hypocrisy. Others recognized, also correctly, that it reflected the kind of compromise between competing interests that is inherent in republican politics: the drafters of the American Constitution, knowing they could never get the southern states to join the Union if they banned slavery, decided that national unity outweighed emancipation. (They might have had some problems as well with slave owners in the northern states that still allowed slavery.)

Many white Americans agreed that slavery was a blot on the nation's conscience and good name. (Almost all black Americans presumably did, too—with the possible exception of those few African Americans who themselves owned slaves.) They were embarrassed to note that slavery had disappeared or was disappearing from most of the modern world. After Britain had abolished slavery in 1833, France did the same in the year of the 1848 revolutions. Portugal phased out slavery across its empire starting in 1858; the Netherlands commenced the process of emancipation five years later. In Latin America, Buenos Aires (Argentina) had led the way toward freedom in 1813, declaring that children born to slaves would be free. Colombia granted freedom at age eighteen to slaves born after 1821. Mexico abolished slavery summarily in 1829—a move that helped touch off the Texas revolution. Most of the other Latin American countries ended slavery during the same period. The two biggest exceptions—Brazil and Cuba, the latter still a Spanish colony—were not the kind of company most Americans liked to keep. Moreover, the domestic European approximation of slavery—serfdom—was also clearly on its last legs. The remaining principal bastions of serfdom were crumbling: in 1848 Austria freed its serfs, followed in 1861 by Russia.

Once a country abolished slavery, it had two reasons for encouraging other countries to do the same. The first was the natural human tendency to impose one's own standards of morality on others. This was especially true regarding the trampling of the rights of defenseless people who needed outside advocates; if you did not help the slaves, who would? The second reason was less high-minded. Employers in countries that abolished slavery feared the competition of countries that still had slaves. British sugar planters in Jamaica, for instance, worried about being undercut by American planters using slaves. Whatever the morality of the issue, for the British government to pressure other countries to eliminate slavery made good business sense.

In most cases the British did not go so far as to meddle with slavery *within* other countries; but they did attempt to suppress the international slave trade. In fact, British attempts to suppress the slave trade predated the abolition of slavery within the British empire. The worst abuses of the slave system occurred in transporting captured Africans across the Atlantic (with the possible exception of the equally horrendous traffic of slaves across the Indian Ocean from East Africa to the Middle East and South Asia). These abuses caused the British to get out of the slave-trading business in 1807. (The same abuses caused the United States to do likewise in 1808.)

But the British (and the Americans) soon discovered that washing their own hands of the slave trade did nothing to diminish its atrocities. On the contrary, British slavers had been comparatively mild in their shipboard treatment of slaves—compared, admittedly, to a pretty unsavory sample of the dregs of humanity. By defaulting their market share to the Spanish and Portuguese and Dutch, the British inadvertently made the atrocities worse. Nor did British efforts to prevent other countries from slave trading do much immediately to improve the lot of slaves. Knowing that some of their vessels would get caught, slavers crammed more slaves than ever onto each so that those vessels that did slip through would keep the slave markets supplied. In addition, slavers who saw the Union Jack appear on the horizon and believed capture to be imminent not infrequently murdered their cargoes and threw the bodies overboard to avert Britannia's wrath.

British attempts to suppress the slave trade brought Britain into conflict with the United States. While most other seafaring nations agreed to let British commanders examine ships flying those nations' flags, to see whether they were illegally carrying slaves, the United States refused such permission. The refusal owed partly to southern objections to anything hinting of additional restrictions on slavery and partly to bad memories of British violations of American neutral rights before the War of 1812. The British nonetheless persisted in stopping vessels flying the American flag, claiming—with some justice—that non-American slavers were illegally using the American flag to prevent capture. American complaints on the topic of the slave trade came to a head in 1841 when slaves aboard an American ship, the *Creole,* en route from Virginia to New Orleans, revolted and seized control of the ship, eventually putting in to port in the British Bahamas. The British released the slaves over the objections of the Tyler administration and the violent protests of American Southerners. Although the Webster-Ashburton negotiations of 1842 resolved the worst of the friction resulting from the disparity between British and American views on slavery, American defense of slavery continued to undercut America's appeal as an exemplar of liberalism.

Americans might have lessened the damage slavery did to their international reputation if they had kept the slavery question quiet in American politics. But by the late 1840s, both the opponents and defenders of slavery were shouting so loudly that almost nothing else could be heard above the din. A central issue in the shouting was the disposition of the territories taken during the Mexican War. In the summer of 1846, Ohio representative David Wilmot had appended to a Polk administration request for war funding (to be specific: a request for $2 million to bribe Santa Anna) a clause declaring that slavery would not be allowed in any territory acquired from Mexico. The Wilmot Proviso fell short in the House of Representatives, but not before polarizing North and South as never before. Northerners denounced as inconceivable the very idea that the United States might reintroduce slavery to California and New Mexico and thereby prove itself more reactionary than backward Mexico. Southerners blasted Wilmot and the North for attacking a cherished southern institution and for treating Southerners as second-class citizens in territory about to be won by southern sacrifice fully as much as northern.

The debate over what to do about California and New Mexico filled the next four years, convincing both sides of the malevolent intentions of the other. Only in 1850 did the leaders of Congress finally jerry-rig a settlement. Like most legislative solutions to difficult problems, the Compromise of 1850 contained something for everybody. The most important partial victories for the North were the admission of California as a free state and the abolition of the slave trade in the District of Columbia. The South received a promise to let states formed out of the rest of the Mexican cession choose slavery if they wished; it also received a tougher fugitive slave law.

Although northern abolitionists decried the 1850 deal as supping with the devil, as a territorial settlement the 1850 compromise favored the antislavery forces. California was the keystone of the Mexican cession, and it was now added to the free column. New Mexico would not amount to much for quite a while and could probably never support slavery economically. Meanwhile, settlers were filling up the northern part of the Louisiana Purchase where slavery was prohibited; eventually the territories there would become free states. Finally, the population of the industrializing North continued to grow at a rate far outstripping that of the agricultural South. Cornered in the southeastern quarter of the country, with few prospects for expansion, the slave holders could not see much of a future for themselves or their institution.

The international climate simply exacerbated the slave holders' fears. Any nation finds it difficult—not impossible, but difficult—to flout a moral consensus of the major countries of the world. The United States, which invented itself as a model of natural rights liberalism, has often been sensitive to international criticism. Americans have usually wanted other people to think well of them. It cut against the American grain to have to justify slavery, an institution most of the rest of the world condemned. Northerners increasingly refused to do so, leaving Southerners feeling more cornered than ever.

As cornered people and animals do, the slave holders struck out. They defended slavery as a positive good, undertaken—to hear their propagandists tell the tale—for the primary purpose of uplifting African savages and bringing their heathen souls to God. Probably some of the slave holders actually believed this rationalization; in any event, it served as their shield against world opinion.

In keeping with this slavery-as-philanthropy argument—and, more important, to escape from their geographical and political corner—slave holders looked south, to Central America and the Caribbean, for new territory into which to expand. They found Cuba particularly attractive, partly because of the richness of that island's agriculture (which nicely complemented that of the American South), partly because Cuba was still a colony of Spain (which meant that the conquest of Cuba could be portrayed as liberation), and partly because slavery still existed there (which allowed would-be conquerors to avoid the odium the idea of restoring slavery to California had raised).

Southern efforts to acquire Cuba began in a serious way at the end of the Mexican War. In 1848 Polk looked into buying Cuba from Spain, but the Spanish refused to relinquish what little remained of their American empire. Neither were the British and French thrilled at the idea of an American Cuba. Until this point, American expansion had been confined to the North American mainland. For the Americans to jump the Florida Strait suggested a major escalation in American plans, something Britain and France—both countries owners of islands in the West Indies—found a bit unsettling.

To divert the Americans, London and Paris proposed a three-way agreement to keep hands off Cuba. One commonly adduced American argument for annexing Cuba was that the United States ought to take the island before some strong European country did. Decrepit Spain did not much threaten American security from Cuba, but Britain or France might. Yet the preemptive argument was more an excuse than a reason, and the American government, feeling full of itself after the victory over Mexico, refused the British-French offer.

In 1852 Americans elected Franklin Pierce president. Pierce came from New Hampshire, which might have meant that he would be a staunch opponent of slavery or at least of its expansion. But Pierce, one of the darkest horses in American political history—he gained the Democratic nomination on the forty-ninth ballot, after the party's heavy hitters had demolished each other—had no political base in the North. Nor did he have an oversupply of principles: he essentially assured southern Democrats a more than fair hearing in his administration in exchange for their support of his nomination. Pierce's secretary of state, William Marcy, a New York spoilsman, likewise knew how to deal.

Pierce and Marcy paid back part of their debt in 1854 when they instructed American diplomats abroad to devise a plan for obtaining Cuba. Three such diplomats—the minister to Spain, James Buchanan; the minister to France,

John Mason; and the minister to Spain, Pierre Soulé—met at Ostend in Belgium to discuss how the Pierce administration should proceed. In a memo of explanation, they asserted that the administration should offer to buy Cuba for a reasonable price, perhaps $120 million. But if Spain refused, the administration should be prepared to use force. Cuba was vital to the security of the United States. Strictly as a matter of self-defense, the United States would be justified in bringing Cuba within the sphere of American sovereignty.

Through the administration's carelessness, this memo—dubbed by headline writers the "Ostend Manifesto"—leaked to the press. Its publication immediately exploded what small chance had existed for an agreement with Spain. It also convinced those few Americans who still needed convincing that a conspiracy of slave holders had captured the Democratic party and would stop at nothing, including war, to extend the territory available to slavery. It ruined the career of Pierre Soulé, whom the administration blamed for the fiasco, but not the career of James Buchanan, who went on to become the next president.

Filibuster Fiascos: Central America

By the 1850s most defenders of slavery were beyond embarrassment on the subject of the peculiar institution, and though the effort to acquire Cuba came to nothing, they soon looked elsewhere for the growing space they believed slavery required. Central America struck the fancy of many. Immediately after independence from Spain in the early 1820s, the countries of Central America had attempted to band together into a larger federal union, but the effort had run up against entrenched local interests; and after a civil war and various other calamities, including a major cholera epidemic, the Central American federalists abandoned the experiment.

Some of the Central American republics survived the crackup better than others. The coffee-producing states of Costa Rica and El Salvador prospered, relatively speaking, as rising world demand for coffee pushed prices up. Guatemala, by contrast, suffered the double disability of unrelieved poverty and the reactionary rule of a right-wing president-for-life. Nicaragua and Honduras became battlegrounds for feuding cattle barons whose ranch hands doubled as cavalry troops.

During their early years, the countries of Central America generally valued the United States government's Monroe Doctrine assertion that Spain and its allies must not try to restore the Spanish empire in the Western Hemisphere. They also appreciated the role of the British navy in putting some muscle behind the American assertion. Yet the Central Americans did not take long to wonder whether the cure was worse than the disease. The British looked on Central America as a possible transit way between the Atlantic and the Pacific. In addition, London fretted that the unrest that seemed to be endemic to the region would spread to British Honduras (Belize) or to the British West Indies.

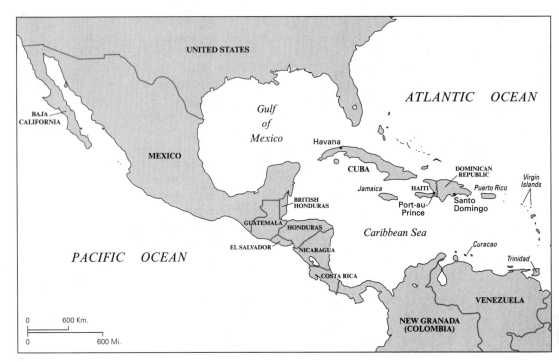

The Caribbean and Central America (1850s)

In the 1840s British troops landed on the Caribbean coast of Nicaragua, apparently intending to stay for awhile.

The interest of the United States in Central America lagged only slightly behind that of Britain. Washington could hardly let the British lock up the best rail and (eventually) canal corridors in Central America. American concern increased dramatically at the end of the 1840s when the United States acquired Pacific frontage in Oregon and California. The 1848 discovery of gold in California rapidly populated America's Pacific coast and made convenient communication with the eastern half of the country all the more critical.

Lest competition over canal rights in Central America derail an otherwise increasingly cooperative relationship between Britain and the United States, the two governments sat down to discuss how they might settle matters amicably. After some effort they devised a treaty—the Clayton-Bulwer Pact of 1850—specifying that neither side would attempt to gain exclusive canal rights across Central America.

The British, reassured that they would not be excluded from any canal-building venture in Central America, gradually lost interest in the area. They pulled back from Nicaragua, leaving that country and the other Central American republics largely to themselves and to the United States.

Americans soon took advantage of the British retreat. The great and growing demand for transportation to California inspired American business interests to invest in Central America. The region was a natural for Cornelius Vanderbilt, a New York steamship magnate who was moving into railroads. Vanderbilt underwrote the construction of a rail line across Nicaragua to connect with his steamships sailing out of New York, New Orleans, and San Francisco. By the early 1850s a traveler could purchase a single ticket to ride in style and comfort from America's financial capital to the East to the gateway to the gold fields in the West.

Although Vanderbilt would go down in American history as one of the "robber barons" of the nineteenth century, he was relatively harmless compared to some other Americans operating in Central America. The most notorious was the filibuster (a term derived from "freebooter") William Walker, a slight man who entertained grand ideas about a Central American empire with himself in charge. Walker made a dry run at empire building in 1853 when he organized a band of soldiers of fortune and marched into Baja California. Walker's adventure caught the Mexican authorities by surprise; they could not figure out why anyone would want to conquer that distant desert. After they recovered from their surprise, they moved against Walker, and when he failed to obtain hoped-for reinforcements from San Francisco, he fled back to the United States.

In 1855 Walker turned his attention to Nicaragua. Some shortsighted members of a liberal faction in that country's continuing civil struggles had heard

Cornelius Vanderbilt, flanked by his steamships, stands atop the Grand Central Railroad Building in New York, straddling two eras of transportation technology. *Brown Brothers*

about Walker, and they invited him to bring some of his ruffians and join the fighting against the reactionaries. Walker complied, and within a brief while he and three hundred of his followers had propelled the liberals into power.

But then Walker and his gang propelled the liberals right on out of power, seizing control of Nicaragua for themselves. Walker assumed the office of president and proceeded to rule by decree. He made English the official language of the country despite the fact that almost no one spoke it besides himself and his desperadoes. In a bid for support from the American South, Walker legalized slavery. The Pierce administration rewarded his efforts by granting diplomatic recognition to his clique as the legitimate government of Nicaragua.

Walker saw himself as the unifier of Central America. He dreamed of drawing the countries and the various factions of the region together in a common purpose. He accomplished his dream, though not quite as he anticipated. Walker so antagonized all parties to the Nicaraguan civil war that they put aside their differences with each other and joined hands to oust him. Likewise the other countries of Central America, which had not been able to agree on anything else for years, agreed with Nicaragua and each other that Walker had to go. By mid-1856 the anti-Walker Nicaraguan forces had proclaimed a "national war" against the American adventurer; Guatemala, Honduras, Costa Rica, and El Salvador soon joined in. For what it was worth, Cornelius Vanderbilt threw his support to the anti-Walker forces as well. Central America was not big enough for two such American egos.

The united opposition succeeded in driving Walker from Nicaragua in the spring of 1857. He fled to the United States, where he spent the next several months plotting his return to Central America and power. But by now his luck had run out. The Buchanan administration decided he was a loose cannon and worked to frustrate his efforts to get back to Nicaragua. The British government trusted him even less and did the same. Despite the American and British opposition, Walker got ashore at Honduras in 1860, only to find himself and his men militarily overmatched. Never one to fight to the finish, he turned himself in to a nearby British official. This representative of London had no desire to shield the Yankee troublemaker and so handed Walker over to the Hondurans. They summarily convicted him of waging war against Honduras and committing other reprehensible deeds. Then they stood him before a firing squad and brought his filibustering career and his life to an inglorious end.

Although William Walker was one of a kind, he had some less capable imitators. A number of Americans signed on with a Venezuelan named Narciso López, who had visions of liberating Cuba from Spanish domination and attaching it to the United States—or so he told those Americans from whom he sought assistance. In the early 1850s López launched a series of ill-fated attacks on Cuba. The last ended when Cuban troops captured López and his band and executed them.

Free Trade at the Point of a Gun: The Opening of Japan

Walker became an embarrassment to the United States more for his failure than for what he attempted. The middle years of the nineteenth century were a bleak period for people who asked for ethical fastidiousness in the conduct of American international relations. Despite the efforts of American apologists to explain away the war with Mexico, most foreign observers saw it as a textbook case of a strong country taking what it wanted from a weak country. The efforts to acquire Cuba cast the United States in hardly more favorable a light. William Walker, though acting as a private individual, nonetheless exhibited the kind of disregard for the rights of Central Americans that made the United States a sometimes scary neighbor to the other countries of the northern half of the Western Hemisphere.

The United States did not confine its bullying to the Americas. After the Opium War crowbarred the Chinese market open to Western merchants, American attention turned to the second most important country in East Asia: Japan. Westerners had begun trading with Japan in the sixteenth century, when Portuguese merchants visited the island kingdom. Catholic missionaries followed close behind the merchants. The missionaries enjoyed much greater success in Japan than in China, partly because the Japanese were used to borrowing ideas and institutions from abroad (usually from China) and partly because certain Japanese political reformers found Christianity a convenient tool for breaking the hold of Buddhist conservatives.

But one person's tool is another's weapon, and by the beginning of the seventeenth century a reaction against Christianity and Christians set in. A rebellion by a Catholic community on the island of Kyushu sealed the fate of Christianity in Japan. The government bloodily suppressed the rebels, and in its fervor to prevent future infection, it slammed the door to outside influences. From 1640 until 1853 the Japanese government banned foreign travel by Japanese nationals and prohibited foreigners from visiting Japan. The sole exception to this hermit policy was a license to call at the port of Nagasaki granted to a small number of Chinese and Dutch merchants—the latter chosen for their lukewarm and relatively nonthreatening Protestantism, as contrasted to the aggressive Catholicism of the Portuguese and Spanish.

The policy of seclusion lasted as long as it did because it suited the interests of the ruling group, the Tokugawa shogunate (the clan of military leaders who ruled in the name of the emperor). The Tokugawa shoguns were intent on pacifying and unifying Japan, which had experienced a centuries-long plague of feudal warfare. They recognized that Christianity and other foreign influences would have an unsettling effect on Japanese society, and they determined to minimize the unsettling by minimizing the foreign influences.

At a later time, when the Japanese population had outstripped the resources of the Japanese islands, isolation from the world would have meant economic death. But during the seventeenth and eighteenth centuries, Japan's population remained well within the country's carrying capacity, and the Japanese people fairly prospered. The capital city of Edo (Tokyo) in 1800 comprised more than 1 million inhabitants, making it larger than London or Paris and far larger than any city in the United States.

The ban on foreign influences was never airtight. The Tokugawas were shrewd enough to see that the rest of the world might have a thing or two to teach Japan, although they intended to allow the spread of foreign ideas only to a compact and reliable group. One eighteenth-century shogun permitted the importation of Western books that did not deal with Christianity. Some especially curious and assiduous Japanese learned to speak and read Dutch to exploit their limited contact with the merchants from the Netherlands. Western items previously unknown in Japan—watches, telescopes, tobacco, potatoes— gradually transformed aspects of Japanese life.

Other circumstances likewise predisposed various factions in Japan to wish for greater contact with the outside world. As part of their plan for pacifying the feudal landlords, the shoguns required the landlords and their henchmen, the samurai, to reside at the court at Edo. This cost the landlords money, which they squeezed from their tenants or borrowed. But there were limits on the tenants' capacity for being squeezed and on the landlords' credit lines, and the landlords began looking for other sources of income. Foreign trade offered possibilities, as did the introduction of manufacturing technology from the West. Moreover, by the middle of the nineteenth century the samurai were restless and poor after a long stretch of Tokugawa-imposed domestic peace (which deprived them of the spoils of war); they were eager for the sort of adventures a more active foreign policy might entail. Japanese merchants, for their part, noted the demand for such Western goods as were let into the country, and they sought opportunities to import more. Japanese intellectuals wanted to travel and study abroad.

Consequently, when American commodore Matthew Perry arrived at Edo in 1853, he found a country ripe for a change in its official attitude toward the rest of the world. Perry's commander in chief, Whig president Millard Fillmore, had three objectives in sending Perry to Japan. The first was to end the mistreatment of American sailors stranded on Japanese shores. In the 1840s and 1850s, American whaling ships roamed the far reaches of the world's oceans; the western Pacific was a favorite hunting ground. But the region was stormy, and the whalers not infrequently foundered. American sailors who suffered the misfortune of washing ashore on Japan were often harshly handled and usually imprisoned, sometimes for years. Perry was to try to secure guarantees of better treatment and swifter repatriation.

Fillmore's (and therefore Perry's) second objective was to arrange for the construction of coaling stations for American vessels. By the 1850s the American navy was well into the switch from sailing ships to steamships. (Two of Perry's four ships were steam driven.) Steamships had cut the travel time across the Atlantic to less than two weeks, across the Pacific to less than three. But the new technology did not come free. In addition to being more expensive to build than sailing ships, the steamships required frequent refueling. Coal is not a very energy-dense fuel, and the steam engines of the day were not very efficient. Without coaling stations at numerous strategic spots around the globe, the American navy would be ineffective. Japan possessed lots of coal; Perry had instructions to see if the Japanese government would make some of it available to American ships. (See map p. 214.)

Perry's third objective was to open the doors of Japan to American trade. The debate that had followed the acquisition of California and New Mexico signaled, at least to the prescient, that the days of America's territorial expansion might be coming to an end. But commercial expansion could continue and indeed pick up where territorial expansion left off. American merchants (with the help of the British) had carved a sizable foothold in China. Japan, logically, should follow. How large the Japanese market would turn out to be, only time would tell; but optimism is the ambitious merchant's stock in trade, and whatever the eventual size of the market, it would surely be larger than it currently was. Perry had orders to try to negotiate a treaty of commerce with the Japanese government.

Perry's mission began inauspiciously. He conveyed greetings from Washington to the Japanese emperor, and he informed the emperor of the objectives of his visit. The Tokugawa officials who actually ruled Japan replied that they could not grant Perry's requests. He should leave.

Perry did, but not before promising to return. In his absence, he said, the Japanese ought to think seriously about changing their position.

By the time Perry got back to Edo in March 1854—with five more ships than before, intensifying the formidable impression his smoke-belching "black ships" had made on their first visit—the Japanese had indeed thought seriously about the matter, and they had decided to accede at least partly to the American requests. The Japanese consented to be more hospitable to shipwrecked American sailors, and they agreed to allow American vessels to refuel and re-provision at two out-of-the-way Japanese ports. They stopped short, however, of granting American merchants broad access to the Japanese market. On this point, despite the formidable presence of Perry's fleet, the Japanese government stood firm.

But two out of three objectives achieved was a reasonably good outcome, considering how the odds had looked before Perry set out. And in fact the American foot Perry stuck in the Japanese door soon sufficed to open the door further. The Japanese government discovered that Western influences were manageable and gradually it agreed to greater foreign access. Two years after Perry's second visit, the Japanese government accepted the appointment of an American consul, who accomplished Perry's third objective: a treaty formally opening Japan to American commerce.

Not everyone in Japan liked the idea of opening up to the West. Two strong-headed nobles, the rulers of the baronies of Choshu and Satsuma, hoped to turn the xenophobia still common in Japan against the Tokugawas, whom they considered illegitimate usurpers. For a while their resistance slowed the pace of Japan's adoption of Western ideas. But in the early 1860s they pushed their program too far. The supporters of Satsuma killed a British subject for a minor violation of Japanese custom. (Like the Chinese, the Japanese had decided to let in merchants from several Western countries so as not to be at the mercy of any one country.) The British government demanded punishment of the offenders, but the shogun had to confess that his power did not stretch as far as Satsuma. The British took matters into their own hands and sent a naval squadron against Satsuma, which the British vessels pounded with cannon fire.

During this same period, the ruler of Choshu ordered his gunners to bombard foreign ships passing along his coast. The foreigners complained to the Tokugawas that the bombardment violated their treaty rights, but their complaints produced no suitable response. Again the foreigners took action on their own: in this case a combined flotilla of vessels from the United States, Britain, France, and the Netherlands meted out the punishment, leveling Choshu's fortifications and sinking most of its ships.

The chastisement at the hands of the West made believers out of the skeptics of Satsuma and Choshu. They concluded that the way to defend Japan against the West was to absorb the technology of the West. Yet even as they accepted certain Western ideas, they used their own harsh treatment at Western hands as another weapon against the Tokugawas. They complained that the shogun had failed to prevent foreigners from attacking Japanese. This failure had disgraced the shogun and the nation; therefore the shogun must resign and restore power to the emperor, to whom power rightfully belonged.

This argument convinced enough people that the shogun did quit. His abdication marked the end of the Tokugawa era and the beginning of the Meiji restoration. Under the Meiji emperor, the Japanese rapidly and successfully adopted many of the attitudes and techniques of the West, especially regarding the application of science to industry and military affairs. So well did Japan learn the lessons of the West that before long many in the West would wonder whether the teaching had really been a good idea.

Nationalists All

The late eighteenth and nineteenth centuries hatched political ideologies like a henhouse: republicanism, liberalism, constitutionalism, conservatism, radicalism, socialism, communism. But for planet-shaking effect, none of the isms matched nationalism. Nationalism asserted that the nation (meaning a people sharing a common culture, history, and, usually, territory) should be the basis for political organization and that each nation ought to have its own state (meaning an apparatus of government sovereign over a particular stretch of land).

The idea of nationalism had been implicit in the unifying, state-building efforts of the kings and queens of England, France, and Spain during the late Middle Ages and early modern period; but nationalism only became an explicit political conception during the European turmoil that followed the French Revolution. As Napoleon's armies marched across Europe, creating an empire that spanned much of the continent, many of the non-French who found themselves under the thumb of Paris objected. Napoleon may have had the best intentions in effecting the reforms he did in the countries he conquered, or he may not have; yet no one likes being reformed at bayonet-point, especially when the soldiers holding the bayonets are foreigners.

Napoleon's empire-building was a kind of internationalism, so it was not surprising that resistance to Napoleon's rule took the form of nationalism. Nationalists have come in all political colorations, from the reddest radicalism to the whitest reaction. This changeable quality has been largely responsible for nationalism's potency in defeating the various ideologies mobilized against it. Typically when the banner of nationalism goes up in a country, as against a colonizing or otherwise occupying power, leftists and rightists join forces to give the foreigners the heave-ho. Equally typically they fall out among themselves after the foreigners are gone, but by then the issue is local politics rather than nationalism. For nationalists, the vital question is: Who rules—the indigenous people or foreigners? The nationalist answer is that the indigenous people must rule, regardless of whether the foreigners are more capable of providing efficient and fair government. A common sentiment among nationalist leaders, repeated in one form or another in various countries, is that it is better to be governed like hell by one's compatriots than to be governed like heaven by foreigners.

During the Napoleonic era, nationalists cropped up all over Europe. Spanish nationalists fought against French occupation of their homeland. Italian nationalists were fewer in number and less violent than their Spanish counterparts, largely because French troops and officials behaved better in Italy than in Spain and because the Italians were more appreciative of Napoleon's liberalizing reforms than were the conservative Spanish; but Italian nationalism was no less potent a force than the Spanish variety. German nationalism took an intellectual and cultural turn during this period, with German writers and musical composers moving from the cool rationalism of the eighteenth-century Enlightenment to the hot-blooded romanticism that characterized much of the nineteenth century.

Although the fall of Napoleon let the air out of some of the nationalist movements, in Germany and Italy nationalism remained strong. Germany in the modern sense did not yet exist; the territory that would become Germany was broken into dozens of small and medium-sized kingdoms and principalities, of which the most important was Prussia. Taught by Napoleon that greatness, even survival, in the modern world depended on strength, German nationalists agitated for the unification of the many German states into a single large and powerful one. Until the latter part of the nineteenth century, their agitation did not produce much in the way of results; the centrifugal force produced by local jealousies and suspicions continued to be greater than the gravitational force of German nationalism. But the desire for unification grew yearly, awaiting only the leader who knew how to marshal it.

Nationalists in Italy likewise had to combat a legacy of division and subdivision. The unity Italy had enjoyed during the days of the Roman empire had dissolved in the invasions that brought Rome down. During the Middle Ages, Italians reorganized themselves into city-states, which gradually expanded into the surrounding areas. But in the early nineteenth century, Italy remained fractioned into more than a dozen political entities. As in Germany, disunity produced weakness, and Italy suffered through repeated insults, invasions, and occupations. The nationalist movement in Italy had the dual goal of reclaiming all of Italy for the Italians and of recapturing the glory that had been Italy's during the days of the Romans. Like the nationalist movement in Germany, Italian nationalism was mostly aspirational at the middle of the nineteenth century. But people who aspire hard enough long enough often get what they want.

Americans were not immune to the siren song of nationalism. The American Revolution was essentially a nationalist rebellion, and to the extent the War of 1812 was an effort to vindicate American republicanism in the face of British provocations and threats, that conflict, too, was a nationalist fight. Some Americans might have liked to describe the territorial expansion of the United States across North America as an outgrowth of American nationalism, but imperialism would be at least as accurate a term if imperialism is taken to mean the forcible extension of the power of one state over other territories and peoples. The Monroe Doctrine was a manifestation of American nationalism, although in its definition of the whole Western Hemisphere as an American sphere of interest it was a very ambitious (and for a time somewhat unrealistic) manifestation.

Another form of American nationalism fit the usual definition more closely. During the 1850s inhabitants of the American South increasingly felt themselves and their way of life endangered by the North. The North's population was bigger and growing much faster than the South's, largely because immigrants shunned the land of slavery. The North's flexible economy was industrializing far more rapidly than the South's comparatively rigid and stagnant economy. Political power was flowing northward: the House of Representatives, where representation proportionally reflected population, had fallen irretrievably into northern hands; the presidency, filled by a vote of the mostly proportional electoral college, was moving inexorably in the same direction.

In the southern view, the attack by the North had already begun. The various attempts to curtail the spread of slavery were one arm of the offensive; laws that favored northern interests over southern in other areas were a second. Of these other laws, those involving economics were particularly galling. Ever since Jefferson had fought Alexander Hamilton over how much assistance government should give business, the South had feared a takeover of the federal government by northern bankers, merchants, and manufacturers. During the 1820s and 1830s, the Bank of the United States became a central issue dividing the capitalists of the North from the planters of the South. The northern business classes backed the bank as essential to the steady growth of the

American economy, while the southern planters (and many Westerners) condemned the bank as a conspiracy against the common people of the country.

The tariff likewise divided North from South, even more violently than the Bank of the United States. At a time when the British were converting to the philosophy of free trade, northern manufacturers held fast to the gospel of mercantilism. The manufacturers liked the tariff for padding their profits; consumers and unprotected producers, including most Southerners, disliked the tariff for raising their cost of living. The battle over the American tariff was even more heated than the fight over the British corn laws. In 1828 Congress passed a tariff so high it promptly received the label "tariff of abominations." Although the tariff was basically a bread-and-butter issue, southern opponents transformed the question into a debate over the question of states' rights versus federal authority. The debate provoked the 1832 nullification crisis, which almost touched off the Civil War thirty years early. The crisis passed only when President Jackson threatened to use the army to force South Carolina to obey federal laws, and the nullifiers backed down.

Though the northern federalists won this round, the southern states rightsers remained unconvinced. Southerners adhered still more strongly to the doctrine of states' rights during the subsequent generation. As the sectional divide deepened, Southerners came to consider theirs a separate way of life from that of the North. Southerners demanded and got separate churches from those serving the North: during the 1840s Methodists and Baptists split into northern and southern wings. A distinctly southern literature developed, glorifying the traditional values of the South and denigrating the crass commercialization of life in the North. *De Bow's Review,* a journal published in New Orleans, became the leading mouthpiece for southern sectionalism. Young southern men of college age increasingly tended to stay in the South for their higher education rather than travel to the North, where they would be exposed to the pernicious doctrine of abolitionism.

What was developing in the South was a form of nationalism not greatly different from that developing in Germany and Italy. Just as the Germans and Italians called for the creation of political institutions that reflected the German and Italian cultural and social identities, so American southerners began to demand political institutions that reflected the distinctive identity of the South. As German nationalism and Italian nationalism derived much of their energy from memories of attack by outsiders (especially the French), so American southern nationalism drew on the perceived (and to some extent real) hostility of the North. Although by the middle of the nineteenth century the German and Italian nationalist movements had become exercises in addition (combining small states into larger ones), each had arisen out of a desire for subtraction (withdrawing from Napoleon's European empire). Southern nationalism likewise started subtractively, with eleven southern states seceding from the Union following the 1860 election of Abraham Lincoln. It then proceeded to the additive phase, with the eleven secessionist states combining to form the Confederate States of America.

The northern response to southern nationalism demonstrated a nationalism of its own. To northern Unionists, the South did not constitute a separate nation at all, just a bunch of selfish soreheads who wanted to live off the sweat of others and who could not stand losing the election of 1860. In the eyes of the Unionists, the issue was not states' rights but the obligation of all citizens to obey the laws of the United States. Secession was an attack on the United States and the principles it stood for; to allow the South to waltz off unmolested would destroy the republican basis of the American experiment. Where German and Italian nationalists sought to create single, strong states from separate elements, northern nationalists sought to prevent their single state from breaking into separate elements. For the German and Italian nationalists, getting what they wanted eventually required war. For the northern nationalists it did, too.

Neutral Rights, Neutral Wrongs: The American Civil War

But Abraham Lincoln did not like to think of the fight to hold the Union together as a war. In the usual sense, wars involve two (or more) sovereign nations hammering away at each other with armies, navies, embargoes, blockades, and so forth. Civil wars are the domestic version: two factions (or more) within a single country choose up sides, form armies, and kill, maim, and impoverish each other as though they were separate countries (except, usually, that the opposing sides claim the same territory). Lincoln preferred to think of the conflict that began in April 1861, when units of the South Carolina militia fired on federal troops at Fort Sumter, as an insurrection rather than a war. Insurrections are internal matters for the countries that suffer them; the issues they raise involve not international affairs but matters of law and order. As president, Lincoln had sworn to uphold the Constitution of the United States; he believed that in requiring the South to obey federal laws he was merely honoring his oath of office.

Lincoln had another motive in treating southern secession as an internal matter. If he could convince foreign powers that the troubles between North and South were simply a family quarrel, he might prevent those foreign powers from assisting the South. Lincoln had studied history, and he knew that the efforts of the American colonies during the 1770s to break loose (secede—though Lincoln shied away from thinking of the actions of the American revolutionaries in such terms) from the British empire had achieved success only with the help of France. If the Union could prevent the South from gaining similar help in the current contest, it would be well on its way to preventing a similar success by the South.

In certain respects, the South needed foreign help during the 1860s even more than the fledgling United States had needed help during the 1770s. The North enjoyed a tremendous advantage over the South in numbers, wealth,

Abraham Lincoln's chief contribution to American diplomacy was preserving the Union, thereby providing the basis for the emergence of the most powerful single country in history. *Library of Congress*

and especially in the industrial equipment and techniques needed to produce modern weapons and supplies. In addition, the North started the war with a near monopoly of naval vessels; for while federal forts and fixed installations could not be removed from the seceding states, federal ships could. The South would have to import much of what it needed to fight, and it would have to export cotton and other goods to finance the imports; the Union's naval advantage would make the importing and exporting difficult and costly.

It was in the matter of cutting off southern commerce that Lincoln ran into trouble regarding his definition of the conflict with the South as a domestic insurrection. Despite the Union's advantage in naval vessels, the American coastline from Chesapeake Bay to the mouth of the Rio Grande was too long and convoluted to seal off without help. The Union's task would be eased considerably if the major European powers could be persuaded not to trade with the South. Almost as soon as the shooting began, Lincoln declared a blockade of southern shipping. The president did so reluctantly and only after Confederate president Jefferson Davis announced a plan to outfit privateers for attacks on northern merchant vessels. Lincoln's reluctance stemmed from the fact that international law recognized blockades only between sovereign countries at war with each other. By proclaiming a blockade of the South, Lincoln implicitly recognized the Confederacy's status as a separate country.

At the same time, though, unless he made some such proclamation, he could not well ask Britain, France, and other countries to refrain from trading with the South or to allow their ships to be searched before entering southern harbors.

The British got a good laugh out of Lincoln's predicament. As long as Britain had been a major sea power, and a frequent blockader, the British government had advocated a broad interpretation of blockading rules, while the United States, a country usually trying to break blockades, had pressed for a narrow interpretation. Now the shoe was on the other foot. The British were happy enough to go along with America's new position, but they did not intend to let Lincoln and company off the hook without sweating a little.

In the war's first months, London declared neutrality between the Union and the Confederacy. This declaration stopped considerably short of the diplomatic recognition the South wanted, but it went a good deal further than Lincoln and Secretary of State William Seward deemed appropriate. Seward, who thought that he should have received the Republican nomination for president in 1860 and often acted as though he had, suggested shortly after entering office that America provoke a fight with one or more of the European powers in order to rally the secessionists back to the Union. Though Lincoln ignored the suggestion and reminded Seward of who actually had won the nomination and the election, Seward continued to fulminate about war against Britain and any other country with the temerity to insult the United States. Lincoln pointed out the folly of unnecessarily adding to the Union's burdens at a time when carrying the ones it already had was job enough. The president settled for a remonstrance to London.

Throughout the war, both American governments—Union and Confederate—made Britain the focus of their efforts overseas, for both understood that Britain's attitude could well determine the outcome of the war. As usual Britain controlled the waves. British factories produced the kinds of weapons the Confederacy needed, and British shipyards built the sorts of vessels the Confederacy required to match the Union on the Atlantic and in the Caribbean. If the British opened their warehouses and yards to Confederate purchasing agents, and if the British navy did not interfere with shipments bound for the South, the Confederacy stood a reasonable chance of offsetting the Union blockade. If the British went further and recognized the independence of the South, the Confederacy would benefit even more. British recognition of the Confederacy would probably provoke a declaration of war by the Union against Britain, and nothing would suit the South better. In such a war the British navy likely would help the South break the Union blockade; at the least a large number of Union ships would have to turn from chasing Confederate blockade runners to fighting British vessels. In addition, the Union might find itself fighting a two-front land war: against Confederate troops in the South and against British troops from Canada in the North.

Confederate leaders had cause for such optimistic daydreams. Britain would not be averse to the splitting of the increasingly powerful United States into two smaller and less powerful pieces, especially since those two pieces would

During the first half of the 1860s, William Seward helped keep the United States from becoming much smaller as a result of southern secession; during the second half of the decade he made it much larger by negotiating the purchase of Alaska. *Library of Congress*

probably be preoccupied with each other for some time. The British could play the balance-of-power game in North America as they played it in Europe. Moreover, Britain's textile industry depended heavily on cotton from the American South: as many as eight bales out of ten that arrived at Britain's mills came from the South. Beyond the hundreds of thousands of workers directly employed in processing southern cotton, millions more drew indirect sustenance—transporting the cotton and the textiles it became, feeding and clothing the textile workers and their families, building the mills, and the like. Southerners were fully aware of Britain's reliance on their cotton, and many of them believed that this reliance would force London to choose the southern side in the Civil War. "King Cotton," as they called it, would prevail.

They turned out to be wrong, for several reasons. First, the American Civil War did not exactly come as a thunderbolt from the blue. British observers, especially British cotton brokers, had watched very carefully as North and South drew closer to the brink, and when opportunities arose, the brokers bought extra cotton as a safeguard against disruptions in supplies. Consequently, when the shooting in America began, Britain's warehouses held enough cotton to get the country's mills through perhaps two years of lean supplies. Second, the cotton plant is an annual that by the 1860s was grown commercially in several parts of the world. Unlike coffee, grapes, or oranges, whose bushes, vines, and trees require years to produce the first crop, cotton yields a harvest after just several months. Expanding production in cotton-growing areas is a relatively easy matter. When the American Civil War broke out, cotton farmers in Egypt and India responded to the war-induced jump in prices by planting more cotton than before. The result was that by the time British warehouses were running low, Egyptian and Indian cotton was available to take up the slack from America. Third, though the Union navy made every effort to intercept cotton leaving the South for Britain (and France, which also had an important textile industry), the Union government quickly sent captured cargoes on their way across the Atlantic. The British (and French) ended up receiving much of the cotton they had contracted for; the shipments just came via a different shipper. In fact, the Confederate government, realizing that it would be in the interest of the Union to adopt such a policy, itself initially halted shipments of cotton. This embargo, like Jefferson's 1807 embargo, was designed to force the Europeans to take a cooperative line. Like the earlier embargo, this one did not work, for the reasons just explained, and the Confederacy soon switched to a ship-all-we-can policy.

Fourth, while British workers spun and wove southern cotton, they ate northern wheat. The 1846 repeal of the corn laws had had much the effect predicted by its opponents: it made Britain vulnerable to pressure from its food suppliers, notably the United States. Even though Britain's dependence on American supplies never became critical—lots of countries grew wheat and other foodstuffs—London had to think twice about antagonizing the Union. Fifth, most people in Britain found slavery abhorrent. Nearly a century of abolitionist propaganda had converted a strong majority of the British to views that made it all but impossible for the British government to ally with the Confederacy. The Lincoln administration almost fumbled this advantage by refusing at first to declare emancipation to be one of its war aims. Lincoln had his reasons, including constitutional scruples and worries about driving the slave states that had not seceded over to the Confederacy. But he swallowed his scruples and figured out how to finesse the border state problem (by decreeing freedom for slaves only in the seceded states), and in September 1862, following a critical Union victory at Antietam, he announced emancipation. Upon this announcement, Britain faced a clear choice on the slavery issue. With the issue unmuddied—and, after Antietam, with the Confederacy an increasingly risky bet—the British could not take the southern side.

Sixth, the American Civil War was not the only thing the British had to worry about. When the secession crisis in America was beginning, the British were at war in China for the second time in two decades. Meanwhile, the Maoris were launching another of several uprisings in New Zealand. In 1861 the Poles staged a rebellion against Russian rule, and though this event did not directly involve British forces, it threatened to upset the European balance of power, which almost certainly would. Prussia got a new king, Wilhelm, in 1861, and in 1862 a new prime minister, Otto von Bismarck. The two made

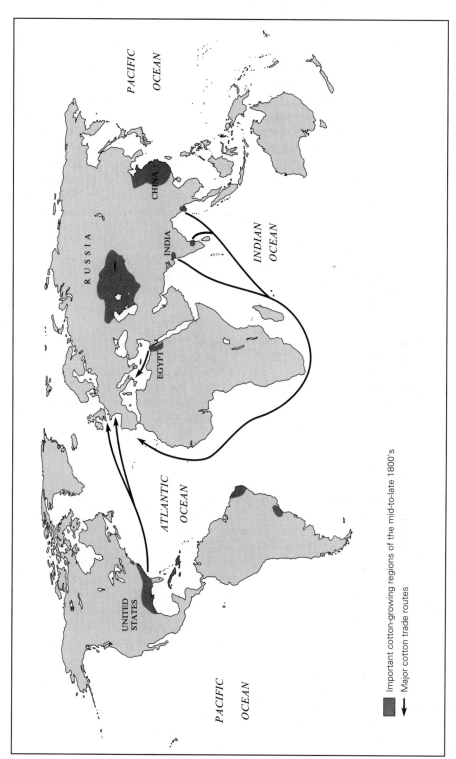

PACIFIC
OCEAN

PACIFIC
OCEAN

RUSSIA

CHINA

INDIA

EGYPT

INDIAN
OCEAN

ATLANTIC
OCEAN

UNITED
STATES

Important cotton-growing regions of the mid-to-late 1800's

Major cotton trade routes

The World in the Late 1800s

a formidable pair and merited close watching. In 1863 a civil war broke out in Afghanistan, which meant that British troops might soon be called on to defend the frontiers of India. In 1863 the French invaded Mexico to install an out-of-work Austrian archduke as emperor. What would come of the Maximilian gambit remained to be seen, but as with most of what the French did, it signaled to the British something suspicious.

For all these reasons, Britain decided not to recognize southern independence. Britain's decision against recognition essentially determined Europe's position on the war. France, the Confederacy's other major hope, chose to be guided on the American issue by the British. Paris might have been willing to tangle with the Union in the shade of British sails and smokestacks, but not on its own. The end result was that the South failed to achieve the primary objective of its foreign policy.

Although Britain's refusal to recognize the Confederacy made the Union's task far easier than it might have been, relations between Washington and London were far from smooth. On several occasions during the war, the British took actions Lincoln and Seward deemed unfriendly. On as many occasions, the British were annoyed at actions taken by the Union. But each time the two sides refused to let the friction develop into hostilities.

About six months after the war started, a Union navy captain caused a fuss between Washington and London when he stopped a British ship, the *Trent*, and seized two Confederate envoys, James Mason and John Slidell. At this stage of the war, Union partisans had little to cheer about, and the *Trent* affair elicited great applause in the North. But the British protested what they considered a violation of Britain's neutral rights. London demanded that Mason and Slidell be released. Lincoln and Seward procrastinated for a while to let the affair slip from the front pages, and they drafted a thoroughly confusing note that surrounded the seizure in a fog of diplomatic precedent and legal technicality. Then they agreed to release the two Confederates, who went on to propagandize and raise money in Europe for the southern cause.

Another brouhaha developed in 1862. The Confederacy was in dire need of a navy, since it had had none when the war began, and the South contained only one shipyard of any size, at Norfolk. To fill the need, Confederate agents contracted with British shipbuilders. British law forbade the construction of foreign warships, but the British yards circumvented the ban by building generic vessels that were easily convertible to Confederate naval use. The ploy fooled no one for long. Yet it did suffice to let one British firm complete most major construction on two vessels, the *Alabama* and the *Florida,* before the American minister in London caught on. The minister, Charles Francis Adams, complained to the British government that by allowing the ships to be built, Britain "to all intents and purposes ceases to be neutral." This time it was the British who found cause for procrastination, allowing the *Alabama* and *Florida* to slip down the ways and out to sea. The British government faced considerable pressure from the shipbuilders and their political allies, who desired to make money off the American war just as American merchants and manufacturers had made money off earlier (and later) European wars. Belatedly, though, the British government conceded the correctness of the American position and restrained further construction; and subsequently it seized two other British-built vessels, known as the Laird rams, on which the Confederacy was counting heavily. But the *Alabama* and *Florida* went on to illustrious careers as wreckers of northern shipping. The aggrieved Union government filed repeated complaints during the rest of the war and for several years thereafter.

In war, as in many endeavors, fortune smiles on the successful. During the summer of 1863, the tide of battle turned in favor of the North. At Gettysburg, Pennsylvania, Union forces threw back the Confederates in the single most important engagement of the war. In the west, Union forces under General Ulysses Grant captured Vicksburg, Mississippi, and gained control of the Mississippi River, thereby slicing the Confederacy in two.

Until this point, European recognition of southern independence had remained a possibility, albeit increasingly slim; after this point the possibility was nil. No European government would be so foolish as to back an obviously

The ranks of the Confederate dead were a formidable argument against British recognition of the Confederacy. *The Granger Collection*

losing cause. Sooner or later the North would win the war and put the Union back together. Already the North had built a powerful military machine, one that could probably hold its own against any European power. When the United States became its old united self again, it would be more powerful still.

Desperate circumstances forced the South to desperate measures. With the handwriting on the wall growing more legible daily, Jefferson Davis sent a special emissary to London in a final effort to obtain British recognition. Davis offered to abolish slavery in the Confederacy if London would recognize southern independence and provide help against the Union. It was a hopeless offer. By now the Union had both committed itself to emancipation and brought victory within sight. The British rejected the Confederate offer without thinking twice. William Gladstone, London's chancellor of the exchequer (finance minister), who earlier had praised southern nationalism in an emotional and widely noted speech, on sober second thought recanted his statement as an error "of incredible grossness."

When the Civil War began, the governments of the major European powers would have been happy for the South to gain its independence. They were not enamored of slavery, but they would have liked to see the United States weakened and humbled. Yet southern independence was not worth the risks involved in giving the Confederacy active support against the North, and as the end drew near for the South, the Europeans resigned themselves to dealing with a single American government again. The foresighted among them guessed that reconstructing the Union would occupy the Americans for some time and would keep them distracted from foreign affairs. They were essentially correct.

Delusions of Empire: France in Mexico

But they were not entirely correct. One reason the French had been content to play second fiddle to Britain with respect to the Civil War was that they had another scheme afoot, one bound to upset the Americans. Even after a century, French pride had not quite recovered from the loss of France's American empire. Napoleon had tried to remedy the loss in Louisiana and failed, but the emperor's namesake and nephew, Louis Napoleon (who now went by the title of emperor and the name Napoleon III), thought he might succeed where his uncle had failed.

The occasion was another round of Mexico's seemingly interminable domestic strife. In 1853 Santa Anna had regained power in Mexico City, and during the next two years he governed about as corruptly and inefficiently as before. In 1855 a reformist movement spearheaded by Benito Juárez deposed the dictator. The reformers attempted a thorough housecleaning, overhauling Mexico's land laws in the process. This antagonized conservatives, as well as the Catholic church, which faced the loss of much of its land. Conservatives branded the reformers "communists"—starting a long tradition of red-baiting in the Western Hemisphere—while the Catholic church excommunicated officials of the reformist government.

A three-year war, descriptively labeled the Three Years' War, followed. Juárez and the liberals won, driving many leading conservatives out of the country. The conservatives headed for Europe, where they pleaded their case to the governments of France, Spain, and Britain. During the recent fighting, property belonging to nationals of the three European powers had been destroyed; in addition, the Juárez government in Mexico City was slow making payments on foreign debts. These offenses provided the pretext the Europeans needed to intervene militarily in Mexico.

The French were the most enthusiastic; the British and Spanish went along as much to watch over the French as for any other reason. In January 1862 a combined military force from the three countries arrived at Veracruz. The British and Spanish withdrew after gaining assurances of future Mexican good behavior and repayment of debts. The French stayed.

They did so largely because the conservative Mexican émigrés convinced Napoleon III that the Mexican people would welcome the reestablishment of a conservative government in Mexico City under the protection of France. Napoleon III in turn convinced Maximilian, the brother of the Austrian emperor, that he was just the man for the job. Maximilian rarely demonstrated much common sense, and he did not now, instead accepting Napoleon III's proposal. In the spring of 1862, a French army drove Juárez out of Mexico City; during that year and the following the French gained control of most of the country's important cities. To reassure Maximilian, the French and their Mexican allies rigged a plebiscite that showed overwhelming enthusiasm for the transplanted Austrian. In the spring of 1864, Maximilian accepted the crown of Mexico in his own name and that of his wife, Carlota.

Maximilian was not quite so pliable as the Mexican conservatives had hoped, and once in office he refused to countenance the most reactionary of their schemes. They began to have second thoughts about this foreigner. Yet at the same time, his efforts to rule as an enlightened monarch failed to satisfy the liberal Juaristas, who continued to harass French and government forces in the countryside. By the beginning of 1865, Maximilian's government was wobbling seriously.

It might have fallen of its own weight, but before it did, it got a push from the United States. The American government had been watching Mexico struggle with its problems during the 1850s, but as long as the Mexicans simply fought among themselves, Washington felt little temptation to get involved. The temptation increased when the Europeans showed up at Veracruz in 1862. Lincoln and Seward did not completely reject the idea that big powers might lean on small powers to collect debts; such a precedent might come in handy. But when the French stayed on after the British and Spanish went home, the president and the secretary of state grew testy. France's occupation of Mexico was as clear a violation of the Monroe Doctrine as any American

Maximilian, still not entirely certain how things turned so bad so quickly, faces his firing squad. *The Granger Collection*

administration was likely to encounter, and Seward protested vigorously. However, with all the Union military forces tied up fighting the Confederates, the administration could not do much more—as the French fully realized.

The Civil War's end changed the situation drastically. Now the French faced the prospect of tangling with the world's strongest army, battle hardened and ready to take on foreigners as a change from fighting fellow Americans. To bring the prospect of war closer, Washington ordered Union troops to mass along the Rio Grande. In the meantime, it reiterated its demands that France get out of Mexico and let the Mexicans solve their problems themselves.

Napoleon III chose to be convinced this time around. The Mexican gamble had seemed worthwhile as long as the stakes were not too high, but it did not warrant hostilities with the United States. Besides, the Prussians were up to no good in Europe. Bismarck was already distinguishing himself for dubious dealings. War between France and Prussia looked alarmingly likely—if not this year, then maybe next.

Napoleon ordered his troops home from France. On their way out they invited Maximilian along, cluing him in to the fact that he was less popular than the phony plebiscite had made him seem. But the Mexican conservatives tugged at his other sleeve. They told him to think of his empire and of all the people who were counting on him. Maximilian pondered the fact that Mexico's throne was probably the only one he would ever occupy, and he decided to stick it out.

It was an imprudent decision. Once the French left, the Juaristas mounted a counteroffensive that chased Maximilian out of Mexico City and across the mountains and deserts of the central part of the country. The liberals cornered and finally captured the Austrian during the spring of 1867. Shortly thereafter Mexico's last emperor fell to a firing squad.

*   *   *

For much of the period since 1776, there had been a certain tentativeness about the United States. No other nation had ever created itself in the self-conscious way the United States did, and many, if not most, foreign observers expected the American experiment in republicanism to dissolve in disarray. During the 1840s and 1850s, the odds of dissolution appeared to increase as North and South drifted farther and farther apart. But at the last minute, Abraham Lincoln and his generals saved the day and saved the Union.

Whether they saved American republicanism was another question. The Confederates certainly did not think so. European liberals were split on the issue, applauding the defeat of slavery even as they questioned the North's denial of the right of self-determination to the South.

Nationalists in Europe and elsewhere learned one lesson above all from the American Civil War. It was the same lesson learned in slightly different contexts by the Japanese who confronted Perry's warships, by the Central Americans who encountered William Walker, and by the French who backed Maximilian in Mexico. The lesson was that although legal, political, and moral arguments could be powerful, military arguments were ultimately more effective. For all the noble sentiments and Enlightenment ideals put forward in Lincoln's Gettysburg Address, what held the Union together was Lincoln's army. Throughout their history, from the days of John Winthrop and the Puritans, Americans had spoken of setting an example for the world. They usually had something else in mind besides the example of the sword. But there it was, and people watching America took note.

Sources and Suggestions for Further Reading

William L. Langer describes the European revolutions of 1848 in *The Revolutions of 1848* (1969); as does Peter N. Stearns in a book also entitled *The Revolutions of 1848* (1974). On the origins of Marxism, consult Ajit Jain and Alexander J. Matejko, eds., *Marx and Marxism* (1984); F. W. Deakin, *A History of World Communism* (1975); Roger S. Gottlieb, *Marxism, 1844–1990* (1992); George Lichtheim, *Marxism: An Historical and Critical Study* (1961); and Peter Worsley, *Marx and Marxism* (1982).

The subject of nationalism has generated hundreds of volumes. Try Benedict R. Anderson, *Imagined Communities: Reflections on the Origin and Spread of Nationalism* (1983); Hans Kohn, *The Age of Nationalism: The First Era of Global History* (1962); William H. McNeill, *Polyethnicity and National Unity in World History* (1986); Hugh Seton-Watson, *Nations and States: An Enquiry into the Origins of Nations and the Politics of Nationalism* (1977); Leonard Tivey, ed., *The Nation-State: The Formation of Modern Politics* (1981); and Liah Greenfield, *Nationalism: Five Roads to Modernity* (1992).

On slavery, a judicious and learned introduction is David B. Davis, *Slavery and Human Progress* (1984). Robin W. Winks, *Slavery* (1972), provides comparisons between American slavery and other versions. See also George M. Frederickson, *The Arrogance of Race* (1988).

Lester D. Langley, *The Cuban Policy of the United States* (1968), deals with the efforts to annex Cuba, while his *Struggle for the American Mediterranean: United States-European Rivalry in the Gulf-Caribbean, 1776–1894* (1976), deals with somewhat larger issues. Robert E. May, *The Southern Dream of an American Empire, 1854–1861* (1973), traces some of the same issues more thoroughly. On the remarkable William Walker, William O. Scruggs, *Filibusters and Financiers: The Story of William Walker and His Associates* (1916) is dated but interesting; Albert H. Carr, *The World of William Walker* (1963), offers a more recent perspective.

On Japan and the opening to the West, Edwin O. Reischauer, *Japan* (1981 ed.) affords a good introduction, concentrating on the Japanese side. Foster Rhea Dulles, *Yankees and Samurai: America's Role in the Emergence of Japan, 1791–1900* (1965), pays more attention to the United States, as does William L. Neumann, *America Encounters Japan: From Perry to MacArthur* (1963). On the Perry mission specifically, two books provide thorough coverage: Samuel Eliot Morison, *"Old Bruin": Commodore Matthew C. Perry* (1967), and Arthur Walworth, *Black Ships Off Japan* (1946).

The diplomacy of the Civil War is the subject of David P. Crook, *The North, the South and the Powers, 1861–1865* (1974), as well as of Philip Van Doren Stern, *When the Guns Roared: World Aspects of the American Civil War* (1965). The best work on the foreign relations of the Confederacy is Frank L. Owsley and Harriet Chappell Owsley, *King Cotton Diplomacy* (1959 ed.). Specific issues engage the attention of Norman B. Ferris, *The Trent Affair* (1977); Stuart L. Bernath, *Squall Across the Atlantic: American Civil War Prize Cases and Diplomacy* (1970); Adrian Cook, *The Alabama Claims* (1975); and Warren F. Spencer, *The United States and France: Civil War Diplomacy* (1970).

Maximilian's misadventures in Mexico are dealt with in Alfred J. Hanna and Kathryn A. Hanna, *Napoleon III and Mexico* (1971), and Thomas D. Schoonover, *Dollars over Dominion* (1978).

Chapter 6

The Age of Steel, 1865–1895

Thehe end of the Civil War marked the beginning of a new era in American international relations. Prior to the Civil War, the United States had been a country of the future—or perhaps two or three or four countries of the future, depending on how the slavery dispute and the related matter of possible secession turned out. The Union victory in the war brought the future much closer. Politically, the war showed that American leaders would stop at almost nothing to secure what they considered to be their country's vital interests. The Union victory cost America more than a half million lives (the unification of Italy and that of Germany came quite cheap by comparison); a government and people willing to pay such a price were not to be trifled with. The economic consequences for American international relations of the Union's victory were even more important, although their importance took longer to become apparent. During the war, heavy government spending boosted investment in factories, railroads, farm machinery, and other productive resources. This investment triggered a boom in the American economy that continued, with a couple of dramatic but brief interruptions, through the end of the century, and made the United States the foremost economic power in the world.

America's unparalleled economic growth during the final third of the nineteenth century dovetailed with developments that during the same period created, for the first time, a genuinely global economy. Innovations in communication and transportation technology allowed goods, money, and people to cross the oceans at unprecedented rates and in unheard of quantities. Americans, now at the cutting edge of technology and industry, actively participated in the global scramble for markets and sources of supply.

Until the late 1890s, however, they refrained from the scramble for colonies that occupied the imperial powers of Europe during this period. Instead Americans concentrated their expansive energies on commercial, rather than territorial, endeavors. The United States purchased Alaska but otherwise added little to the national domain.

Yet even as the territorial expansionists took a rest, they and others fashioned a body of ideas regarding America's role in the world that provided the basis for a renewal of territorial expansion. Some of these thinkers stressed what they conceived to be America's religious obligation to spread the blessings

Chronology

1866	Border skirmishes between American Irish and Canadians
1867	Alaska purchased from Russia; Maximilian executed in Mexico; Canada gains home rule
1868	Meiji restoration in Japan; Burlingame treaty with China
1869	Suez Canal opened; American transcontinental railroad completed
1870	Attempt to annex Santo Domingo fails; Franco-Prussian War begins; revolt in Paris
1871	Treaty of Washington with Britain; Stanley meets Livingstone in central Africa; Paris Commune; unification of Germany
1873	Financial panic spreads from Austria across Europe and to America
1875	Reciprocity treaty with Hawaii approved; Ten Years' War in Cuba begins
1876	Telephone invented
1877	Díaz takes power in Mexico; Satsuma revolt in Japan suppressed
1878	Samoan treaty
1880	Edison invents practical electric lights
1882	Chinese Exclusion Act; Hague Convention stipulates three-mile limit for territorial waters; British occupy Egypt
1883	American (and Canadian) railroads adopt four standard time zones across North America; Congress authorizes construction of three steel cruisers; Bismarck introduces health insurance in Germany
1884	Berlin conference on Africa
1885	Shift in immigration patterns to United States: from northern and western European origins to southern and eastern
1886	First meeting of Indian National Congress
1887	Pearl Harbor treaty with Hawaii approved
1889	Samoan treaty with Britain and Germany; Pan-American conference in Washington
1890	McKinley tariff; Mahan's *Influence of Sea Power upon History*
1893	Monarchy of Hawaii overthrown by Americans on islands; Franco-Russian alliance

1894	Sino-Japanese War begins
1895	Venezuelan crisis with Britain; Cuban war of independence breaks out; radio telegraphy invented

of liberty to other lands and peoples; others concentrated on the lessons of history and the implications of such lessons for modern Americans. The expansionists' ideas contributed materially to a burst of American reassertiveness during the 1890s. The first signs of the reassertiveness appeared in dealings with Hawaii and with Britain regarding Venezuela. Subsequently the ideas would provide the intellectual justification for the evolution of foreign policies that would fit American ambitions to American economic strength.

A World Economy

Between 1865 and 1898 American production of corn more than tripled, as did wheat production. American production of refined sugar quintupled. Output of coal multiplied ninefold; steel rails, sixfold; crude oil, eighteenfold; steel ingots and castings, more than four hundred–fold. In 1865 the United States trailed Britain by half in overall manufacturing output; by 1898 Americans manufactured more than the British by nearly a third.

America's economy would have grown even if it had been utterly detached from the rest of the world; to a larger extent than any other country, the United States contained the materials and markets its economic growth required. (Only Russia came close, and Russia fell short in markets.) As it happened, however, America's economic growth was closely tied to changes in the world economy. While America supplied itself with most of what it needed to produce what it did, in critical areas—especially capital and labor—it imported substantially; and while Americans consumed a majority of what they produced, they increasingly relied on overseas markets to clear their warehouses and grain elevators.

The most important change in the world economy during the last third of the nineteenth century was the continued improvement of transportation and communication. Steamships constantly gained ground, or water, on sailing vessels, although until the mid-1870s, cargoes crossing the Atlantic were as likely to be driven by wind as by coal. And few steamships could match the American clipper ships, the thoroughbreds of sail, for speed when the wind was right. But despite their clunkiness and cost of their fuel—as opposed to wind, which comes free—the steamships kept better schedules and made more money for their owners. Customers likewise benefited as shipping costs fell. By the end

It wasn't pretty, but it made people rich and America powerful: the oil country of western Pennsylvania during the late 1860s. *The Bettman Archive*

of the century, those sailing ships that had not been converted to steam were steering a course for oblivion.

The transition from sail to steam was merely evolutionary, with improvements in speed and reliability being matters of modest degree. By contrast, innovations in communication during the middle and late nineteenth century were genuinely revolutionary. For the first time in history, it became possible to communicate over long distances at a rate faster than humans could travel. There had been a few previous exceptions to this rule—carrier pigeons, signal fires—but nothing of consequence. The introduction of the telegraph, which the American inventor Samuel Morse made practical during the 1840s, allowed nearly instantaneous communication at distances of thousands of miles, even across—or rather under—oceans. Telegraph lines spanned Europe by the 1850s and North America by the 1860s. As the Civil War was beginning, specially outfitted ships laid a cable under the Atlantic. Later in the same decade, India plugged into a Eurasian telegraph net.

The clicking telegraph wires greatly facilitated the development of world markets in commodities such as wheat, cotton, and coffee. Grain brokers in Liverpool now monitored market-influencing developments in North Dakota, Ukraine, and Australia on a daily basis. If the monsoon failed in India, cotton buyers could increase their orders from Texas. A threatened revolution in Brazil immediately sent coffee prices up around the world.

Samuel Morse (standing, with white beard nearly brushing the bald head in front of him) and a group of venture capitalists consider how to lay a telegraph cable beneath the Atlantic. *AP/Wide World Photos*

Swift communications were not an unmixed blessing. At moments of great tension, enforced reflection can calm things down. The uproar that surrounded the Union seizure of the *Trent* during the Civil War illustrated this principle. When the crisis was approaching its hottest point, the Atlantic telegraph cable fortuitously failed. Leaders and people in both Britain and America were deprived of the opportunity to hear the nasty things each side was saying about the other, which facilitated the eventual peaceful resolution of the affair.

The global information network made it easy for investors to keep track of investments in the far corners of the globe. By the late nineteenth century, the opportunities for investment in Europe had been fairly thoroughly picked over. Pounds sunk into British mills, francs into French factories, and marks into German mines tended to yield lower returns than funds invested in relatively underdeveloped countries. As a consequence, investment capital flowed out of industrialized Europe and into the United States, Canada, Latin America, Africa, Asia, Australia, and New Zealand, speeding the development of the countries that received it. The American railroad industry, for example, benefited greatly from British investment, and the American economy benefited greatly from the growth of American railroads. Through the late nineteenth century, the United States remained a fertile field for foreign investors. Until the First World War, America was a net debtor nation: foreigners had a greater claim on the American economy than Americans had on foreign economies.

Investors invest in the enterprises they do for the money they expect to receive in return, and when they put pounds or francs or marks into a foreign enterprise, they want to know they can get their pounds or francs or marks back out again, with interest. But the foreign enterprises do not usually do business in pounds or franks or marks; an American railroad company, for instance, pays its contractors and workers in dollars. For this reason, convenient convertibility between currencies is essential to the expansion of foreign investment. During most of the nineteenth century, the international economy operated on a gold standard. The strongest currencies were pegged to gold at a fixed rate, which in effect implied that they were fixed against each other. Consequently, investors did not have to worry about whether their dollar investments would depreciate relative to pounds, or franc investments relative to marks. When investors worry, they invest less; eliminate a worry and they invest more.

The gold standard had a drawback, however. There was no guarantee that the world's supply of gold would grow at the same rate as the world economy. If gold and other goods multiply at the same rate, the prices in gold of those other goods stay stable. If gold multiplies more rapidly, prices go up; if gold multiplies more slowly, prices go down. (Imagine an economy in which 100 gold coins are the only currency and 100 horseshoes the only commodity. Horseshoes then cost 1 gold coin each. If the currency expands to 200 gold coins while the supply of horseshoes sticks at 100, the price per shoe rises to 2 coins. If the supply of horseshoes doubles to 200 while the currency holds steady at 100, each shoe costs half a coin.)

During most of the final third of the nineteenth century, the output of the world economy grew faster than the supply of gold. This occasioned a fall in the world price level. Creditors tend to like falling prices because each dollar or pound repaid next year buys more than it would today. Debtors dislike deflation (another name for falling price levels) for the same reason. (A farmer who borrows 1000 dollars when wheat costs $1 per bushel has to grow and sell 1000 bushels to pay the debt. If wheat falls to 50 cents per bushel, he or she has to grow and sell 2000 bushels.) Europeans lending money to American businesses were creditors, so they did not mind the falling prices and kept lending—except during the recurrent "panics" when they lost confidence in dollar-denominated bonds and notes and fled for the security of gold.

Europe's investment of capital provided one element necessary to the rapid growth of the American economy; equally important was Europe's investment of labor. During the latter part of the nineteenth century, more people migrated across the surface of the earth than during any comparable period of time in previous history. One cause of all the movement was simply the increase in the sheer numbers of people on the planet. Between 1850 and 1900 world population grew by more than a third, from 1.2 billion to 1.6 billion. In other words, 400 million more people had to figure out how to make a living in 1900 than had had to do so fifty years earlier.

In terms of continents, the biggest absolute increase occurred in Asia, chiefly because Asia contained the most people. Europe's increase came second and in fact mattered more than Asia's because Europe's extra millions were more mobile than those of Asia. Roughly 60 million Europeans migrated to other continents in the century after 1840. More than half went to the United States, about a quarter to Latin America, and lesser numbers to Canada, Asiatic Russia, Australia, New Zealand, and South Africa.

Other waves of migration, smaller than the tides pouring out of Europe, also changed the demographic landscape of the earth. Tens of thousands of Chinese merchants and farmers left their homeland to resettle in Southeast Asia; thousands of Japanese did the same. Tens of thousands of Chinese and thousands of Japanese workers emigrated to the United States, until the American Congress closed the door. Afterward they continued to emigrate to other parts of the Western Hemisphere. Indians moved to the various regions touching the Indian Ocean, ranging from East Africa to Southeast Asia; a few made it to the Americas.

Asian immigrants to the United States helped dig the gold and silver that came out of western mines after the 1848 strike in California, and they built much of the western half of the transcontinental railroad system; but it was the far more numerous immigrants from Europe who played the largest role in the industrialization of America. Immigrants provided an endless source of labor, unskilled but willing to work cheaply (to the dismay of union organizers trying to raise wages). They operated the machines in the factories; they laid the stones on the roads; they cut the timber in the forests; they bore the children who swelled the populations of the cities that furnished the markets for the goods that the American economy churned out at a record pace.

Beyond their effects on the American economy, the swelling numbers of immigrants from previously exotic (to America) countries had a cultural impact that soon made an impression on American international relations. One reason American foreign policy had centered so long on Britain was that most Americans were of British descent. When almost no one in America was from Italy or Russia, why should Americans care about happenings there? Through the mid-nineteenth century, northern and western Europe—especially the British Isles, including at that time Ireland—supplied most of the immigrants to the United States. But during the last third of the century, more and more immigrants came from southern and eastern Europe. Although nearly all the immigrants eagerly embraced the country of their adoption, few forgot the countries of their origin. Consequently, when Abyssinian forces fought and defeated Italian troops during the 1890s, Italian-Americans paid close attention. Anti-Jewish pogroms in Russia produced demands that the United States do something to stop the violence and aid the victims.

If the increasing internationalization of American culture pushed the United States toward greater involvement in world affairs, the increasing internationalization of the American economy pushed even harder. During the last third

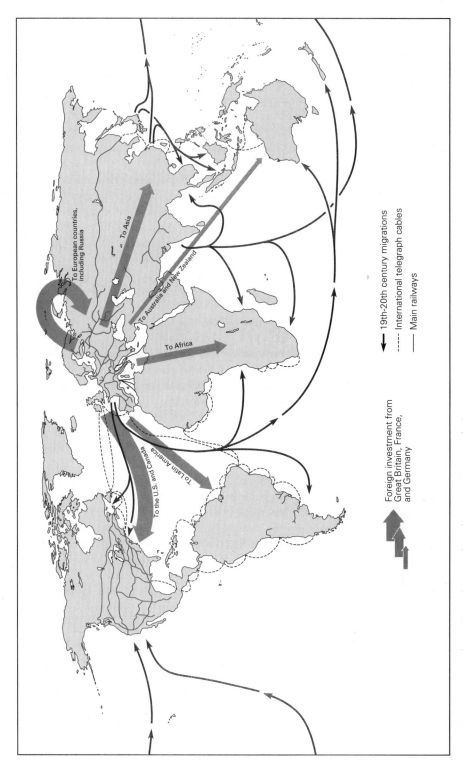

To European countries,
including Russia

To Asia

To Australia and New Zealand

To Africa

To the U.S. and Canada

To Latin America

Foreign investment from
Great Britain, France,
and Germany

19th-20th century migrations

International telegraph cables

Main railways

World Migration of People and Capital in the Late Nineteenth Century

Chinese and American laborers take a break from trying to get rich in the California gold fields. Here the Americans seem comparatively content to have the Chinese around; often they weren't. *California State Library*

of the nineteenth century, the American government began making special efforts to secure foreign markets for American manufactured goods and American farm commodities. The period of American industrialization was marked by intense economic crises. The American economy produced panics, as economic shakeouts were called in those days, on a cycle nearly as certain as sunspots. The panic of 1837 was followed by the panic of 1853, which was followed in turn by the panics of 1873 and 1893. Lesser malfunctions sometimes occurred between the major breakdowns, for example during the early 1880s. Various events triggered the different panics (unfavorable changes in the trade balance, crop failures, manipulation of the stock market, frights among foreign lenders), but the economic depressions they produced had one characteristic in common: people did not spend enough money to buy all the goods American farms and factories were spewing forth. The consequences included business bankruptcies, foreclosed farms, and destitute out-of-workers.

The obvious solution was to increase demand for American goods; one promising method was to open foreign markets. Sometimes the opening occurred peacefully and relatively benignly. During the late 1880s and early 1890s, President Benjamin Harrison and Secretary of State James G. Blaine negotiated reciprocity treaties with several countries of Latin America, by which the United States lowered tariffs on imports from Argentina, Chile, and the like in exchange for lowered tariffs in those countries on exports from the United States. This was not as much freedom as free traders in America wanted; they thought markets should be opened without conditions. But it was more freedom than was desired by the holdover mercantilists, who wished to keep foreign goods out. Such compromises are standard practice on dollars-and-cents issues like trade, which lend themselves to difference-splitting (compromise comes harder on matters of moral principle).

In cases where diplomatic negotiations did not suffice to pry open markets, the American government was not averse to force. In China, the force had been supplied by the British; American merchants simply took advantage of it. In Japan, the United States provided the force in the shape of Matthew Perry's warships.

Reciprocity and gunboat diplomacy were examples of wholesale market penetration; Americans also worked at the retail level. A primary job of American consuls in foreign countries was to spy out opportunities for American businesses. Consuls sent home information regarding market niches that might be filled by American goods, and they arranged introductions to appropriate foreign officials when American salespeople came calling. During the nineteenth century, at a time when American diplomatic relations with many foreign countries were low key and relatively inconsequential, consuls were often the most important Americans in any given country. They formed a separate consular corps (as opposed to the diplomatic corps of ministers and, later, ambassadors), and they were judged for advancement and raises on how well they promoted American commercial activity abroad.

Expansionism on Ice: Alaska

While Americans during the three decades after the Civil War directed most of their expansive energies into commercial endeavors, American territorial expansion did not cease—though, contrary to many expectations, it did slow down considerably. Numerous foreign observers had expected that the war, by settling the slavery issue, would lead to a new wave of American land-grabbing. It did not, for several reasons.

First, acquisition of either of the two closest targets of American expansion—Mexico and Canada—remained more or less out of the question. The Mexicans continued to make clear that they would not join the United States voluntarily, and after all the carnage of the Civil War, few Americans wanted to fight another Mexican war. The Canadians were equally uneager to join the United States, and hostilities against Canada were equally unpalatable to most Americans.

There were some exceptions regarding Canada, however. In the two decades before the Civil War, Irish men, women, and children fleeing the potato famine in their home country came to America by the millions; along with their hunger, most brought an undisguised hostility toward Britain. The Irish exodus included many members of the Fenian society, a sometimes-terrorist underground movement dedicated to the termination of British colonial rule in Ireland. While the Fenians at home waged direct action against British soldiers and colonial officials, Fenians in America operated indirectly. They calculated that a war between Britain and the United States might give Irish nationalists an opportunity to toss the British back across the Irish Sea, just as American nationalists in the 1770s and 1780s had capitalized on Britain's troubles with France to gain independence for the United States. To provoke such a war as well as simply to get in a few licks at the British, the Fenians in 1865 and 1866 staged raids into Canada—then still controlled by Britain—from the American side of the border. The raids did not come close to provoking the war the Fenians wanted; almost no one in America besides some of the Irish wanted to fight the British, and certainly not so soon after the Civil War. The American government condemned the raiders' actions and took measures to suppress their continuance.

The Fenian raids did have one salutary effect—but for Canadians rather than Americans. The raids gave the final push to Britain to grant Canadian self-government. In 1867 Parliament passed the British North America Act, which created the self-governing dominion of Canada out of several of the British North American colonies (several others joined subsequently). The grant of self-government eliminated nearly all the appeal of attacks against Canada for anti-British types like the Fenians, who now would have to find some other way to hit at evil England (this was part of the reason for granting self-government). An additional effect of self-government was to make the Canadians more determined than ever to resist amalgamation into the United States. Until this point, Americans coveting Canada could offer something the Canadians did not have: the right to rule themselves. Not many Canadians had ever found the offer appealing, so long as it required membership in the United States. But now that they had self-rule, the offer was even less appealing than before (which was also part of the reason for self-government: the British had no desire to see Canada joined to the United States).

A second reason for the failure of American territorial expansionism to revive in a big way after the Civil War had to do with the shift in American economic development from agriculture to industry. With the emphasis increasingly on industry, land per se meant less to Americans than it had earlier. When Jefferson bought Louisiana, the vision of a nation of yeoman farmers and their families was thoroughly believable, for it approximated reality reasonably closely. But by the post–Civil War period, that reality had given way to a new one in which the nation's wealth increasingly came from factories rather than farms and in which people lived less on the soil and more in the cities. It was not that land no longer mattered; it just did not matter as much as it had. Some people still held to the Jeffersonian vision, but they were not making American policy.

A third reason related to the second. In the late nineteenth century, American politics was falling under the sway of business classes that had no desire to extend the country geographically. Acquiring new territory cost money, whether the territory was purchased peacefully or taken in war. Business people generally did not like government to spend any more money than necessary since lots of government spending required high taxes. Administering new territories likewise cost money, and with exceptions such as gold-rich California, the new territories usually did not pay for themselves for years. Rather than foreign territory, the business classes wanted foreign markets. The latter, they pointed out, did not require the former.

Finally, the empire-building mindset of the era of Manifest Destiny had required a sense of mission. Americans needed to be able to feel that they were doing good for other people in extending America's boundaries. This philanthropic feeling may not have been the actual driving force behind the efforts to gain Texas, California, and Oregon, but it did serve as a necessary veil to keep Americans' less admirable motives from their own eyes. The Civil War and Reconstruction exhausted Americans morally, as wars tend to do. By the end of Reconstruction in 1877, most Americans had no desire to save the world. They wanted to stay home and get fat and rich.

Yet if most Americans no longer coveted their neighbors' land as much as before, some still coveted it a little. Those looking south cast their eyes on Santo Domingo (the Dominican Republic). Santo Domingo had been independent for several decades and possessed many of the attractions of Cuba without the troublesome ties to Spain. It sat amid the sea lanes of the Caribbean, lanes that gained importance with the increasing possibility of an Atlantic-Pacific canal across Central America. It possessed a fine harbor for both naval and commercial use. It grew timber, sugar, and rope-grade hemp. The best part of all was that the Santo Domingans were crying out for annexation to the United States.

Or so said the American supporters of the project. These individuals included some old-style expansionists who simply liked to see more of the United States on maps of the Western Hemisphere, as well as advocates of a big American navy who wanted a naval station in Santo Domingo. Supporters also included some rather shady characters who intended to make a great deal of money out of annexation. These last had convenient access to the Grant administration, the most corruption-riddled in American history. The Grant insiders worked on the president to get him to support their plan. Grant knew a good cigar when he smoked one, which may have enhanced his interest in the Caribbean (it also evidently shortened his life: he died of throat cancer); but he could not tell a crook from a rocking chair. (Grant's private secretary was a member of the notorious Whiskey Ring, which bilked the government of millions in liquor taxes. His vice president channeled government railroad funds into his own pockets. His secretary of war sold exclusive concessions to trade with American Indians to friends who kicked back the purchase price. His brother-in-law conspired to corner the country's gold market.)

Grant's "advisers" on the Santo Domingo issue supplied him with the results of a bogus referendum purporting to show that Santo Domingans desired attachment to the United States, by a proportion of more than 999 to 1. The pro-annexationists also convinced him—or at least his public statements indicated they had—that if the United States did not grab Santo Domingo, some potentially unfriendly foreign power probably would.

In the autumn of 1869, the Grant administration negotiated a treaty of annexation with the president of Santo Domingo—whose talent for working fast and loose with his nation's finances made him an appropriate negotiating partner. The administration then presented the treaty to the Senate. Despite Grant's personal lobbying, several senators objected. Charles Sumner, the chairman of the Senate foreign relations committee and a prominent moralist who despised Grant and the spoilsmen who dominated the administration, denounced the treaty as a conspiracy to defraud the American people of their tax money (annexation would not come free, which was why the corruptionists were so interested) and the Santo Domingans of their independence.

Sumner's efforts proved more effective than those of the administration. In June 1870 the Senate voted against ratification. Grant got back at Sumner by engineering the chairman's removal from the foreign relations committee, but the ouster came too late to salvage the agenda of the annexationists. For better or worse, Santo Domingo was left to its own devices.

American expansionists had greater luck acquiring territory in the opposite direction from the Caribbean. During the first half of the nineteenth century, the government of Russia gradually came to realize that administering Alaska was a losing proposition. The colony was at the far end of a communication line that spanned the wastes of Siberia and the storm-battered North Pacific, and though Alaska produced furs in abundance, it never paid its way. It was sparsely populated and would almost certainly never attract many Russian settlers, on account of its distance and climatic inhospitability (the Russians could find all the cold and snow they wanted without leaving home). St. Petersburg sporadically tried to keep foreign merchants out of Alaska, but never with much luck. The few Russian settlers there had to live, and when the czar's government proved stingy regarding provisions, they dealt with foreign traders on the sly.

During the 1840s and 1850s, the Russian government came to accept that Alaska was almost indefensible. The Americans showed by the Mexican War that they would not stop short of armed force to take what they wanted; if they turned their guns against Alaska, Russia would be hard pressed to hang on to it for more than a month or two. Britain posed an even greater immediate threat, in that the British had a better navy than the Americans and could shut off access to Alaska from Russia almost at will. During the Crimean War of 1853–1856, which pitted Russia against Britain (and France and Turkey), the British left Alaska alone, but only as part of a general decision to keep the conflict confined to the area of the Black Sea.

The Crimean War also demonstrated to the Russian government the need to cut expenses and streamline government operations. The retrenchers were assisted by the fact that the czar who started the war, Nicholas I, died halfway through it; his successor, Alexander II, could acknowledge the need for new policies without suffering personal embarrassment. Alexander's most significant domestic reform was freeing Russia's serfs; from the American perspective, his decision to liquidate Russia's Alaskan enterprise was more important.

Alexander's initial intimation of a desire to sell Alaska came shortly before the American Civil War, but that conflict prevented the American government from responding in any meaningful way. Upon the Confederacy's defeat, the Russians again came calling. William Seward welcomed the opportunity to buy such a prime piece of property, but he did so circumspectly so as not to drive up the price. In Seward's view, Alaska could serve as America's way station to Asia (a geographically sound position, as is plainly evident on a spherical globe of the earth, if not on direction-distorting flat maps). Alaska's harbors could shelter an American North Pacific fleet; American merchant vessels could refuel and reprovision there.

But Seward was in a distinct minority in desiring Alaska. Most Americans could not place it within five thousand miles, and far fewer could identify its positive attributes. To avoid stirring up opposition, Seward conducted talks with the Russian minister behind closed doors. Eventually they cut a midnight (literally) deal by which Washington would pay St. Petersburg slightly more than $7 million for somewhat in excess of a half million square miles of land. As usual in such transactions, the indigenous inhabitants of Alaska were not consulted.

Seward would have been happy to consummate the deal secretly if the American Constitution had allowed. It did not, though, and the Senate had to give its approval. Selling the idea of buying Alaska was not easy given the low level of public awareness of the territory's finer points. But the Russian minister knew how the American political system worked in the age of the spoilsmen, and he set about wining and dining and lining the pockets of wavering legislators. The American public paid the bill—the Russians simply charged their expenses against the Alaskan purchase price. The Senate approved the treaty of transfer, and the House of Representatives, after further palm greasing, voted the money to pay the Russians (and its own members).

The New Imperialism: Europe in Africa, America on the Sidelines

Though Americans lost much of their appetite for territorial expansion during the second half of the nineteenth century, they would regain it by century's end; and they would do so in significant part as a result of the ravenous example other countries were setting. For a variety of reasons, imperialism as both a philosophy and a practice of international relations enjoyed an enthusiastic resurgence during the 1880s and 1890s. To some extent the new vogue of imperialism was an outgrowth of European nationalism. The failure of the revolutions of 1848 had knocked European nationalists down but not out. In Italy the movement for national unification gained momentum during the 1850s, culminating in the victorious 1860 march of Giuseppe Garibaldi (a filibustering type who had taken refuge in the United States after the collapse of the 1848 uprising) through the Kingdom of the Two Sicilies, and the 1861 proclamation of the establishment of the Kingdom of Italy under Victor Emmanuel II. It took the Italian people a while to appreciate what had happened. "We have made Italy," said Gabriele d'Annunzio, the poet of Italian nationalism. "All that remains is to make Italians." As a means of making Italians, some Italian leaders decided on foreign adventures; these presumably would foster a sense of national pride and unity. In the 1880s and 1890s, Italian troops forayed south and east, seizing territory on the Horn of Africa where the Red Sea meets the Indian Ocean (but being rebuffed in Abyssinia, later known as Ethiopia).

German imperialism likewise grew out of German nationalism. While Italian nationalism looked back to the Roman empire of the Caesars, German nationalism recalled Charlemagne's Holy Roman Empire—admittedly a poor substitute (having been, in Voltaire's deriding description, "neither holy nor Roman nor an empire"), but the best the Germans had. Prussia, the largest of the German states, and Bismarck, the iron hand at Prussia's helm, succeeded by threat, force, and guile in extending their authority over most of the German-speaking lands outside Austria. The last major piece of the German puzzle fell into place during the Franco-Prussian War of 1870–1871, near the end of which Bismarck's boss Wilhelm was proclaimed German emperor. The crowning took place in France in the palace built by Louis XIV at Versailles—a fact that festered in French minds for forty years.

Like Italy, Germany proceeded after unification to look abroad for new territories to conquer. The Germans went farther south than the Italians did, staking a claim to Tanganyika (Tanzania, after merging with Zanzibar) and Southwest Africa (Namibia).

The Italians and Germans were latecomers to the field of imperialism in Africa, which was why they got the comparatively slim pickings they did. The British and French had led the way earlier in the nineteenth century. For the British especially, the new imperialism of the late nineteenth century differed significantly from the old imperialism of the seventeenth and eighteenth centuries. Settlement had been a major theme of the first round of British imperialism; colonists had gone out from the British Isles to New England, Canada, Australia, and New Zealand looking for homes. The United States owed its existence to the settlement theme of the first round of British imperialism. The second round had little to do with settlement; few British left home in the 1880s and 1890s to take up housekeeping in Africa.

The new British imperialism was an imperialism based on trade. The British, as the most aggressive traders in the world, initially penetrated Africa during the first half of the nineteenth century when British merchants established spheres of economic interest around the mouth of the Niger River. At a time when the British navy was trying to suppress the slave trade, British merchants needed an alternative source of revenue. So did local leaders who had served as the procurers of the slaves and who were not especially happy at the Europeans' sudden conversion to humanitarianism. Both groups found palm oil to be a workable substitute for slaves, and by 1880 British traders were well entrenched along the West African coast.

France arrived in West Africa from the north. The French occupied Algiers in 1830; subsequently they chopped a foothold near the mouth of the Senegal River. The French were not uninterested in trade, but in characteristically French fashion they preferred glory to mere profits. (Napoleon once sneered at Britain as "a nation of shopkeepers.") Many of the French considered it a shame and a disgrace that the British were spreading Anglo-Saxon civilization around the globe more energetically than the French were spreading French civilization. To remedy the problem, France set out to establish colonies and spheres of interest where the natives would learn to speak French, partake of French culture, and appreciate the superiority of the French way of life over not only their own but also that of the British and other lesser Europeans.

Until about 1880, the competition between Britain and France for Africa was muted and more or less gentlemanly (for the Europeans; for most of the Africans involved it was never much of a bargain); but the last two decades of the nineteenth century saw a mad scramble for colonies and protectorates in the great continent to Europe's south. To some degree, the scramble was triggered by the sudden coming-of-age of Germany and Italy. Until the appearance of unified Italy and Germany, British and French leaders could tell themselves that there was no hurry to divide up Africa; after the appearance of these new competitors, there was no time to waste. To some degree, the scramble resulted from advances in geographical knowledge regarding the interior of the African continent. In the 1860s European explorers found the source of the Nile; in the 1870s they reached the head of the Congo. As the Europeans' knowledge regarding Africa increased, so did their cupidity. To some degree, the race for African colonies started accidentally. In the early 1880s a nationalist revolt broke out in Egypt against foreign influence in the Cairo government. The British, concerned about the security of the Suez Canal, their principal passageway to India, sent troops to occupy the canal zone and its environs. The French, Italians, and Germans thought Britain's move might portend a major land grab; they mobilized to grab some land themselves.

At least as important as any other factor in triggering the African land rush was the continued development of technology. The same technological changes that were tying the United States more tightly into the world economy had a like effect on Africa. Steamships brought the coast of West Africa much closer to European ports; the construction of the Suez Canal, which opened in 1869 (the year of the completion of America's first transcontinental railroad), cut weeks to months off travel time to East Africa. Technological change had other effects as well. The Europeans' steel ships, their rapid-firing machine guns, and their accurate artillery gave them a military advantage the Africans could not counter. Their increasingly efficient European factories produced trade goods that drove traditional items out of African markets. Their newly discovered medicines for the first time afforded them protection against previously (and still occasionally) lethal tropical diseases.

But often the factories of the industrial countries produced more than consumers in those countries would buy. The same problem of overproduction that afflicted America plagued the western Europeans. The Europeans had things worse in this regard than the Americans because the European powers had less potential for internal growth than the United States did. To an influential group of European leaders, the key to continued European economic growth lay in Africa and such other distant regions as East and Southeast Asia. Africa might be to Europe what the frontier West was to America.

Africa beckoned also as a field for European investment. Already returns on investment from America were beginning to decline; Africa looked like the next great frontier for capital. There were railroads to be constructed, mines to be opened, plantations to be developed. In order to facilitate and safeguard investments, European investors and their agents pressured governments to stake claims to Africa.

The United States had little directly to do with the scramble for African colonies, although connections did exist between America and certain parts of the African continent, dating from the era of the Atlantic slave trade. The suppression of the trade early in the nineteenth century cut direct links between America and Africa, but African Americans retained cultural traditions that tied them to their ancestral land. To many Americans, Africa seemed a logical refuge for freed slaves who wished to leave the United States (and to the many whites who wished them to go). In 1821 the American Colonization Society helped found what would become the republic of Liberia, on the West African coast. The country's purpose was to furnish a home for emancipated slaves, about fifteen thousand of whom eventually settled there.

American traders continued to call at African ports even after the end of the slave trade, but the trade they found never matched slaving in profitability. As the Europeans constructed exclusive spheres of influence and later colonies, American visits grew still less profitable and accordingly less frequent.

Americans paid some attention to the efforts by Europeans to explore the interior of Africa. A New York newspaper sent explorer-reporter Henry Stanley to cover the travels of explorer-philanthropist David Livingstone, a British doctor who had plunged into the remotest recesses of the continent and disappeared from view (the view of Europe and America, that is; the Africans whose territory he and his entourage passed through could not miss him). A few American big-navy enthusiasts and chamber of commerce boosters warned that the United States was losing a good opportunity by not seizing harbors and penetrating markets more aggressively. But most Americans who looked acquisitively abroad tended to look west and south, to Asia, Central America, and the Caribbean, rather than east. To the east was the world of the past, the world Americans' forebears had left behind.

Otto von Bismarck was called the Iron Chancellor for his belligerent policies, not for all the metal he liked to wear. *The Bettman Archive*

American interest perked up slightly during the 1880s when the European imperialists got together to talk about how to divide Africa among themselves. In 1884 Germany's Bismarck invited the interested European powers, the Ottoman empire, and the United States to Berlin. (Bismarck did not think it necessary to invite any Africans.) The delegates agreed on a set of rules regarding the partitioning of Africa. The Americans liked the rule declaring the Niger and Congo river basins to be free trade areas, which meant that American merchants would not be shut out—assuming the signatories played by the rules, which they often did not. Less important to the United States but more important to the non-present Africans was the rule specifying that claims to territory did not count unless the claimants put people on the ground in the claimed territory. First sightings and early exploration no longer sufficed to keep the flag waving over some river basin or inland lake; troops and traders were what was needed. This rule effectively fired the starting gun in the race for African colonies, as each country rushed to beat the rest in getting its people to the choice spots.

American president Grover Cleveland declined to seek Senate approval of the Berlin agreement. Cleveland's reservations apparently did not have anything to do with uneasiness about a deal that went far toward determining the fate of tens of millions of people not consulted; his reservations instead had to do with the American tradition of avoiding foreign commitments. Cleveland did not want to be branded as the president who broke George Washington's

Grover Cleveland pondering
what to do about Queen
Lilioukalani. *Brown Brothers*

rule about steering clear of permanent alliances, who violated Thomas Jefferson's dictum about eschewing entanglements with foreign powers, or who overstepped the dividing line between the New World and the Old World laid down in the Monroe Doctrine. Besides, Democrat Cleveland was not quite as solicitous of the health of American business as the Republicans of the time were. Assuring access to the Africa market was not a political priority. Moreover, Cleveland could see that the Berlin agreement hardly needed America's approval for its enforcement. If it suited the European imperialists to abide by the Berlin rules, the rules would hold; if some Europeans saw advantage in breaking the rules, the rules would break. American wishes would carry little weight in the matter.

As the Americans stood on the sidelines, the Europeans spent the 1880s and 1890s dividing nearly all of Africa into colonies, protectorates, and spheres of influence. By 1900 hardly a square foot remained without some European flag flying overhead. The example afforded a powerful lesson to all those watching, including Americans.

The New Imperialism: American Ideology

Although Americans mostly kept out of Africa, they were subject to many of the same impulses and imperatives that triggered the outburst of European

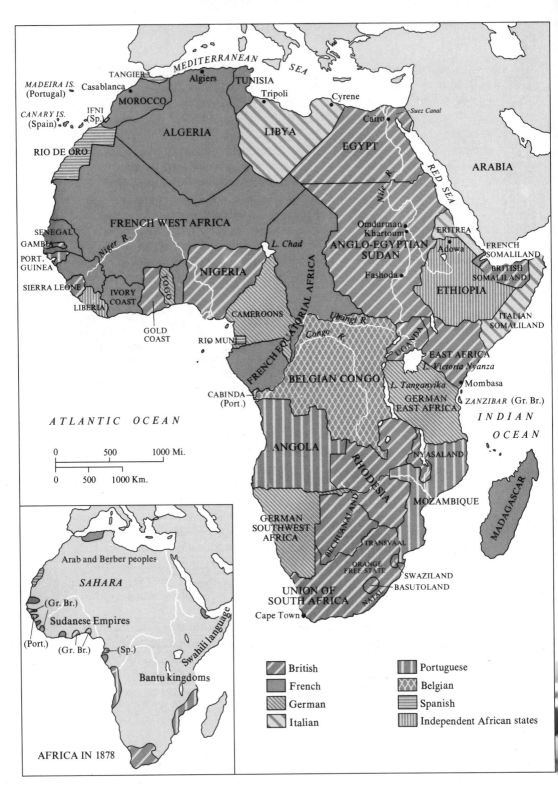

Africa Before and After Partition

imperialism. Americans were as nationalistic as the next people (although the American conception of nationalism differed from, say, the German conception. Germans thought of nationality as a matter of birth: once a German always a German. Americans saw nationality at least partly as a matter of choice: anyone could become an American simply by coming to the United States and adopting American values and ways of living.) Americans felt the spur of competition from the other great powers—of which the scramble for Africa was Exhibit A. American expansionists repeatedly urged haste lest all the choice locations for naval bases, coaling stations, and spheres of influence be appropriated by rivals. Technological innovations provided Americans with the same advantages over potential colonial peoples that the Europeans enjoyed. American industry poured forth merchandise that needed, like European merchandise, to be sold.

Americans put their own peculiar gloss on certain chapters of the imperialist gospel. To one degree or another, all the imperialists thought they were doing the people they imperialized a favor. The British prided themselves on bringing good government to Egyptians, Kenyans, Nigerians, and Indians; the French congratulated themselves on introducing Algerians, Senegalese, and Vietnamese to French language and culture; the Germans patted themselves on the back for introducing Tanganyikans to notions of modern efficiency.

American imperialists of the late nineteenth century took their cue from the Manifest Destinarians of midcentury. America's mission was to spread democracy, Christianity, and prosperity—not necessarily in that order. American publicists such as John Fiske and Josiah Strong declared that God wished Americans, as the most enlightened and progressive wing of the Anglo-Saxon race, to share the gifts he had bestowed on them with the less favored peoples of the earth. For Americans to hoard their blessings, to hide their light under a bushel basket, would be sinfully selfish. The unfortunates of the world cried out for regeneration. "The work which the English race began when it colonized North America," Fiske proclaimed, "is destined to go on until every land on the earth's surface that is not already the seat of an old civilization shall become English in its language, in its political habits and traditions, and to a predominant extent in the blood of its people." Britain had initially led the way toward the world's regeneration; now the torch had passed to America, which would spread its influence "from pole to pole" and "from the rising to the setting sun." Josiah Strong was equally adamant that the future of humanity rested with America. "It is fully in the hands of the Christians of the United States during the next ten or fifteen years to hasten or retard the coming of Christ's kingdom in the world by hundreds and perhaps thousands of years," Strong declared. "We of this generation and nation occupy the Gibraltar of the ages which commands the world's future."

The new imperialists in America had an arrow in their quiver that the Manifest Destinarians had lacked. By the late nineteenth century, Darwin's theory of evolution was firmly established as the model of scientific thinking. Like many grand theories, Darwin's was dragooned into service in areas that would have bewildered its originator. Apologists for the status quo of devil-take-the-hindmost capitalism trotted out Darwin's notion of the survival of the fittest to justify the current distribution of power and wealth in society. In the view of the Social Darwinists, those individuals who had risen to the top of society and the economy within particular countries, and those countries that had attained preeminence internationally, had done so on account of their special fitness to modern conditions. The captains of industry in the industrialized countries owed their wealth and influence to their brains and drive; the great powers of the world owed their global reach to the collective superiority of their inhabitants over the inhabitants of the lesser states.

Social Darwinism, like genuine Darwinism, had first gained a vogue in Britain. Philospher Herbert Spencer popularized Social Darwinist ideas, which did double duty justifying both the laissez faire order of political economy within Britain and British imperialism overseas.

Spencer's thinking soon caught on in America. The most effective broadcaster of the Social Darwinist message was William Graham Sumner, a sociologist and political economist at Yale University. Sumner carried Spencer's ideas to their logical conclusion: he contended that efforts by government or other institutions to alleviate poverty were misguided and pernicious. Only the goad of hunger and the fear of falling by the wayside kept people at their tasks; only these tasks separated the capable and willing from the incompetent and dissolute. Of the latter, Sumner said, "They constantly neutralize and destroy the finest efforts of the wise and industrious and are a dead weight on the society in all its struggles to realize any better things." To mitigate the lot of the poor would be to reward the wrong class of people and would burden future generations with that class's offspring.

Sumner and other Social Darwinists highly valued the competition of capitalism. They judged it to be capitalism's most valuable feature. (Although the capitalists themselves usually voiced support for Social Darwinist ideas, in practice they were not especially enamored of competition. Corporate titans such as John Rockefeller, Andrew Carnegie, and J. P. Morgan spent much of their time trying to *eliminate* competition by swallowing or merging with their competitors.) The Social Darwinists similarly applauded competition among nations, judging it to be the most valuable characteristic of international relations. Since war was the sharpest form of international competition, they tended to glorify or at least approve of war. Not for them the peaceful negotiations that settled disputes without conflict; only by war was the mettle of countries and peoples truly tested.

Social Darwinism also lent an air of scientific respectability to the racism that pervaded American society (and most other societies) during the late nineteenth century. The end of slavery had not brought an end to the widespread belief among white Americans that they were superior to persons of darker skin in intelligence, moral rectitude, and the other important measures of human worth. This superior attitude prevailed within the United States, blocking the advancement of African-Americans and excusing (in the view of most whites) the harsh treatment meted out to the American Indians. It applied also in American dealings with foreigners. Americans treated most Europeans as their racial equals, although the Slavs of eastern Europe and the peoples of the Mediterranean basin were often treated as only marginally equal. Latin Americans, thought to combine the traits of the Spanish and Portuguese with those of the aboriginal peoples of the Americas, were placed a couple of rungs lower on the ladder of civilization. Asians—Turks, Indians, Malays, Chinese—were farther down. Africans were at the bottom.

The racial argument cut both ways: in favor of imperialism and against it. Imperialist racists contended that Americans had a right, even an obligation, to impose their will on backward, inferior peoples; and in imposing their will, Americans might legitimately use more force than they ought to get away with in dealing with civilized peoples. Anti-imperialist racists asserted that the United States should have as little as possible to do with the lower races; Americans owed them nothing and would only be corrupted by contact with them.

While American imperialists shared much of their expansionist argument with European imperialists, one facet of their case was specific to the United States. An obscure historian named Frederick Jackson Turner, perusing the American census report of 1890, was struck by a statement that the American frontier, statistically speaking, had disappeared. The population had spread so widely across the American landscape that it was impossible to distinguish settled territory from unsettled territory. To Turner, this fact was tremendously significant, for it seemed to him that the frontier—a place of readily available land, where people could go to remake their lives and win their fortunes—had been the distinguishing feature of American history. "The existence of an area of free land, its continuous recession, and the advance of American settlement westward, explain American development," Turner declared. But now the frontier had vanished. With its passing, the first era of American history ended.

American imperialists quickly appropriated Turner's idea and put it to their own use. The frontier might have disappeared within the United States, they argued, but it still existed overseas. If the frontier had been responsible for the development of American democracy, self-sufficiency, and egalitarianism, as Turner said, then the United States must find another frontier lest Americans lose all those admirable traits. Turner spoke of the continual American advancement westward; just because Americans had reached the Pacific was no reason to stop advancing. Perhaps, as Turner said, an era of American history was ending; but another era, even more glorious, might be beginning.

Alfred Thayer Mahan distilled a different message from history than Turner did. Mahan, an instructor at the Naval War College, believed that history—world history, not just American history—demonstrated that those countries that possessed naval superiority sooner or later acquired other forms of superiority as well. Naval superiority required not simply powerful ships (he favored a few large battleships over more numerous smaller cruisers) but also the support facilities needed to maintain them. In the modern day, this implied coaling stations and repair facilities located strategically in the various oceans of the world. Mahan put his thoughts to paper in the 1890 *Influence of Sea*

Power Upon History and subsequent books with the same theme; these became overnight bestsellers. Mahan's ideas quickly caught on with expansionists in America, including the likes of Theodore Roosevelt and Henry Cabot Lodge; they gained an equal following abroad. Translated into several languages, Mahan's books were required reading in naval colleges and admiralties around the world. Britain honored Mahan with honorary degrees from Oxford and Cambridge; Japan's Meiji reformers embraced his teachings as the latest in usable Western ideas; Germany's Kaiser Wilhelm ordered all his naval officers to familiarize themselves with Mahan's work. In the long run, Mahan's books helped trigger the naval weapons race that contributed significantly to the outbreak of war in Europe in 1914; in the shorter term, they prepared Americans for a revival of territorial expansion.

Making Waves in the Pacific

One reason for Mahan's popularity was that he promulgated his theories at a time when Americans were looking out across the world's largest ocean more seriously than ever before. Looking seriously, however, did not necessarily imply looking perceptively; and when Americans gazed across the Pacific, they often did so with the same narrow-minded, self-congratulatory attitude that typified their perceptions of much of the rest of the world. One might have thought that as American merchants and missionaries gained familiarity with China and Japan, they would come to respect the ancient and sophisticated civilizations of those countries. But it is often the case that to appreciate sophistication one has to be sophisticated—throwing pearls before swine, and all that. Americans in the late nineteenth century tended to be rather unsophisticated, and whatever was different they usually interpreted as inferior. In fairness to Americans, the Chinese acted quite arrogantly at times, treating foreigners as barbarians who had to be suffered only because they were strong. Nor were the constricted relations that accompanied American contacts with East Asia of a kind likely to impress either side with the wisdom and magnanimity of the other.

Contrary to the hopes of American merchants, the China market remained depressingly small through the end of the nineteenth century. Part of the problem was China's debilitating poverty. There might be hundreds of millions of Chinese, but taken together they lacked the purchasing power (for American goods, at any rate) of a medium-sized city in the American Midwest. American sales representatives could pitch their products night and day, but until the average Chinese family got its hands on more disposable income, they would be wasting their breath.

Part of the problem was the unwillingness or inability of American merchants to tailor their products to Chinese tastes. American Christian missionaries sometimes solicited financial support in the United States by pointing out that they were teaching their converts to wear American clothes, thereby creating a market for American textile products. Given the dismal record of the missionaries in attracting converts, this was not much of a marketing strategy. American merchants spent little effort to determine what the *Chinese* wanted, as opposed to what the missionaries and other China-watchers thought the Chinese ought to have. To some extent, the problem was circular: because Chinese demand was so low, tailoring products to the China market often did not make marketing sense; but a principal factor in keeping the demand so low was the absence of specially tailored products.

For whatever reasons, American goods did not become particularly attractive to the Chinese; yet *America* did. In fact, America became so attractive that tens of thousands of Chinese broke Chinese laws to leave their country for the United States. Some came for the personal freedom America offered, but most came for the money. Young Chinese men flocked to the gold fields of California and Nevada and the railroad construction camps of several western states with the intention of striking it rich and returning home wealthy. Until they returned, they sent money back to their families.

Not many of these Chinese intended to settle in the United States. This was just as well because most of the Americans they encountered did not want them to settle. The Chinese labored under the triple burden of being of the wrong race (any but Caucasian), the wrong religion (non-Christian), and the wrong economic class (poor and therefore willing to work for wages that, though far higher than anything available in China, were union-bustingly low by American standards). In California a group calling itself the Workingmen's Party advocated and practiced anti-Chinese measures. The party agitated for an end to Chinese immigration to the United States; while impatiently awaiting action by Congress, party members terrorized Chinese already in America. Anti-Chinese riots became a regular feature of life along the American West Coast from California to Washington and far into the interior. One of the worst outbreaks of violence occurred at Rock Springs, Wyoming, in 1885, when white railroad workers killed more than two dozen Chinese workers who crossed picket lines during a strike.

Not surprisingly, the violence damaged relations between the United States and China. In China, resentment often took the form of hostility toward American missionaries. Not that the Chinese needed much encouragement to be hostile; xenophobia was even stronger in China than in the United States, and contending political factions used their opposition to foreigners as a way of demonstrating their reverence for traditional Chinese values. American officials in China demanded protection for Americans there. Chinese officials responded by demanding protection for Chinese nationals in America. Neither side got much in the way of satisfaction, despite various diplomatic efforts to resolve the problem.

In 1882 the China-baiters in the United States persuaded Congress to call a halt to Chinese immigration. Chinese immigrants to America at this point numbered somewhat more than two hundred thousand—which was about two hundred thousand too many for the Workingmen's Party and other nativist organizations. Employers such as railroad companies and mine owners initially opposed legislation restricting immigration. The employers often cited America's historic openness to the oppressed of foreign lands as reason for their opposition to immigration curbs, but the bread-and-butter side of their case was a desire to keep wages down by keeping immigration up. Although the employers successfully resisted meaningful across-the-board restrictions on immigration until well into the twentieth century, the hostility toward the Chinese was more than they could counteract. The Chinese Exclusion Act of 1882 suspended immigration of Chinese laborers for ten years, subject to renewal. The act was duly renewed, and the ban on Chinese immigration became effectively permanent.

The United States treated Japan with somewhat greater respect during this period. One reason was that there were not as many Japanese migrating to America. Another was that Japan was becoming a major power in East Asia. The Meiji restoration had set the Japanese on the modernizing road; within only a few years their proficiency at learning the lessons the West had to teach was showing. Various social reforms freed the Japanese people from anachronistic constraints, while the adoption of Western technology freed them from some of the burdens and inefficiencies of preindustrial life. Japan's industrialization followed a course different from that of most of the West. Government bureaucrats directed investment and other aspects of the industrialization process in a way that would have been politically impossible in laissez faire Britain or America. But the Japanese method obviously suited the Japanese, and by the 1890s Japan boasted the strongest economy and the most formidable military establishment in East Asia.

This was what worried the American government. A cardinal objective of American diplomacy toward Asia had long been the maintenance of access to markets on a footing at least equal to that afforded other countries. When the countries of the region had been weak, achieving this objective had not been especially difficult and had chiefly involved preventing any of the European countries from gaining an advantage. Japan's rise complicated things.

The complication became a source of concern when Japan fought China in the Sino-Japanese War of 1894–1895. The occasion of the war was a dispute over the status of Korea. For centuries, off and on, China had controlled Korea as a protectorate. By the late nineteenth century, Chinese control was mostly off, with the Chinese concentrating less on Korea than on their own country's stagnation. Japan looked at Korea as the entryway to mainland Asia, especially to China's resource-rich northeastern province of Manchuria. In 1894 Japan decided to challenge China's position in Korea. Japanese troops smashed China's feeble resistance, rooting Chinese forces out of Korea and commencing an occupation that lasted until 1945.

The outcome of the Sino-Japanese War altered American perceptions of the three Asian states involved. It made American leaders think that Korea might be a lost cause in American foreign policy. For three decades American officials had tried to open Korea, which was shut as tightly as Japan had been before 1854. After some Koreans in 1866 killed the crew of an uninvited American merchant ship, the American navy retaliated with a bombardment that left hundreds of Koreans dead. The incident left many ill feelings in Korea, but eventually, in 1882, the Korean government signed a treaty of commerce with Washington. Yet when Korea fell under Japanese control in the 1890s, all bets regarding the future of American commerce in Korea were off.

The outcome of the Sino-Japanese War also altered American views of China. For years the chief question regarding China had been how long that country could hold up under the combined weight of external Western pressure and internal domestic discontent. Would the sick man of Asia recover his strength? If not, was the illness mortal? China's quick loss to Japan suggested that the malady might indeed be mortal and that the end was nearer than most observers had reckoned.

As to Japan, the war with China demonstrated that the Japanese were a power to be contended with, if not immediately then soon. For millennia Japan had been China's poor relation; now the poor relation had battered down the rich relation's front door and looted the parlor. What else Japan had in mind was unclear. What the United States could or would do about it likewise was unclear. American policy toward East Asia had been premised on a balance of weakness among the indigenous states and a balance of distance among the Western imperialists. No single country had been able to dominate the region because the local governments were weak and the strong governments were far away. Now one of the locals had gotten strong, and the balance in the area seemed to be in jeopardy.

Events elsewhere in the Pacific worked more to America's advantage. The idyllic (before the Westerners got there anyway) island group of Samoa provoked a mini-scramble among three of the big powers. During the 1870s and 1880s, naval forces from Britain, Germany, and the United States paid periodic visits to Samoa, with each country's representatives promising wealth and happiness to the Samoans if only they would ally their islands with the representatives' respective governments. For a while it seemed as though the contest for naval bases in the archipelago might bring the big powers to blows. Amid considerable posturing and pontificating, the three powers agreed to meet in Berlin in 1889 to determine Samoa's fate. (Naturally the Samoans were not invited.) As if as a reminder that even countries with steel-hulled, steam-powered warships were not omnipotent, a hurricane roared through the islands just when the delegates were preparing their position papers. By the time the wind died down and the waves receded, Samoa seemed much less worth a wrangle. In short order the three powers cut a deal dividing access to Samoa three ways.

Hawaii was closer to the American West Coast than Samoa, much farther north, and therefore more on the way to places of interest to Americans. (Samoa was on the way only to British-controlled Australia and New Zealand.) American traders had been visiting Hawaii en route to China since the late eighteenth century. American whalers subsequently made it a customary port of call. American missionaries arrived to redeem the Hawaiians from the

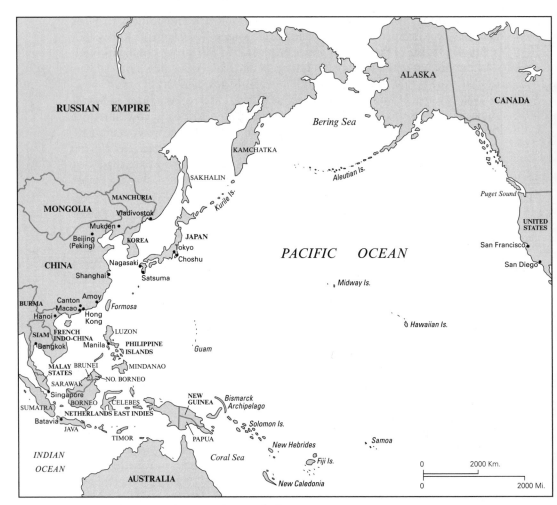

The Pacific Rim in the Late Nineteenth Century

wicked ways the merchants and whalers had introduced them to, as well as any they might have stumbled into on their own. American planters followed the missionaries. While the missionaries did fairly well harvesting souls, the planters did even better harvesting sugar and pineapples.

Most of the Americans in Hawaii looked favorably on closer formal relations between the United States and Hawaii. The merchants, whalers, and missionaries expected greater predictability and security under an American government than under Hawaii's monarch; the planters did, too, but in addition the planters hoped to get their exports, particularly sugar, admitted to the American market duty-free. An 1875 reciprocity treaty, which reduced the

American tariff on Hawaiian sugar, gave the planters most of what they wanted. Nevertheless, they and the other groups desired annexation.

The Hawaiians did not desire annexation, though, and neither did the British or the Japanese desire that Hawaii be annexed. Britain for many years had coveted Hawaii, particularly Pearl Harbor, the best shelter for ships in the central Pacific. The British objected to America's growing influence in Hawaii, and when Washington in 1887 acquired rights to develop Pearl Harbor as a naval base, they got more irritated still. The Japanese disliked America's deepening entrenchment in Hawaii for the same reasons the British did. The Japanese were additionally sensitive to Hawaii's affairs because people of Japanese descent constituted a large minority of Hawaii's population. Americans on the North American mainland had shown themselves to be almost as racist toward Japanese as toward Chinese, and there was little indication that the Americans would be much broader minded toward Japanese in Hawaii. As a matter of national honor—a more serious matter to Japan than to many other countries—the Japanese government felt required to look after Japanese abroad.

British irritation and Japanese sensitivity, however, only encouraged the Americans in Hawaii to attach Hawaii more closely to the United States. The going was not easy. American planters who competed with Hawaiian sugar lobbied to have Congress rescind Hawaii's favored treatment, and after considerable jawboning and arm twisting they succeeded. To add insult to injury, Congress granted special treatment to sugar from Cuba—where American growers also controlled production.

Having been jilted, temporarily at least, by Uncle Sam for a Cuban sweetheart, Hawaii's sugar faction pushed harder than ever for annexation to the United States. Americans in the islands, who by the 1890s numbered some three thousand out of a total population of perhaps ninety thousand, began plotting against the government of Queen Liliuokalani. The queen detected the unrest and suspended the Hawaiian constitution, thereby revoking some of the rights the planters had squeezed out of her predecessor. This only exacerbated the plotting, and in January 1893 a group of the most prominent members of the American community staged a coup that forced Liliuokalani from her throne. The American minister in Hawaii, John Stevens, effectively guaranteed the success of the coup by ordering marines ashore from an American warship anchored at Pearl Harbor. The new rulers of Hawaii, led by Sanford Dole, requested annexation to the United States.

From the perspective of the Americans in Hawaii, annexation promised that Hawaiian sugar and other products would enter the American market duty-free. In light of the increasingly competitive nature of world commodity markets, free access to the American market could well make the difference between prosperity and bankruptcy for Hawaiian producers. Annexation also promised protection against pressure from Britain and Japan, both of which looked on the new pro-American government in Hawaii with distrust tending toward hostility. Finally, annexation would make the Americans in Hawaii, greatly outnumbered by indigenous Hawaiians as well as Japanese and

Queen Lilioukalani weighing what to do about Grover Cleveland. *Brown Brothers*

Chinese, feel more comfortable about their personal future in the islands. The Americans would be a minority in Hawaii for a long time, perhaps forever. But if the United States annexed Hawaii, they would become part of the larger white majority in America. In unity there often seems to be strength, especially in matters of racial psychology. This was doubly true during an era when racial thinking was as prevalent as it was during the 1890s.

From the perspective of the United States, annexation was not such an ob- viously good idea. The strategic significance of Pearl Harbor was apparent, as was the importance of keeping the harbor out of British, Japanese, or possibly even German hands. But the same sugar interests that had blocked easy entry of Hawaiian sugar into the United States still wanted to keep the sugar out. Nor did the psychological worries of Americans in Hawaii much concern Americans on the mainland.

The administration of Grover Cleveland, just returned to office for a second (nonconsecutive) term, had special difficulties with annexation. Democrat Cleveland was a long-time supporter of clean government, especially as a con- trast to the spoilsmanship of the Republicans. He had campaigned on the slo- gan "Public office is a public trust," and he was loath to contradict himself in office. Hawaiian annexation seemed to Cleveland suspiciously like a payoff to Dole and the American coup makers in the islands. The United States, he be- lieved, should not get into the business of assisting in the overthrow of foreign governments in order to capture their countries. Cleveland also worried about the racial problems involved in annexing a territory inhabited mostly by non-

Caucasians. It was hard to conceive that such a territory would become a state, equal to all the rest. But did Americans desire to maintain a territory in a condition of permanent inferiority?

Cleveland decided against annexation. Briefly he pondered assisting Lili-uokalani to regain her throne, but ultimately he dropped the idea. It was one thing for a president to refuse to deal in stolen property; it was another for the leader of the world's largest democracy to restore a monarchy. Cleveland already was under fire for putting the interests of Hawaiians ahead of those of Americans, and he preferred not to invite any more volleys.

As a result, the Hawaiian question went on the shelf, much as the Texas question had done during the late 1830s and early 1840s. Pulling it off the shelf awaited a change of mood in the United States and a change of administration in Washington, again much as had happened with Texas fifty years before.

A Last Twist of the Lion's Tail: Cleveland, Olney, and Venezuela

If Cleveland thought Hawaii was trouble, he had not seen anything yet. In the spring of 1893, the American economy imploded. An adverse balance of American trade had left foreigners holding more dollars than they wanted; to dump the dollars, the foreigners exchanged them for gold from the American treasury. Financial tremors in London further encouraged British investors and speculators to get out of dollars (and other currencies) and into gold, and the consequent additional drain on America's gold supply caused it to dwindle dangerously. The dwindling touched off a panic in the American stock and bond markets, which triggered the worst depression to date in American history. To stanch the bleeding, Cleveland negotiated a deal with J. P. Morgan for shoring up the treasury's gold reserves. The deal helped avert a collapse of the government's finances, but it provoked charges that Cleveland had sold out the country to the biggest of the big bankers.

Stymied on the home front, Cleveland not surprisingly looked for victories abroad. One possibility presented itself across the Caribbean in Venezuela. For many years the boundary between Venezuela and the neighboring British colony of Guiana had been a matter of dispute. But for most of that time the dispute had not been a very serious one since the only thing at stake was some jungle nobody much cared about. In the 1880s, however, prospectors discovered gold in the disputed region, which immediately elevated the dispute to world-class. The Venezuelans began demanding that their claims be honored; the British told the Venezuelans it would be a cold day in the rain forest before Britain retreated. Venezuela then appealed to the United States to defend a fellow American republic against this European bullying. The Monroe Doctrine had pledged the United States to just such a defense, the Venezuelans said. Did the American government intend to honor its pledge?

Until Cleveland took up the issue, Washington had mumbled distractedly to the British about arbitrating the dispute; now the president decided to speak more clearly and forcefully. On his direction, Secretary of State Richard Olney fired off a loud message to London (Cleveland satisfiedly likened it to a "twenty-inch gun") telling the British to leave Venezuela alone and to remember that in the Western Hemisphere the United States made the rules. "Today the United States is practically sovereign on this continent," Olney said, rhetorically annexing South America to North America, "and its fiat is law upon the subjects to which it confines its interposition."

American superpatriots loved the Cleveland administration's performance. Henry Cabot Lodge, embarking on a long senatorial career devoted to furthering his often grand views of American interests overseas, applauded the administration's determined stance. Theodore Roosevelt, another up-and-coming Republican, similarly bared his chest and war-whooped. Irish-American politicians, always eager for a swipe at the British, cheered the president and secretary of state.

Had the British chosen to take umbrage at the American posturing, something serious might have come of the incident. The British prime minister, Lord Salisbury, did not suffer fools gladly and American fools least gladly of all. But Salisbury had even bigger fools to deal with in the British empire. While the dispute over Venezuela's border was brewing, trouble was afoot in South Africa. For most of the nineteenth century, British colonists at the Cape of Good Hope had lived uneasily alongside the neighboring Boers, the descendants of Dutch colonists who had arrived a couple of hundred years before the British. Despite intermittent friction, nothing had happened to escalate the uneasiness to the point of open conflict until, at about the same time gold was discovered in the Venezuela border region, gold was discovered in the Boer republic of Transvaal. British (and other) gold diggers descended on the Boers, who did not do much to make the intruders feel welcome.

Boer discrimination against British nationals and, more important, Boer possession of gold mines the British lusted after led to various schemes to capture Transvaal and its twin, the Orange Free State. In 1895, when the Americans were thundering about Venezuela, a British adventurer named Jameson led a raid into Transvaal. The raid failed and Jameson was captured, to the tremendous embarrassment of Salisbury and the British back home. Reddening Salisbury's cheeks further (one has to assume: the cheeks in question were hidden under a bumper crop of whiskers), German Kaiser Wilhelm sent a letter of congratulations to the Boers. Berlin intimated that the Boers might expect German help in case of more serious trouble with the British.

For the British government, the Jameson fiasco and the German meddling in South Africa constituted a crisis, by comparison to which the Venezuelan affair was merely an annoyance. Salisbury put off the Americans for as long as he could, then finally agreed to negotiate. The American warhawks were disappointed, but not Cleveland, who really did not want to go to war over some half-century-old surveyor's mistake. When London agreed to refer the matter to an international tribunal, the Cleveland administration declared victory for itself and for its generous interpretation of the Monroe Doctrine. By the time the international panel in 1899 awarded most of the territory in question to the British (but granting to Venezuela control of the mouth of the Orinoco River, mistakenly thought by some to be the gateway to an important future South American trade), the dispute had largely been forgotten. At least it had been forgotten by the Americans, who had just finished fighting a war with Spain and were still fighting a war in the Philippines. It had also been forgotten by most of the British, who were fighting the Boers. The Venezuelans had not forgotten, but the Americans and British had forgotten them.

Britain's simultaneous difficulties with the United States over Venezuela and with Germany over South Africa, and London's decision to resolve its double troubles by placating the Americans reflected an incipient shift in the balance of world power. For a century, the United States had been rising to a position where it could challenge Britain's interests in the Western Hemisphere and perhaps elsewhere. Since unification in 1870, Germany had been shouldering its way to a position where it could challenge Britain's interests in Europe and elsewhere. In 1895, faced with a choice of rivals, Britain chose Germany—which meant that it chose the United States as a collaborator.

Two considerations motivated the choice. First, Europe counted more in British calculations than the Western Hemisphere did, and while Britain could live with a Western Hemisphere dominated by some other country, it could not live with a Europe dominated by someone else. Second, just as Americans felt a cultural affinity to the British, so the British often felt a connection to their English-speaking cousins. Americans and British had often been competitive, but more often (at least since 1815) they had been cooperative, if sometimes grudgingly so. Alexander Hamilton had said that Americans "think in English"; if the British did not quite think in American, they found that language and the attitudes it conveyed more understandable and less threatening than Germany's. For three generations Americans and British had found common ground. The tacit agreement that had long underwritten the Monroe Doctrine, the amicable compromise on the Oregon question, and Britain's refusal to recognize the Confederacy showed that Washington and London could get along without insurmountable difficulty.

So had an 1871 settlement, the Treaty of Washington, that tied up several loose ends between the United States and Britain. These included claims resulting from British construction of the *Alabama* and other Confederate warships, questions relating to fishing and sealing rights in the North Atlantic, and a dispute over the location of the main channel in the Strait of Juan de Fuca in the Pacific Northwest. After some political posturing on both sides, the two governments agreed to arbitrate the major differences, which the arbitrators ended up splitting, some more in favor of the United States, some to Britain's advantage.

It was a reasonable solution to several nagging problems between the British and Americans (and the principal achievement of American secretary of state

Hamilton Fish, the best of Grant's bad lot of advisers). On this and the other evidence, there seemed little reason to think America and Britain could not get along in the future as they had in the past.

*   *   *

Britain's acceptance of the American position in the Venezuela case furthered friendly Anglo-American relations and laid the cornerstone for the most enduring alliance (informal at first, later formalized) of the twentieth century. Americans did not all catch on to the British game right away—and the British at times, as during the early years of the First World War, did a clever job concealing their strategy. But British leaders, foreseeing trouble ahead with Germany, started building up credit with the Americans, to be redeemed when the trouble arrived, which it did within two decades.

London's decision to cultivate the United States reflected America's increasing influence in world affairs. The three decades after the Civil War were a comparatively quiet time in American international relations. The United States fought no foreign wars (domestic wars against the Indians continued and concluded at the 1890 battle, or perhaps massacre, of Wounded Knee). Such sizable new territory as Washington acquired—namely, Alaska—was obtained only by peaceful purchase. But this period was also a time during which the American economy expanded rapidly, as a result both of internal developments and of America's integration into the world economy. With growing economic strength came a growth in the power the United States was able to bring to bear against other countries. As of 1895, this power remained largely potential. Converting the potential to actual, however, would not take long.

Sources and Suggestions for Further Reading

Two surveys of American foreign relations in the late nineteenth century are Robert L. Beisner, *From the Old Diplomacy to the New, 1865–1900* (1986 ed.), and Charles S. Campbell, *The Transformation of American Foreign Relations, 1865–1900* (1976). Other general works include Milton Plesur, *America's Outward Thrust* (1971); and Foster Rhea Dulles, *Prelude to World Power* (1968). Studies of particular administrations and diplomats include Allan Nevins, *Hamilton Fish: The Inner History of the Grant Administration* (1957 ed.); Ernest N. Paolino, *The Foundations of American Empire: William Henry Seward and U.S. Foreign Policy* (1973); Alice F. Tyler, *The Foreign Policies of James G. Blaine* (1927); and David M. Pletcher, *The Awkward Years: American Foreign Policy under Garfield and Arthur* (1962).

James Foreman-Peck, *A History of the World Economy: International Economic Relations since 1850* (1983), is a survey. W. W. Rostow, *How It All Began: Origins of the Modern Economy* (1975), is opinionated. D. K. Fieldhouse, *Economics and Empire, 1830–1914* (1973), relates changes in the world economy to the rise of European imperialism. On the international demographics of the late nineteenth century, try Carlo M. Cipolla, *The Economic History of World Population* (1962).

Walter LaFeber, *The New Empire* (1963), provides a provocative introduction to American economic foreign relations during the decades after the Civil War. William A. Williams, *The Roots of the Modern American Empire* (1969), does too. Other works elucidating economic aspects of American foreign relations are Fred V. Carstensen, *American Enterprise in Foreign Markets* (1984); Robert B. Davies, *Peacefully Working* to Conquer the World (1976); Tom Terrill, The Tariff, Politics, and American Foreign Policy, 1874–1901 (1973); Emily S. Rosenberg, Spreading the American Dream: American Economic and Cultural Expansion, 1890–1945 (1982); Edward P. Crapol, America for Americans: Economic Nationalism and Anglophobia in the Late Nineteenth Century (1973); and Mira Wilkins, The Emergence of the Multinational Enterprise (1970).

The ideology of American expansion shows up in David Healy, U.S. Expansionism: The Imperialist Urge in the 1890s (1970); Richard Hofstadter, Social Darwinism in American Thought (1955), and The Paranoid Style in American Politics and Other Essays (1966). Alfred Thayer Mahan receives his due in Robert Seager, Alfred Thayer Mahan (1977).

Archie W. Shiels, The Purchase of Alaska (1967), and Ronald J. Jensen, The Alaska Purchase and Russian-American Relations (1975), fairly well cover that subject, although Paul S. Holbo, Tarnished Expansion (1983), adds some juicy tidbits, and Howard Kushner, Conflict of the Northwest Coast, provides background.

The efforts to acquire Santo Domingo are well aired in Charles C. Tansill, The United States and Santo Domingo, 1798–1873 (1938), as well as in Lester Langley's Struggle for the American Mediterranean. Dexter Perkins, The Monroe Doctrine, 1826–1867 (1933), and The Monroe Doctrine, 1867–1907 (1937), cover the Western Hemisphere more broadly.

Since its publication in 1961, the jumping-off point for most excursions into the new imperialism has been Ronald Robinson and John Gallagher, Africa and the Victorians. Also insightful are Fieldhouse, Economics and Empire; Wolfgang J. Mommsen and Jurgen Osterhammel, eds., Imperialism and After (1986); Tony Smith, The Pattern of Imperialism: The United States, Great Britain, and the Late–Industrializing World since 1815 (1982); and Phillip Darby, Three Faces of Imperialism: British and American Approaches to Asia and Africa, 1870–1970 (1986). American connections to Africa specifically are explored in Peter Duignan and L. H. Gann, The United States and Africa (1984); and Clarence Clendenen, Robert Collins and Peter Duignan, Americans in Africa, 1865–1900 (1966).

The works by Spence, Fairbank, Hunt, and Reischauer mentioned in the previous chapter contain much information on American relations with China and Japan during the late nineteenth century. Additional books on American-Asian relations include David L. Anderson, Imperialism and Idealism: American Diplomacy in China, 1861–1898 (1986); Stuart C. Miller, The Unwelcome Immigrant (1969); Fred H. Harrington, God, Mammon, and the Japanese: Horace N. Allen and Korean-American Relations, 1884–1905 (1944); and Yur-Bok Lee, Diplomatic Relations between the United States and Korea, 1866–1887 (1970).

The Samoan affair is the subject of Paul M. Kennedy, The Samoan Tangle: A Study in Anglo-German-American Relations (1974), while Hawaii is the topic of discussion in Merze Tate, The United States and the Hawaiian Kingdom (1965), and William A. Russ, Jr., The Hawaiian Revolution, 1893–1894 (1959). The Venezuela dispute with Britain kicks off Bradford Perkins's book, The Great Rapprochement: England and the United States, 1895–1914 (1968). Another dispute involving a Latin American country forms the raison d'etre of Joyce S. Goldberg, The Baltimore Affair: U.S. Relations with Chile, 1891–1892 (1986).

Chapter 7

Democratic Imperialism, 1895–1914

T he twentieth century started early for the United States. The opening gun was the outbreak of war with Spain in the spring of 1898, though the war was merely a symptom of something larger. Americans had fought Europeans before: the British twice and the French once. Each fight had been a stiffer contest than the bout with Spain proved to be. Nor were the stakes of the Spanish-American War especially vital. Some American property in Cuba had suffered damage in the preceding turmoil, but hardly enough to warrant a war. Had the McKinley administration chosen to ignore Madrid's ill-treatment of its Cuban subjects, Americans might simply have gone on about their affairs; other imperial powers routinely oppressed their colonials. For America's part, Washington had nothing to boast of in its treatment of native Indians.

The significance of the Spanish-American War lay in the fact that it represented a willingness on the part of the American government and the American people to use American power for purposes not immediately related to American security and to do so at a great distance from home. This was what most plainly distinguished the twentieth century in American international relations from the eighteenth and nineteenth centuries. Americans had not shied away from the use of force during the earlier period, but force had always borne a direct and obvious connection to vital American interests. During the Revolutionary War, America's national existence was on the line. During the undeclared naval war against France in 1798–1800, Americans fought to avenge past attacks on American shipping and prevent future attacks. The War of 1812 had a variety of causes, but they clustered around a felt need to enforce respect by the British for American rights and interests. The other foreign war to date—the Mexican War—had less to do with American security than the others, but took place right next to the United States.

Although the Spanish-American War started over events in Cuba, some of the most important fighting occurred halfway around the globe in the Philippines. By carrying the contest to the Philippines, the American government signaled America's intention to join the ranks of the world's great global powers. The joining did not come without complaints: from the Filipinos who resisted the extension of American control over their islands, from American anti-imperialists who denounced the establishment of an American empire in the far Pacific, and from Americans generally who believed that the warnings of George Washington, Thomas Jefferson, and John Quincy Adams about keeping clear of entanglements with other countries and peoples still ought to guide American foreign relations. The complainers lost this round of the debate, as, for most of the twentieth century, would those who advocated a modest and circumscribed role for the United States in world affairs.

The energies of the United States for the first decade and a half of the twentieth century continued to concentrate on East Asia and the Caribbean basin. In East Asia, the American government sought to prevent any other country from gaining inordinate influence. The term "open door" catch-phrased the policy devised to prevent such a happening. The policy had both political and economic connotations and referred especially to China. Politically, the Open Door aimed to keep China from being partitioned among the European imperialists and perhaps Japan; economically, it attempted to forestall the closing of China to American trade by the Europeans or Japanese.

In the Caribbean basin, the policy of the United States had the same overall objective as in Asia—maximizing American influence against competing claims—but employed quite different tactics. If the label Open Door captured the American approach to Asia, "closed door" could have summarized American policy toward the Western Hemisphere. First by the Roosevelt corollary to the Monroe Doctrine, and subsequently by the "dollar diplomacy" of the Taft administration, the American government attempted to secure much of Latin America as a United States sphere of influence. Only in Puerto Rico did Washington explicitly colonize territory to its south, but American leaders acquired influence in many parts of the region that made formal control almost superfluous.

That the United States did *not* claim more territory—Cuba being the most likely candidate—resulted from two factors, one that reflected well on America's national conscience and one that did not. Many Americans felt it unbecoming, indeed disgraceful, for the country that had invented modern democracy to forcibly deny other countries the right to govern themselves. This strain of thinking had been evident earlier in American history, notably during the Mexican War; but it gained adherents and influence during the controversy that followed the Spanish-American War. This appeal to America's better nature did not prevent the annexation of the Philippines and Puerto Rico, but it did help prevent the emergence of a full-blown American colonialism. The anticolonial factor that did not reflect well on Americans had also been evident during the nineteenth century. Many opponents of an American overseas empire shrank from association with the dark-skinned peoples such an empire would include. The majority of those who felt this way did not have much use for African-Americans in the United States, and they thought that (white) Americans would only be asking for more trouble to take other colored people to their bosom.

Underlying the controversy over America's new role in international affairs were fundamental questions of how to reconcile democracy with global power. Could a democracy rule an empire and remain a democracy? Were spheres of influence more compatible with democracy than outright colonies? What

Chronology

1895	Venezuelan crisis with Britain; Cuban war of independence breaks out; radio telegraphy invented
1898	Spanish-American War; Hawaii annexed
1899	Philippines annexed; Philippine war begins; first Open Door note; Samoa partioned between United States and Germany; Boer War begins
1900	Boxer Rebellion in China; second Open Door note; first radio broadcast of human voice
1901	Platt amendment to Cuban constitution; Hay-Pauncefote treaty with Britain; oil discovered in Texas
1902	Anglo-Japanese alliance
1903	Panama gains independence with American help; Hay-Bunau Varilla treaty with Panama regarding canal
1904	Russo-Japanese War begins; Roosevelt corollary to Monroe Doctrine
1905	Taft-Katsura agreement with Japan; Treaty of Portsmouth between Russia and Japan
1906	American troops occupy Cuba; Algeciras conference regarding Morocco
1907	"Gentlemen's agreement" with Japan; J.P. Morgan stops run on U.S. gold supply; Roosevelt sends fleet on around-the-world cruise
1908	Root-Takahira agreement with Japan; Henry Ford introduces the Model T car
1909	Payne-Aldrich tariff
1910	Japan annexes Korea; Mexican revolution begins
1911	Qing dynasty in China falls
1912	U.S. troops land in Nicaragua; Sun Yatsen founds Guomindang party in China
1913	Balkan war
1914	American troops occupy Veracruz; First World War begins; Wilson proclaims neutrality; Panama Canal opened to traffic

obligations did a great democracy have to its colonies or to the countries within its sphere? What effect would America's new role in the world have on its institutions at home? Americans wrestled with these questions at the beginning of the twentieth century; in one form or another, they have been wrestling with them ever since.

Cuba Libre!

Although Grover Cleveland could interpret Britain's agreement to submit the Venezuelan dispute to arbitration as a diplomatic triumph, the Democrats remained in the ditch the depression of the 1890s had got them into. Foreign-policy successes almost never make up for domestic debacles, and they did not for the Democrats in Cleveland's day. The presidential campaign of 1896 turned on a homegrown issue: silver. The Democratic candidate, William Jennings Bryan, knew almost nothing about international affairs (which nonetheless would not disqualify him, older and only slightly wiser, from being named secretary of state in 1913); but Bryan did not bother with foreign affairs, instead training his booming voice on what he discerned as America's need to debase the currency by remonetizing silver. Bryan naturally did not put the matter so directly—but the Republicans did. Republican candidate William McKinley promised sound money, meaning gold, and a return to prosperity. The voters preferred McKinley's promises to Bryan's.

McKinley entered the White House with no compelling agenda for international affairs (in fact, so leery was he of seeming forward on foreign topics that when visiting Niagara Falls he refused to walk more than halfway across the bridge connecting the United States to Canada lest he be the first president to leave American territory while in office). McKinley initially thought it would be enough for him to get the American economy back on track again. But events overseas—and reactions to those events in certain American quarters—soon demanded his attention.

The most pressing of those events took place in Cuba. Early in the nineteenth century, when most of the rest of Spain's American empire was breaking free of the mother country, Cuba had remained loyal. The Cubans' loyalty did not indicate so much a deep-seated affection for Spain as an attachment to the prosperity the island was enjoying. The anti-French revolt in Haiti, which had contributed to Napoleon's decision to get rid of Louisiana, sparked protracted unrest that destroyed Haiti as a major sugar producer; primacy in sugar production shifted to Cuba. The Cuban population grew tremendously, as did Cuba's wealth. A large portion of both consisted of the slaves who worked the sugar plantations. Elsewhere in Latin America, independence from Spain had produced strong pressure for emancipation of the slaves. Cuba's slave holders had no desire to give up their slaves or the riches the slaves were bringing them; they sought to avoid the pressure for emancipation by eschewing independence.

Looking neither like a warmonger nor particularly like an imperialist, William McKinley was accused of being the one and convicted himself of being the other. *Brown Brothers*

But the slaves, predictably, did not like the situation, and on several occasions during the first half of the nineteenth century, they rose in rebellion. None of the rebellions succeeded, but they did rattle the Cuban status quo. Over time, the dissatisfaction spread to other groups in Cuba, including the Creoles (Cubans of Spanish descent), who held most of the positions of power in the island—and only some of whom owned slaves. The Spanish government was growing increasingly corrupt, and decisions affecting Cuba often were dictated by court politics in Madrid. When a sharp economic depression in the 1860s added to Cuba's distress, a group of Creoles decided that continued loyalty was costing too much, and they determined to split from Spain. In 1868 they declared Cuba's independence and prepared to defend it by armed struggle.

The Spanish government responded to the declaration by sending a huge army to Cuba: ten times the size of the force it had sent to deal with the revolts in all of Spanish America earlier in the century. For ten years, war—labeled the Ten Years' War—ravaged the island and exhausted both the Cubans and the Spanish. Finally in 1878 the two sides called it quits. Madrid granted greater autonomy, short of full independence, to the Cubans; the Cubans pledged continued allegiance to Spain.

As part of the peace package, Spain freed Cuba's slaves. Emancipation was designed to win the gratitude of Cuba's large black population, which to some extent it did. But it had the additional effect of cutting the Creole slave holders'

If conditions in Cuba had always been as pleasant as in this drawing, there probably wouldn't have been uprisings there or a war between the United States and Spain. *The Bettman Archive*

last tie to Spain. Formerly independence had threatened to deprive the planters of their slaves; now, with their slaves lost, independence held no such threat.

Moreover, Cuba was falling into the American economic sphere. During the latter half of the nineteenth century, American investors purchased farms and other property in Cuba, slowly at first and then faster. By the mid-1890s Americans had sunk some $50 million into Cuba's economy. American interests gained control of the Cuban sugar industry, aided by the McKinley tariff of 1890, which eliminated duties on sugar imports to the United States from Cuba (while applying duties to Hawaiian sugar). Cuba became the third leading supplier of foreign goods to America (after Britain and Germany). The United States was far and away the largest market for Cuban exports.

The growing American stake in Cuba caused Americans to pay more notice than before when the Cuban independence movement revived in 1895. The chief revivalist was José Martí, a Cuban exile who after the Ten Years' War had spent more than a decade in New York writing and agitating in favor of Cuban independence. In the spring of 1895, Martí and a small band of followers landed on the Cuban shore and once again raised the banner of revolt. Though Martí was killed shortly thereafter (he would become a hero to subsequent generations of Latin American revolutionaries), the insurgency grew swiftly.

Spain's response to the renewed revolt could hardly have been more inept. The Spanish employed tactics that were harsh enough to alienate most of the Cuban people but not harsh enough to stamp out the insurgency. The most infamous tactic was that of *reconcentrado,* a brutal, albeit logical, effort to terminate the guerrilla activities of the insurgents. The insurgents attempted to blend in with the population at large while staging nighttime raids and hit-and-run ambushes. The Spanish forces, led by General Valeriano Weyler, countered by concentrating the Cuban peasants into camps where they could be closely supervised and by declaring much of the rest of the countryside a free-fire zone. Anyone found outside the camps was assumed to be an insurgent and could be captured or killed summarily. Not surprisingly, the *reconcentrado* policy made Spain many enemies. Ordinary people who merely wished to be left alone were uprooted and treated as criminals. Conditions in the camps were miserably unsanitary; thousands of Cubans died of disease.

The Cubans' plight quickly became a hot issue in the United States. Part of the reason was that the fighting between the Cuban insurgents and the Spanish troops destroyed American property: American businesses and individuals who saw their investments torched wanted the war to end. If neither the Spanish nor the Cubans could put a finish to the fighting, then perhaps the United States should step in. Another part of the reason for the American interest was the brilliant success with which the Cuban insurgents broadcast their propaganda in the United States. Building on the contacts José Martí and others had established during the 1880s and early 1890s, the rebels made sure that their side of the story was carried by most important newspapers in the United States.

It helped the cause of the insurgent propagandists that American newspapers, especially in New York City, were engaged in fierce battles for readers. The battles reflected recent changes in printing technology that allowed newspapers to be printed more efficiently and sold more cheaply than before. But the new presses cost money, and publishers sought to recoup their investment by attracting advertisers to their papers. The advertisers demanded large readerships: hence the newspaper wars. William Randolph Hearst and Joseph Pulitzer, whose papers dominated the New York market, were happy to publish the most lurid stories about Spanish atrocities in Cuba. The tone of Hearst's *New York Journal* was typical when it described General Weyler as a "fiendish despot" and an "exterminator of men." The *Journal* added, "There is nothing to prevent his carnal animal brain from running riot with itself in inventing tortures and infamies of bloody debauchery." If the characterizations were overdrawn and the stories were not always entirely true, Hearst and Pulitzer persuaded themselves that moderation and scrupulousness did not sell papers.

President McKinley, pressured by his Republican capitalist friends with Cuban connections and by an American public opinion that increasingly backed the Cuban insurgents against Spain—and finally by American expansionists who hoped to add Cuba and perhaps other Spanish possessions to American territory or at least an American sphere of influence—began speaking out. McKinley did not want war if war could be avoided. The American economy was finally beginning to recover from its disastrous slump, and the president did not wish to do anything that might shake the confidence necessary for the recovery to continue. In December 1897 he called on Spain to pay heed to the legitimate demands for more self-government, and he suggested that the United States might feel obliged to intervene if the situation in Cuba did not improve. But he resisted demands from warhawks for American belligerency, and he refused to grant diplomatic recognition to the insurgents' provisional government.

The situation in Cuba did not improve. It only got worse. Loyalists in Cuba (that is, opponents of Cuban independence), resenting what they saw as American meddling, attacked American property and threatened American nationals. McKinley responded by ordering an American battleship, the *Maine*, to Havana in January 1898. This infuriated the loyalists even more. In February an explosion tore through the hull of the *Maine*, killing hundreds of American sailors and sending the ship to the bottom of Havana's harbor. Although the cause of the explosion was unknown at the time (much later an investigation called it an accident), fire-eaters in the United States immediately pinned the blame on Spain and the loyalists. "Remember the *Maine!*" resounded across America.

Though the cause of the explosion that sank the *Maine* was unknown, the chief effect was soon apparent: increased shouting in the United States for war against Spain. *The Bettman Archive*

A Spanish diplomatic (or rather undiplomatic) blunder increased the momentum toward war. The Spanish minister in Washington, Enrique Dupuy de Lôme, wrote a letter to an associate in the Spanish government describing McKinley unflatteringly as a "bidder for the admiration of the crowd" and predicting that the Americans could be appeased with reforms that were more cosmetic than substantive. The part about McKinley wishing for popular admiration was true enough—as it would have been true of nearly any politician. But diplomats are supposed to be more tactful than to say so, at least in correspondence that might be pilfered by enemies. The insurgents got hold of de Lôme's letter and leaked it to American newspapers. The uproar against Spain grew louder than ever.

McKinley was not one to buck a strong tide, and despite persisting reservations about the wisdom of war, he issued an ultimatum to Spain that proved to be more a justification for American intervention than an honest effort to end the fighting in Cuba. The most important part of the ultimatum implied that Spain must grant Cuba independence.

The Spanish government had numerous problems of its own, and for it to knuckle under to the American demands almost certainly would have been politically fatal. For a time the Spanish government looked to the other European powers for help. Public opinion in Europe toward American meddling in Cuba ranged from disappointment to outrage; almost no one took the Americans at their word regarding concern for the welfare of oppressed Cubans. Among some of the European governments there existed strong sentiment in favor of warning the Americans off. Germany's Wilhelm saw a conspiracy between the Americans and the British to aggrandize themselves at the expense of the rest of the world and considered American pressure on Spain to be part of the plot. Wilhelm declared that it was "high time" the monarchs of Europe jointly offered their assistance to Spain "in case the American-British Society for Theft and Warmongering looks as if it seriously intends to snatch Cuba from Spain."

Unfortunately for Spain, the other powers did not agree with Wilhelm (neither did all of Wilhelm's own ministers). None of the other powers wanted to see the United States take Cuba, and none particularly wanted to see Spain humbled. But neither did any of them especially desire to tangle with the Americans over an issue that was peripheral to essential European interests. Britain was having more trouble than ever in southern Africa, where the Germans were still aggravating the situation; the British and French were at loggerheads in central Africa and were about to go to the brink of war over a spat at Fashoda on the upper Nile; the British, Germans, French, and Russians were fretting over the Japanese and each other in northeastern Asia. Although the Europeans made a largely pro forma gesture of urging moderation on the Americans, they refused to offer Spain the sort of support Madrid needed to withstand the American pressure. The British, most notably, refused to jeopardize their recently improving relations with the Americans. British prime minister Salisbury thought the Spanish government hoped to get the British navy to do Spain's dirty work and thereby spare Spain the trouble; he declined the honor, saying that the British should resist entreaties "to offer ourselves as candidates for the post of Archibald Bell-the-Cat."

When the Europeans left Spain to its own devices, and when Madrid refused to grant Cuba independence, McKinley on April 11 asked Congress for authorization to employ military force against Spain. "The present condition of affairs in Cuba is a constant menace to our peace," he said, exaggerating. Congress granted the president's request, and shortly thereafter Spain and the United States traded war declarations.

The Spanish-American War

The war against Spain came at a convenient time for the McKinley administration and the Republicans. The party of the administration had elections coming up in the fall, and though it seemed almost impossible that the Republicans would do as well this time as in their thorough trouncing of the Democrats in 1896, the war would be a good issue to campaign on.

It would be, that is, if the war went quickly and well. Skeptics had reason to doubt that Spain would be a pushover. The oldest among the naysayers could remember the Mexican War and how the American army had needed two years to get the overmatched Mexicans to give up. Middle-aged doubters recalled that both sides in the Civil War had expected that contest to be far shorter than it proved to be. Spanish power was not what it had been, but it was not obviously something to sniff at either. Americans attacking Spanish forces in Cuba would be mounting a difficult amphibious operation, the likes of which no living American soldier had ever accomplished (nor any dead ones, for that matter).

The skeptics turned out to be wrong, however, and the American contest against Spain turned out to be not much of a contest. Although the Spanish navy looked reasonably strong on paper (much the way the Mexican army had looked in 1846), its ships were old and poorly maintained. The smaller American navy was newer and faster and packed more punch—chiefly because of the influence of A. T. Mahan and his disciples on congressional appropriations during the 1890s. The American army was typically unready for war when Congress declared it, but the overall fighting capacity of the United States enormously exceeded that of Spain. And a generation of young men weary of hearing their fathers and grandfathers talk about the glorious days of the Civil War, when men were really men, flocked to arms to test their mettle.

Theodore Roosevelt desired more than most others of his generation to prove his manhood. Many American leaders (and many more leaders of other countries) have sought the fruits of war, but the majority of them would have preferred that the harvest not include all the killing and dying that war inevitably brings. Roosevelt adopted the—thankfully uncommon—view that war is

Theodore Roosevelt was never happier than when contemplating the glories of war. *Brown Brothers*

to the nation what calisthenics are to the individual: a means of eliminating flab and toning muscles. "No triumph of peace is quite as great as the supreme triumphs of war," he declared; and he spoke glowingly of that moment in the warrior's life "when the wolf begins to rise in his heart."

As soon as Congress declared war against Spain, Roosevelt began rounding up a volunteer cavalry unit. Several years earlier he had spent time in Dakota Territory, where he was smitten by the romance of the American cowboy; now he contacted some of his old partners and talked them into taking their ponies and six-shooters to Cuba to clean out the dastardly Spaniards. He also lined up some polo-playing buddies from his days at Harvard. This unusual mix gathered at San Antonio before moving to Florida, where Roosevelt and fellow officer Colonel Leonard Wood pulled strings to get the Rough Riders, as they called themselves (having rejected other monikers proposed by the press, such as "Teddy's Terrors" and "Teddy's Texas Tarantulas"), booked onto transports for passage across the Florida Strait.

Well they might have wanted to get out of training camp and into combat. Battle deaths in the Spanish-American War were very light as wars go: less than four hundred Americans fell to enemy fire. American soldiers faced far greater danger from tropical diseases contracted on the way to the battlefield than they did once they got there. Ten times as many succumbed to malaria, yellow fever, and dysentery as to Spanish bullets and bayonets.

Outfitting the troops (many in wool winter uniforms since there were not enough summer khakis to go around), arranging for provisions (including, as

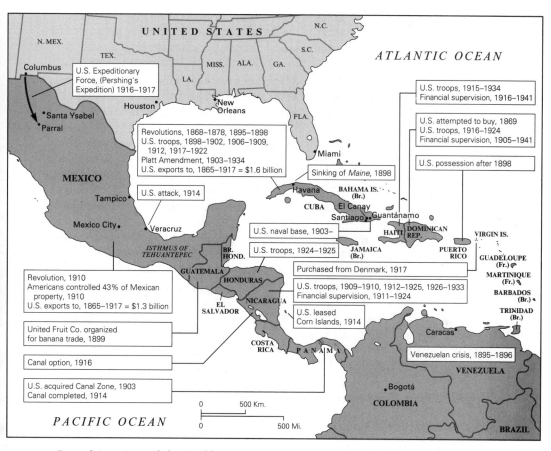

Central America and the Caribbean

it turned out, some poisonously putrid meat that laid hundreds of American soldiers low), training the men (using officers who had not seen regular combat for more than thirty years, if at all), putting them up (in camps that often showed an abysmal ignorance regarding basic principles of cleanliness), and transporting them to Cuba (several weeks into the Caribbean hurricane season) required until the middle of June. During the latter part of that month, some eighteen thousand troops of the American expeditionary force landed in Cuba. The Spanish commander on the island chose not to challenge the landing, preferring to save his troops for later battles.

When those later battles came, their results showed that he should not have waited. At San Juan Hill (where Roosevelt and the Rough Riders gave a good account of themselves), El Canay, and, ultimately, Santiago, American forces soundly defeated the Spanish. The capture of Santiago in July, shortly after the American destruction of the Spanish fleet harbored there, effectively ended the

Cuban phase of the fighting, although the details of an armistice required another month to work out.

Part of the reason for the delay was that the war had spread far beyond the Caribbean. Despite the fact that the situation in Cuba had dominated headlines in the United States, American military strategists well understood that a declaration of war against Spain would make Spanish possessions around the world fair game for American soldiers and, especially, sailors. Before the war started, the Navy Department had formulated contingency plans for dealing with the Spanish; the plan in effect at the time of the war's outbreak called for the American Asiatic fleet under Commodore George Dewey to steam to the Philippines and destroy the Spanish naval squadron at Manila.

As soon as the fighting commenced, Dewey weighed anchor from Hong Kong, where the British had been kind enough to allow him to provision, and set off for Manila. On arrival, he engaged the handful of Spanish ships in the bay and destroyed them within a matter of hours without loss of American life or craft. By noon on May 1, Dewey commanded the waters near the Philippine capital.

Conquering the land in the area and in the rest of the Philippines was much harder and took far longer. Dewey had to wait for reinforcements of ground troops to arrive from the United States. The outcome was never in doubt: since American ships controlled the approaches to the Philippines, Dewey could ensure that American reinforcements got through and Spanish reinforcements did not. The only question was how much resistance the Spanish would put up.

Actually, there was another question as well. For several years the situation in the Philippines had mirrored the situation in Cuba: local nationalists, upset at their treatment as inferiors by the Spanish colonial authorities, had waged a revolt. But in the Philippine case the revolt had fizzled out just before the United States declared war on Spain. The leader of the insurgents, Emilio Aguinaldo, had surrendered and gone into exile.

The onset of hostilities between Americans and Spanish seemed to Aguinaldo an opportune moment to resume the fight for Philippine independence. He hurried to intercept Dewey, about to embark for Manila, and hitched a ride back home. Because Dewey lacked ground troops, the American commodore calculated that Aguinaldo might help speed Spain's surrender by remobilizing his freedom fighters. Confusion later clouded the issue of what sort of bargain Dewey and Aguinaldo struck: Aguinaldo claimed that Dewey promised to support Philippine independence in exchange for collaboration against the Spanish; Dewey denied doing any such thing. No paper trail traced the negotiations, such as they might have been. Aguinaldo said that when he had suggested something in writing, he had been assured that the word of an American naval officer was guarantee enough. Traveling aboard an American warship, still separated from his fighting forces, the Filipino leader was in no position to insist.

During the several weeks after Dewey's victory in Manila Bay, Aguinaldo's troops succeeded in wresting control of most of the Philippines from the Spanish. At the beginning of August, only the city of Manila remained in Spanish

The Philippines During the
Spanish-American War

hands. By this time sufficient numbers of American ground forces had arrived
to allow a landing and an attack. The Spanish found themselves confronting
two armies: the American and the Filipino. The two armies were now coop-
erating only in the sense of sharing Spain as an enemy; the Filipinos had caught
on that the Americans might have aims in the Philippines besides Philippine
independence, while Dewey took care not to make any (more?) commitments
binding the United States past the end of hostilities against Spain.

The Spanish commander, weighing considerations of Spanish honor and his
own, judged that it would be less humiliating to acknowledge the termination
of more than three hundred years of Spanish rule in the Philippines by handing
his sword to a general of the United States army than to surrender to the rebel
Aguinaldo. The Filipinos guessed that something like this might happen, and
they assaulted the city. The Spanish stoutly resisted the Filipino attack but
offered only token opposition to a simultaneous American assault. After a curious battle in which the Spanish barred Manila's front gates to the Filipinos
even as they let the Americans in at the back, the Americans wound up in
possession of the city, and the Filipinos wound up frustrated. Rendering the
whole affair more ironic was the fact that the battle of Manila, like the 1815

Dewey's victory at Manila in 1898 was almost as easy and one-sided as this illustration suggests. *The Bettman Archive*

battle of New Orleans during the War of 1812, took place after the diplomats had negotiated a formal end to the fighting. In this case, however, the delay of the news was deliberate, or at least the result of a deliberate act, rather than the consequence of a technological shortfall: Dewey earlier had cut the telegraph cable in order to disrupt Spanish communications.

Getting from the armistice of August 12 to the Treaty of Paris of December 10 required much talking and evaluating of options. The principal American options involved how much to claim as spoils of war. At the beginning of the conflict, American anti-imperialists, who doubted warhawk claims of solicitude for the welfare of oppressed Cubans, had called the war faction's bluff and inserted into the war resolution an amendment barring the United States from annexing Cuba. The war advocates had to accept the Teller amendment (named for Colorado Republican senator Henry Teller) or else admit the selfishness of their motives. They ground their teeth and went along with the maneuver.

But they had their revenge regarding the Philippines. It had not occurred to Senator Teller to include that distant archipelago in his disclaimer; as a result, the McKinley administration enjoyed the option of taking title to the Philippines from Spain. McKinley evidently struggled with the issue before deciding that he ought to exercise the option. The alternatives were not especially promising. To leave the islands in Spanish control would create a tumult in the United States. If the Spanish had not been fit to govern Cuba, what fitted them to govern the Philippines? Besides, though American casualties in the Philippines had been relatively light, the McKinley administration would have had serious problems justifying those casualties and the expenses of the Philippine campaign if it merely restored the status quo.

Granting the islands independence made sense to many Americans but not to the administration. McKinley and his advisers contended—with good reason—that given the predatory atmosphere of the times, an independent Philippines would not last long. Germany already was lurking in the area. Japan was likewise seeking to extend its grasp. Britain or France might move simply to preempt Germany, Japan, or each other. Some persons suggested Philippine independence under an American protectorate. This suggestion presupposed greater altruism than Americans possessed toward the Filipinos: it would saddle the United States with the liabilities of defending the Philippines against foreign attack without availing the United States of the benefits of ownership. The protectorate proposal went nowhere.

The administration settled on annexation. American navalists, led by Mahan, liked annexation because it gave the United States control of Manila Bay—and, even better, the deeper and more protected harbor of Subic Bay. Commercial expansionists saw the Philippines as an entrepôt to the Orient, especially to the China market. (Just weeks earlier, amid the applause for Dewey, the navalists and commercial expansionists had finally persuaded Congress to annex Hawaii.) Missionaries—Protestant missionaries, that is—viewed the Filipinos, 90 percent of whom were Catholic, as constituting a field of souls awaiting harvest. McKinley later claimed to have arrived only reluctantly at his decision to annex. He said he had sweated and prayed over the issue long and hard before receiving divine guidance. "There was nothing left to do," he said of the islands and their inhabitants, "but take them all, and educate the Filipinos, and uplift and civilize them."

Inducing the Spanish to agree to American annexation of the Philippines was not particularly difficult, since Spain had few cards left to play. To soften the blow, the United States agreed to pay Spain $20 million, in keeping with the American diplomatic conceit that the United States never stole, only purchased, territory. The Paris treaty also transferred Puerto Rico and Guam, two islands that had similarly escaped the attention of Senator Teller, to the United States. Last but certainly not least, the Spanish consented to clear out of Cuba.

The Wages of Empire: The Philippines

The 1898 Treaty of Paris was hardly the last word on the issue of Philippine annexation. The Senate still had to approve the treaty, and approval was no sure thing. While the war was going on, the glorious news from the front drowned out the complaints of American anti-imperialists, but once the shooting stopped and the bargaining began, the anti-imperialists commenced a campaign against annexation. The anti-imperialist movement was a diverse coalition, including Republicans (Teller and Massachusetts senator George Hoar, among others), Democrats (most conspicuously William Jennings Bryan, the past and twice-future presidential nominee), captains of industry (steelman Andrew Carnegie) and of labor (Samuel Gompers of the American Federation of Labor), denizens of the ivory tower (Presidents Charles Eliot of Harvard University and David Starr Jordan of Stanford), journalists (E. L. Godkin of *The Nation* and Carl Schurz of *Harper's*), other writers (Mark Twain), and many more besides.

Some of the anti-imperialists made their case on the ground that an American takeover of the Philippines would deprive the Filipinos of their right to govern themselves; but this argument did not persuade very many people since it seemed to imply that the Filipinos would do a better job governing Filipinos than Americans could. To most Americans, such a contention sounded absurd. How could Filipinos, who had no tradition of self-government, know as much about governing as Americans, who had been running their own affairs for more than a century—and were Caucasians to boot?

Besides, selfless arguments almost never win in American politics (or the politics of other countries). Americans (and other people) considering a particular course of action want to know what is in it for them. Regarding the Philippines, the anti-imperialists replied: Nothing but expense and worry. To take the Philippines would cost Americans piles of money at the least. The United States would have to increase the size of its army and navy and prepare to fight the Germanys and Japans of the world. If war preparations did not suffice to warn off aggressors, the cost would escalate much further as Americans died defending Filipinos. Such entanglements were what the sages of American foreign relations—Washington, Jefferson, John Quincy Adams—had warned about from the start. Adams, in particular, had also warned that enlisting in the causes of others would corrupt American institutions, demoting liberty as an American priority and elevating force. The anti-imperialists considered this the most pernicious effect of annexation. Endlessly they recited the example of republican Rome, which had lost its virtue when it acquired an empire. An imperial America might gain the world but would lose its soul.

The anti-imperialists slipped from this high moral ground when some among them injected the specter of race mingling into the debate. What in the world did America need with millions of colored people, they asked, when it had not figured out what to do with the colored folk it already contained? American blacks at least had a chance of making something of themselves, being surrounded by the higher civilization of whites; Filipinos, in their backward native environment, would be nearly hopeless. Furthermore, if the Spanish experience afforded any example, annexation would invite miscegenation. Filipinos might be happy and pleasant people by their own standards, many Americans conceded. But would you want your daughter to marry one?

The imperialists rebutted each of the anti-imperialist arguments. Depriving Filipinos of the right of self-government was no more serious than depriving children of the right of self-government. Someday the Filipinos would be able to look after themselves; in the meantime, the United States was justified in acting in loco parentis. An imperial policy would be expensive but no more expensive than a policy that ignored America's global interests. Whether the anti-imperialists liked it or not, the world was an increasingly competitive place, and those who did not join the competition would find themselves at the mercy of those who did. By fearing for America's republican future, anti-imperialists betrayed a lack of confidence in the strength and resilience of democracy. American democracy had survived repeated foreign and domestic crises, including a civil war; it would not be destroyed because the American flag waved proudly in the breeze over some islands far away. Nor would the political attachment of the Filipinos to the United States corrupt American society. And who said anything about marrying?

The imperialists won the debate, but not by much. And their victory only followed a torpedoing of the anti-imperialist case by one of the antis' leaders, William Jennings Bryan. Though Bryan had convincingly lost the 1896 presidential election to McKinley, he was an unregenerate optimist and hoped to even the score in 1900. Bryan wished to clear the deck of the Philippine issue, which he throught would cloud the campaign. Besides, as he pointed out, if the Senate rejected the Paris treaty, America would remain technically at war with Spain, an awkward situation for both countries. By accepting the treaty, the Senate could detach the issue of the Philippines' future from the issue of the war with Spain. Then the American government could deal with the Philippines on that country's separate merits.

From this combination of reasons, Bryan directed his followers in the Senate to support the Paris treaty. The Bryanite votes provided just the margin the McKinley administration needed for victory. Yeas outnumbered nays by 57 to 27—1 more yea than the necessary two-thirds. On February 6, 1899, six months after the fighting ceased, the Spanish-American War formally ended.

It ended not a moment too soon. Several hours before the Senate approved the Paris treaty, a new conflict broke out in the Philippines. For some time after the August battle of Manila, the Filipinos had hoped that the Americans would live up to their democratic traditions and grant Philippine independence. Filipino diplomats traveled to Washington to make their case to McKinley and then to Paris to urge their views on the American negotiating team. They contended that Spain could not convey ownership of the Philippines to the Americans since Spain had never acquired legitimate title; title remained with the Filipinos, as title to any country invariably remains with that country's inhabitants. All the Filipino envoys got for their trouble was a runaround by the McKinley administration; the administration had decided to annex, and that was going to be that.

But the Filipinos had not exhausted their arguments. Unheeded in Paris and Washington, they took to the mountains of the Philippines to continue the debate with bullets. Ignoring injunctions to lay down their arms, they launched a war of independence against the Americans.

The Philippine War, the direct result of the Spanish-American War, lasted far longer than that conflict and produced much more in the way of death and destruction. The majority of the deaths and most of the destruction befell Filipinos, a fact that did little to endear America's new subjects to their new rulers. After unsuccessfully challenging the Americans in regular combat, the Filipino soldiers adopted a guerrilla strategy. Like most guerrilla contests, this one brought out the worst in both sides. Filipino fighters requested, then demanded, the support of Filipinos living in the countryside. If they did not receive enough of it fast enough, they punished the laggards, often harshly. The Americans discouraged Filipinos from assisting the guerrillas, by means including torture. The technique that gained the greatest notoriety was the "water cure," in which a subject being interrogated was forced to swallow more water than his stomach could hold and then had his stomach pummeled or kicked until he chose to cooperate with the interrogators, or occasionally died. Ironically for the Americans, and tragically for the Filipinos, the American military commanders in the Philippines felt themselves compelled to resort to the same reconcentration tactics the Spanish had used in Cuba, and which Americans had condemned as barbarous. The results of the American policy in the Philippines, in terms of lives lost among the persons reconcentrated, were comparable to those of the Spanish policy in Cuba.

Gradually most of the Filipinos decided that they could not win and that continuing the war compared unfavorably to accepting American rule. American officials made this decision easier than it might have been by offering educated Filipinos, even some who had taken part in the fighting, a share in the islands' government. This policy of attraction drew all but the hardest core of the nationalists out of the mountains and back into civilian society; by 1901 the resistance had lost most of its energy. When Aguinaldo fell into an American trap and was captured, and soon thereafter publicly swore allegiance to the American government, the fighting all but ceased. What little resistance remained caused the Americans no trouble.

Progressives and Imperialists

The American policy of coopting the Filipino nationalists was not entirely cynical. Despite Americans' preoccupation with what served American interests, they were not immune to considerations of what might benefit the Filipinos. The good of the Filipinos never weighed more in the scales of American policy making than the good of Americans, but when American interests did not dictate one course of action over another, Filipino interests sometimes tipped the balance.

Besides, Americans at the turn of the twentieth century were sufficiently self-centered to believe that what served American interests usually served Filipino interests as well. Rarely in history have American leaders been so sure they knew what ailed humankind and how to fix it. The period of the presidencies of Theodore Roosevelt, William Howard Taft, and Woodrow Wilson was the great age of progressivism. The progressives came from both major political parties and from various occupations, but they all believed that the ills of life in a modern industrial society could be substantially mitigated by intelligent people acting through government on behalf of society as a whole. The progressives placed much store in education, being convinced that understanding a problem was halfway to solving it. They revered democracy, often saying that the cure for democracy's shortcomings was more democracy. They were whiggishly optimistic, judging that nearly any problem could be cured by progressive legislation or other social action. On the whole the progressives were a pretty sunny bunch of confident, energetic, and capable people.

But there was also a darker side to progressivism. When progressives touted education, what they often had in mind was not an open-ended seeking after truth but an instilling of the values of well-educated America into less fortunate groups. The progressives particularly targeted recent immigrants, who brought their own sets of values and customs across the ocean with them. The progressives promoted education as a means of "Americanizing" such people: that is, making them over in the pattern of the progressives. When progressives glorified democracy, they had a particular kind of democracy in mind. Not for them the democracy of the urban political machines, of Tammany Hall and its imitators in other cities, despite the fact that the big-city bosses (or often their front men) were duly elected and reelected by their constituents. The progressives had a much more genteel vision of democracy: they conceived of scrubbed and schooled voters casting their ballots against Boss Tweed and his henchmen and in favor of good-government reformers—candidates much like progressives themselves. The progressives were optimistic, yet not uniformly so. Certain social problems might be too much for people to solve of their own free will. In such cases, people could use the assistance of the strong arm of government coercion. The movement to prohibit alcohol, for instance, represented an effort by progressives (and others) to enforce respectable middle-class behavior on working-class, tavern-frequenting types.

It was no coincidence that the same period that saw the blossoming of American progressivism also witnessed the flowering of American imperialism. Much of what the imperialists were trying to accomplish abroad, in places like the Philippines, was what the progressives were trying to accomplish at home. In fact, many of the most imperialistically minded American leaders were also the most progressively minded. Albert Beveridge purpled the Senate chamber with a rousing proannexation speech during the debate over the Philippines; Beveridge later helped organize the Progressive party. Teddy Roosevelt, that advocate of the martial virtues, wielded his Big Stick as energetically against corporate malefactors at home as against rival foreigners abroad. William Howard Taft, the first American governor-general of the Philippines, as president busted even more trusts than Roosevelt. Woodrow Wilson belonged to the wrong party to be an overt imperialist (Democrats attacked imperialism in large part as a means of breaking the Republican lock on the presidency); but in intervening in the Mexican revolution, in the First World War in Europe, and in the Russian Revolution, Wilson showed himself to be as militantly assertive as the most flagrant American imperialist. Historically, Wilson is commonly considered the greatest progressive president.

"Progressive" has never been a dirty word in American politics; "imperialist" usually has. Yet in certain respects, American imperialism was simply American progressivism gone international. Chronologically, progressivism began at the level of the cities, where reformers took on corrupt bosses and graft-ridden machines. Progressivism advanced to the state level when civic reformers realized that state governments set the tone and the ground rules for much of what went on in the cities. After reform slowed at the state level and the progressives discovered that many problems were too big for the states to handle, progressivism hit the national stage. Finally, progressives—especially progressive presidents Roosevelt and Wilson—became convinced that the realm of international affairs had to be progressivized if America as a nation were to live in peace and prosperity. Roosevelt's corollary to the Monroe Doctrine conferred on the United States police power for the Western Hemisphere, imposing American ideas of order and fair dealing on America's neighbors; Wilson led Americans to war in 1917 to make the world, as he put it, "safe for democracy."

China and the Open Door

American progressives looking for evidence that the world required remaking did not have to look any farther than China—which admittedly was rather far from the United States in miles but which with ongoing improvements in ocean travel and telegraphic communications increasingly seemed part of America's Pacific neighborhood. (Upon American annexation of the Philippines, East Asia became even more a part of America's neighborhood.) China during the late 1890s was nearly at the end of its rope. The rope in question was quite long, stretching back more than 250 years as it related to the current Qing (or Manchu) dynasty and more than 2,000 years as it related to a unified China under a central authority. As the nineteenth century drew to a close, both the Qing dynasty and the concept of a unified China were at serious risk. Since the Taiping Rebellion of midcentury, China had continued its slow process of disintegration. The presence of foreign merchants and soldiers in the treaty ports exacerbated the process by capitalizing on China's weakness to extract and enforce concessions. The Chinese were of two minds regarding contacts with the Western countries. Some Chinese sought to shut the Westerners out entirely; others argued for using Western technology to defend China against the West. The latter group, waving the banner of "self-strengthening," gained the upper hand during the 1860s and 1870s and adopted a program of importing selected Western products, studying Western languages and ideas, and building a Western-style army and navy.

But Chinese conservatives opposed the self-strengtheners. To some extent, their opposition reflected an honest Confucian regard for precedent. It would be unfilial of the emperor, they said, to alter traditions established by his predecessors; it would be equally unfilial of the Chinese people at large to overturn the ways of their ancestors. To some extent, the conservatives' opposition reflected the natural inclination of those in power to resist whatever might diminish their power. Getting ahead in Chinese officialdom was a trying process, and having invested their careers in learning to play by one set of rules, Qing bureaucrats were reluctant to see the rules change. Against this entrenched opposition, the efforts of the self-strengtheners made progress only slowly.

Too slowly, as it turned out. Japan's defeat of China in the Sino-Japanese War of 1894–1895 precipitated a psychological crisis in China. To have to bend to the will of the Westerners had been hard enough for Chinese to accept, but to be humiliated by Japan, which for centuries had existed in China's shadow, was too much to bear. The terms of surrender included, besides the acceptance of Japanese primacy in Korea, the loss of Taiwan to Japan and an

Beijing looks calm in this picture, but the troop column that these American soldiers were part of had to fight its way to the city in 1900 to relieve the foreign community trapped there in the Boxer rebellion. *The Bettman Archive*

indemnity that amounted to three times the Chinese government's yearly revenues.

The European powers had attempted, with some effect but not enough for the Chinese to notice, to get the Japanese to soften their demands. No love of China motivated the Westerners; they simply wanted to prevent Japan from taking so much from China that there would not be anything left for anyone else. Japan's pressure on China prompted the Europeans to increase their own pressure; as they did so, it looked as though China might go the way of Africa, sliced into pieces by the imperialists.

Chinese reformers made a last-ditch effort to salvage their country and their culture from the barbarian assault. A group of several hundred examination candidates (bureaucratic hopefuls) petitioned the Guangxu emperor to make major changes in China's system of education, economy, and government. The emperor mulled the matter over—for three years—and agreed to implement many of the reformers' demands.

But conservatives retreated only to counterattack. They persuaded the young emperor's aunt, the empress dowager Cixi, to force her nephew into premature retirement. She then threw her support to the standpatters, leading to the rout of the reformers. Many fled to other countries; some died on the barricades.

American leaders observed China's vicissitudes with concern. Although the China market had never lived up to the expectations of American merchants, they continued to hope it would. But clearly it would not if the Japanese and the Europeans partitioned the bulk of China into colonies or exclusive spheres of influence. Therefore, the merchants opposed such partitioning. Meanwhile, American missionaries kept the attention of another influential sector of the American public—evangelical Christians—focused on events in China. The missionaries did not like to see the Chinese victimized by European and Japanese imperialists; in addition, the missionaries suspected that if the Europeans and Japanese partitioned China, they would not leave much room for American missionaries.

Both the merchants and the missionaries appealed to Washington to do something to prevent the sundering of China. Like all persuasive arguments in matters of foreign policy, this one joined self-interest to altruism. Preserving China from the imperialists would benefit both American merchants, who could continue to hawk their wares in China, and American missionaries, who could continue their efforts to save Chinese souls. It would benefit the Chinese, who would be able to buy American products and join American churches and who did not want to have their country stolen out from under them by the foreign imperialists.

The merchants' and missionaries' arguments found a sympathetic hearing within the McKinley administration. McKinley's secretary of state was John Hay, formerly personal secretary to Abraham Lincoln and a man who had cut his teeth in government during the tenure of the archexpansionist and Pacificist (as definitely distinguished from pacifist) William Seward. Hay proposed a strategem reminiscent of the promulgation of the Monroe Doctrine. Hay had reason to believe that the British would support a warning to the other powers

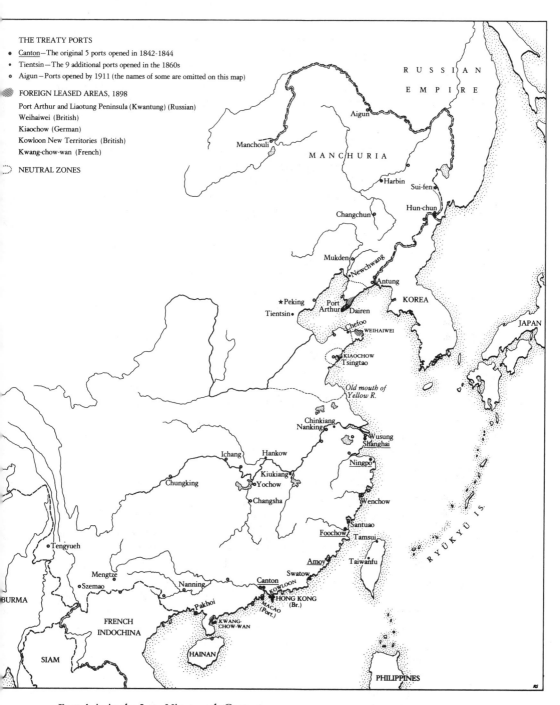

THE TREATY PORTS

- **Canton** — The original 5 ports opened in 1842-1844
- **Tientsin** — The 9 additional ports opened in the 1860s
- Aigun — Ports opened by 1911 (the names of some are omitted on this map)

FOREIGN LEASED AREAS, 1898

Port Arthur and Liaotung Peninsula (Kwantung) (Russian)
Weihaiwei (British)
Kiaochow (German)
Kowloon New Territories (British)
Kwang-chow-wan (French)

NEUTRAL ZONES

East Asia in the Late Nineteenth Century

to lay off of China, just as the British had supported the Monroe administration's warning to lay off of the Western Hemisphere. Hay's reason for this belief was that the British had broached the idea of just such a warning, much as they had broached the similar idea in Monroe's day. And just as John Quincy Adams and James Monroe had declined a joint Anglo-American statement in 1823, leaving the British to recognize their own interests in the affair, so John Hay and William McKinley decided to go it alone in 1899 and let the British tag along.

The vehicle Hay chose to declare the American policy was a diplomatic note circulated to the governments of the great powers. This first Open Door note started its rounds in September 1899 and declared American adherence to the principle of "equality of treatment of all foreign trade throughout China." Tariffs, transportation charges, and the like should be the same for every comer. The point was to prevent the powers from enforcing spheres of economic interest in China to the detriment of merchants from the United States. Hay requested that the powers announce their backing for such a policy of fair dealing.

It was a clever ploy. Hay knew the British would accept the Open Door principle; they had indicated as much, and with all their troubles in South Africa and elsewhere, they did not want to have to join a scramble for China. The Japanese were still trying to digest their meal from the Sino-Japanese War and were not itching for a tussle with Westerners just yet. The French were fairly well satisfied with the colonies they had recently seized in Indochina and were not eager to push north. Although the leaders of Britain, Japan, and France did not appreciate Hay's putting words in their mouths, none sufficiently opposed the American position to denounce it publicly. Their diplomats muttered in their beards, producing equivocal replies that committed them to nothing—but allowed Hay to claim their assent.

Russia and Germany caused more worries. Both countries had recently grabbed bits of Chinese ocean frontage, and both seemed hungry and aggressive enough to try to grab more. But as things happened, neither St. Petersburg nor Berlin cared to start something in East Asia that might spread to other regions, particularly Europe, where the balance of power was growing more precarious by the day. With a conspicuous lack of grace, the Russians and Germans acquiesced in Hay's statement.

Hay had little time to congratulate himself on his shrewdness. As rulers beleaguered at home so often do, the Chinese empress dowager tried to shift blame from herself to outsiders. She joined forces with a xenophobic secret society known as the Boxers and in 1900 declared war on foreigners in China. The Boxers killed those foreigners they could catch in the countryside and then marched to Beijing to besiege the foreign quarter there. A massacre appeared imminent. But the foreigners dug in and managed to keep the Boxers at bay. The Western and Japanese governments hastily put together a rescue force, including American troops pulled from the Philippines, and directed the rescuers to fight their way to Beijing from the sea. They succeeded in doing so, lifting the siege after two months with little additional loss of foreign life, but more than a little of Chinese.

With large numbers of foreign troops now on the ground in China, and with the foreign governments hopping mad, partition appeared more probable than ever. This was especially true in light of the fact that the foreign governments could reasonably claim that the Chinese government no longer possessed the power to enforce its own laws, including those that should have protected foreign nationals.

As before, John Hay sought to prevent such a fate befalling China—and American interests there. In July 1900 he circulated a second Open Door note, which amplified the first and explicitly called for continued "Chinese territorial and administrative entity": in other words, no partition.

As before, the Europeans and the Japanese acceded to the American position, less out of respect for the Americans or the Chinese than out of fear of each other. To them, China just was not worth fighting over at this stage.

The McKinley administration's establishment of the Open Door policy toward China had two effects. The first was to put the other great powers on notice regarding where the United States stood with respect to China. From the narrow perspective of 1900, it did not really matter much where the United States stood; Americans were not ready to put steel and lead behind their views on China. Yet for future reference this was worthwhile knowledge.

The second effect was to delude the American people into thinking that their country exercised more power in East Asia than it actually did. The Republicans were not above claiming a moral and diplomatic victory for the McKinley administration: the administration had spoken forthrightly in defense of China, and the other powers had backed off. *Post hoc ergo propter hoc.* Gradually at first, but significantly over time, Americans came to consider themselves the protectors of China. This attitude and the fact that it was based on specious reasoning eventually had very large consequences.

No-Fault Imperialism: Latin America

American policy toward East Asia was in the classical tradition of power balancing, of keeping competitors at bay by keeping them preoccupied with each other. Wars do not usually happen when two opponents are evenly matched or think they are; governments tend not to start wars they might lose or even need a long time to win. (Civil wars and revolutions—conflicts fought by entities other than sovereign governments, at least on one side—are a different story.) Wars usually break out when one country thinks itself sufficiently stronger than its rivals that it can defeat them fairly easily. Sometimes such countries are wrong; the bad guessers lose or expend an excessive amount of energy winning. The point of power balancing is to keep potential enemies from getting too confident. This was the approach the British took in Europe through most of the nineteenth century, and it was the American approach in East Asia at the beginning of the twentieth.

The other common way to prevent wars is for one country to be so much stronger than all its rivals that none of the rivals will risk crossing it. If governments do not like to start wars they *might* lose, they like even less to start wars they are *sure* to lose. No country has ever established hegemony all around the world; the best any country has been able to manage is regional hegemony. During the heyday of the Roman empire, the Romans controlled a big territory centered on the Mediterranean; within this region there prevailed a *pax Romana*, or Roman peace, the result of would-be upstarts knowing that Rome's legions would quickly quash any peace breaking.

The Monroe Doctrine represented an effort by the United States to establish hegemony—a *pax Americana*—in the Western Hemisphere. The effort lacked teeth until late in the nineteenth century, but by the time of the Venezuelan boundary dispute and the Spanish-American War, it was starting to bite. The war with Spain demonstrated that the United States was far and away the dominant military power in the Americas. The chief question that remained was what the United States intended to do with its dominance. Washington annexed Puerto Rico, making it an American colony. As for Cuba, the precipitant of the war and the prize of the Caribbean, that island's fate was complicated by the self-denying Teller amendment.

When the war ended, American forces occupied Cuba, effectively controlling as much of Cuban life as the officers of the occupation chose to. American authorities were pledged to Cuban independence, but they were determined to take their time delivering it and to ensure that Cuban independence would not damage what they conceived to be American interests in the area. Partly because of the existence of the Teller amendment, and partly because the Cuban revolutionaries were exhausted after years of battling the Spanish, no insurgency against the American occupation developed, such as in the Philippines. The Americans had promised to go home and leave Cuba to the Cubans; until the Americans showed plainly that they were reneging on their promise, there was no percentage in picking a fight with them.

The American occupying force was commanded by Roosevelt's friend General Leonard Wood, and it set about putting Cuban life on a soundly progressive footing. The first order of business was repairing the damage wrought by war and Spanish neglect. This required time but was well under way within a couple of years. As part of this reconstructive effort, Wood's engineers and doctors (Wood himself had an M.D.) undertook to wipe out yellow fever by attacking the mosquitoes that transmitted it. American educators revamped the school system the Spanish had left behind, making it possible for millions of Cubans to learn to read and write ensuring that what they read—at least in the schools—instilled the values of middle-class America. Although instruction took place in the Spanish language, many of the texts were translations of books written for students in places like Boston and Kansas City.

Wood and the Americans sought to foster conditions that would produce political stability in Cuba, which in turn, they believed, would produce economic stability and growth. Cuban prosperity and happiness, to the American way of thinking, depended on close economic ties between the United States and Cuba. The American economy at this time was one of the wonders of the world; by hitching a ride with the Americans, the Cubans likewise would enjoy the benefits of economic advancement. Cuba should be opened to American investment, which would provide jobs for Cuban peasants, besides guaranteeing continued American interest in Cuba's security and welfare.

Wood oversaw the gathering of a Cuban constitutional convention that had the purpose (for the Americans) of making sure that the good work of the occupation forces would not be undone by Cuban carelessness and (for the Cubans) of convincing the Americans to leave sooner rather than later. The constitution the conventioneers drafted met the Americans' requirements—which was not particularly surprising, since Wood kept them writing until they came up with a document he and his superiors in Washington liked. The final draft included provisions that closely circumscribed the independence the Teller amendment was supposed to have promised the Cubans. The most important provision was the so-called Platt amendment (named for American senator Orville Platt of Connecticut but actually composed by Secretary of War Elihu Root), which gave the United States the right to intervene in Cuba to preserve Cuban independence, to defend lives and property, and generally to look after American security needs. Most Cubans disliked the Platt amendment for obvious nationalistic reasons; but if such was the price of ending the American occupation, they were willing to accept it.

America's limited grant of independence to the Cubans left the United States in a position other imperialists could only envy (and attempt to emulate, as some did). By relinquishing authority over the day-to-day running of Cuban affairs, Washington absolved itself of responsibility for what befell the Cubans. Were Cubans poor? That was not America's problem. Were Cuba's leaders corrupt and brutal? Tough luck. But by retaining ultimate power over Cuba's foreign and economic policy, Washington ensured that American interests were well looked after. Did foreign powers threaten America's favored position in Cuba? Cite the Platt amendment and the Monroe Doctrine and chase them off. Did some Cuban government threaten the security of American investments in Cuba? Send in the marines.

Responsibility without power is an unenviable combination: you get blamed for problems you have no way of fixing. Responsibility with power is a fairer deal: you have to cope with the problems, but you have tools for doing so. Power without responsibility—what the United States enjoyed in Cuba—is what only children and great powers can get away with: you do what you want and let others clean up the mess you leave behind.

The American domination of Cuba soon came under political assault in the island. Most Cubans objected to the duress under which the Cuban constitution had been written and contended that the Platt amendment had no validity. A 1903 trade treaty between the United States and Cuba, which slashed tariffs between the two countries and tied the Cuban economy more closely than ever to the American economy, raised additional objections. Cuba was dependent on the United States not only politically, the critics charged, but also economically. Easy access to the American market for Cuban sugar was a mixed blessing at best: though it provided jobs for Cubans, it warped the Cuban economy by pushing it toward the production of a single crop. American investors bought up a great amount of farmland in Cuba and planted it to sugar, displacing producers of food crops, who in any event were being undercut by cheap imports from the mechanized farms of the United States. Cuban industry did not stand a chance against competition from American factories. Boosters of close Cuban-American economic relations might point out that the average income of Cubans increased with increasing trade between the two countries, but the critics countered by contending that averages masked wide disparities between the few wealthy of Cuba's cities and the many poor of the countryside. Besides, the economic colonization of Cuba by American capital was too high a cost to pay for marginally higher incomes.

Cuban resentment at American influence led to protests against the government the departing American troops left behind. That scandals and corruption surrounded the activity of the government did not help matters. In 1906 a rebellion broke out. President Taft responded by ordering American forces back to Cuba. A former judge himself (his real ambition, later achieved, had always been to be Supreme Court chief justice rather than president), Taft appointed a Minnesota judge, Charles Magoon, to head a provisional Cuban government. Somewhat like Solomon, Magoon offered to split the spoils of office between the leaders of the rebels and the incumbents. Unlike the real mother in the Solomon story, the rebels and the incumbents accepted Magoon's offer.

In buying off the insurgents, Magoon paved the way for the withdrawal of American troops, which took place early in 1909. At the same time, however, he helped institutionalize corruption in Cuban politics. Cubans dissatisfied with the status quo came to see that although the United States would tolerate no serious revolution–making in Cuba, Washington would not object to spoilsmanship and pocket lining by those in office. So the pockets got lined, and the revolution got postponed.

Cuba felt the weight of American hegemony more directly than any other Latin American country, but it was not alone in the kind of treatment it received. During the early years of the twentieth century, the United States broadened and deepened its influence in the southern two-thirds of the Western Hemisphere. In the rest of Latin America, as in Cuba, what Washington desired most was stability, usually defined to mean security for American investments and the prevention of undue European influence. These two objectives meshed with each other: conditions that jeopardized American investments usually jeopardized European investments as well, tempting European governments to act as bill collectors for their nationals and otherwise try to increase their influence.

Although Theodore Roosevelt and his associates in the executive branch of the American government were progressives, they were also Republicans. This implied that they placed great importance on contracts and financial obligations. If Latin Americans borrowed money, they ought to pay it back; if they resisted paying, they ought to be made to. Roosevelt had a hard time complaining too much when the Europeans dunned tardy regimes, even by threat of military force.

But such threatening violated the Monroe Doctrine. Roosevelt would not have been Roosevelt had he not insisted that other nations respect this hoary article of American international relations. To square the two principles—that governments ought not to be allowed to default on debts and that the Europeans ought to observe the Monroe Doctrine—Roosevelt devised a principle of his own. In 1904, following some brusque treatment of Venezuela by Germany, France, and Britain and concurrent with an impending default by the Dominican Republic, the president enunciated what came to be called the Roosevelt corollary to the Monroe Doctrine. The Roosevelt corollary asserted that to prevent other countries from enforcing proper behavior on the Latin Americans, Washington would undertake the duty itself. The United States would exercise an "international police power" to see to it that the Latin American countries met their obligations.

Predictably, most Latin Americans did not acquiesce kindly to the idea of the United States acting as the cop of the Western Hemisphere. They had not liked the idea of European intervention either, but most people, when given a choice, prefer bullies who live far away to ones who live next door.

As always, though, there were persons willing to adjust to the new power reality to claim a piece of the action. The Roosevelt corollary led to American military intervention in several countries—Cuba, Haiti, the Dominican Republic, Nicaragua, Honduras, Mexico—during the next three decades. In each country American officials looked for and eventually found locals who could accomplish, for a while anyway, the delicate feat of appeasing Washington without thoroughly alienating the masses of people in their own country. Those who undertook this assignment commonly comforted their consciences with the typical collaborator's rationale: that somebody has to do it, and if not me, then probably someone worse. They comforted their bank accounts by skimming taxes and shaking down officeholders. The American government usually looked the other way unless the grafting got so bad that the grafters' opponents took up arms. Then Washington sent in the marines and found a new set of collaborators.

There was one problem with the policy outlined by the Roosevelt corollary, though; it required too much effort on the part of the United States. Roosevelt himself never complained about the effort; he liked the exercise. But to many Americans, there seemed something incongruous about American troops acting as collection agents for European bankers. The Europeans made money off their loans, while American taxpayers picked up the tab for the cost of collection.

Roosevelt's successor Taft, who was smarter than most people gave him credit for being, had a better plan. Washington should encourage the Latin Americans to curtail their financial obligations to Europe in favor of closer ties to the United States. In particular, the Latin American governments should retire their European debts by taking out loans from American banks. This way the profits from the loans would flow north instead of east across the Atlantic, and there would be fewer objections in the United States to using American force to collect late payments. In fact, if Washington played its hand shrewdly and used American money to back regimes that arranged their priorities correctly—placing prompt payment at the head of the list—intervention might rarely be necessary. Moreover, the expansion of American loans and investments would contribute to hemispheric solidarity—always important in Washington's thinking—and encourage development of the Latin American economies. Economic development would benefit both the Latin Americans, who would see their living standards rise, and American farmers and manufacturers, who would watch their exports to Latin America increase.

Taft and Secretary of State Philander Knox practiced this dollar diplomacy toward several countries of Latin America (and less successfully toward East Asia). The best example of how the policy worked involved Nicaragua. In 1909 the Nicaraguan government of José Santos Zelaya faced a revolt by the numerous persons and groups he had antagonized during the course of his dictatorial rule. The Taft administration disliked Zelaya's policies, which included close financial connections to Europe; Zelaya had equally little use for Taft's policies. The decisive break between Washington and Managua came when Zelaya ordered the execution of a pair of Americans caught with the rebel forces. Washington responded by severing diplomatic ties to Zelaya's government and by providing support to the rebels, who proceeded to defeat Zelaya's troops and take power.

The Taft administration then resumed diplomatic relations with Nicaragua, now headed by the friendly and cooperative Adolfo Díaz, formerly an employee of an American company in Nicaragua. Díaz reversed his predecessor's pro-European policies, granting Americans favored treatment and borrowing from American banks to pay off his country's European creditors. When a new group of rebels rose up against Díaz in 1912, the United States again intervened, but this time on the side of the government. Washington sent marines to put down the revolt and safeguard Díaz—and American investments and loans.

The Big Stick and the Big Ditch: Panama

Although Americans tended to think of Latin America as a whole—for the purposes of the Monroe Doctrine, for instance—in practice the American government has always paid closest attention to Mexico, Central America, and the Caribbean basin. One reason for this extra attention has been proximity: people are naturally concerned about what happens nearby. The other reason has been the long-standing American interest in canal transit between the Atlantic and the Pacific. From the early nineteenth century onward, it was clear that any such canal would be built in Mexico or Central America; ships approaching or leaving the canal would pass through the Caribbean. The canal would be vital to the economic health of the United States, and American naval vessels would need to traverse the canal. (The perceived need for a canal increased greatly during the Spanish-American War when the battleship *Oregon* had to go clear around South America to get from the American west coast to Cuba and almost missed the fighting.)

After early flutters of interest in Mexico's Tehuantepec isthmus, Nicaragua and Panama (the latter still a province of Colombia) had become the prime possibilities for an interocean canal. The French trencher Ferdinand de Lesseps, fresh from his triumphal excavation of the Suez Canal, started slicing across Panama in the late 1870s, but mountains, jungles, and yellow fever forced him to abandon the project. The attention of canal builders then shifted to Nicaragua. The shift occurred, not because the Nicaraguan route was easier, shorter, or less expensive, which it was not, but because the French company that held the rights to dig in Panama wanted an extortionate price for surrendering those rights.

At the turn of the twentieth century, the French company's board of directors hired two agents, French engineer Philippe Bunau-Varilla and American lawyer William Cromwell, to represent the board. Bunau-Varilla and Cromwell first convinced the board to cut the asking price by more than half, to a mere $40 million, and then convinced the American Congress to authorize payment of $40 million for the rights.

There were two flies in the ointment, however. The first was Britain, which by the 1850 Clayton-Bulwer Treaty possessed a veto right over a Central American canal. The Roosevelt administration swatted this fly by negotiating a new treaty, the Hay-Pauncefote pact of 1901, which allowed the United States to build (and fortify) a canal on its own.

The second fly was the Colombian government. The Colombians did not want to approve the transfer of canal rights to the United States, chiefly because the French company's concession would expire in 1904, causing the rights and the $40 million or whatever the rights were worth to revert to Colombia. Bunau-Varilla and Cromwell were painfully aware that their hopes for a commission would expire at the same time; they redoubled their lobbying efforts.

At this point, their interests and those of the Roosevelt administration, which wanted to get started digging a canal as soon as possible, fell into line with the interests of nationalists in Panama. Colombia's hold on Panama had never been very firm; from Colombian independence in 1821 through the end of the nineteenth century, various Panamanian factions had averaged almost one rebellion against Colombian rule every year and a half. At the beginning of the twentieth century, a bitter civil war wracked Colombia, encouraging the Panamanians to try again.

The Roosevelt administration likewise encouraged the Panamanians. When Bunau-Varilla told Roosevelt in the autumn of 1903 that an uprising was near, the president hinted strongly that the United States would look favorably on self-determination for the Panamanian people.

This was good enough for Bunau-Varilla, who relayed the message south. In November the rebellion began. American warships conveniently positioned nearby—under the terms of an 1846 treaty granting the United States transit rights across Panama—made sure that Colombia was unable to land troops to quell the uprising. (It was one of many ironies in the affair that the 1846 treaty had been designed to protect Colombia, then called New Granada, against outside aggression; now it was being invoked against Colombia.) Two days later Washington extended diplomatic recognition to the new government of Panama. Secretary of State Hay and Bunau-Varilla quickly devised a treaty by which the American government would guarantee Panama's independence and pay $10 million at once and $250,000 per year in exchange for rights to a ten-mile-wide canal zone across Panama.

The affair turned out well for all involved except Colombia. Panama got its independence, although later it would have second thoughts about relinquishing control of the canal zone. The United States got its canal—the Senate ratified the Hay–Bunau-Varilla Treaty at the beginning of 1904; construction

By the time they got to the bottom of this mountain range, some of the engineers and construction workers were wishing the great canal had gone through Nicaragua rather than Panama. *AP/Wide World Photos*

commenced a few months later; and the canal opened to traffic in 1914. Bunau-Varilla and Cromwell got their commission. Indeed, the two agents got more: Bunau-Varilla went on to serve as the Panamanian minister to the United States, while Cromwell was appointed Panama's fiscal representative in the United States, a post he held for more than thirty years.

Though Roosevelt was mightily pleased with the outcome of the affair, the president could not escape a certain nagging of conscience regarding his role in fomenting a revolution against the Colombian government. At a cabinet meeting shortly after the event, he strenuously supported his actions—against no particular challenge. "Have I defended myself?" he demanded of those present. "You certainly have, Mr. President," Elihu Root replied. "You have shown that you were accused of seduction, and you have conclusively proved that you were guilty of rape."

Roosevelt Wins Peace Prize!
(Japan and Northeast Asia)

The Panama Canal's primary importance was economic. It speeded water transportation from one coast of the United States to the other and from some foreign countries to some American ports. Its secondary importance was strategic. It allowed the American navy to conserve ships by making it easier to shift vessels from the Atlantic to the Pacific and vice versa. (The fact that the canal had to be defended, thus adding to the navy's tasks, partially offset the convenience it afforded.)

The strategic element increased in significance during the ten years of the canal's construction. In Europe, the Germans were acting more bellicose by the month, causing the European powers to divide into two armed camps: Germany and Austria-Hungary against Britain, France, and Russia. The slightest incident, it seemed, might precipitate a bloodbath. If war came, the United States would be hard pressed to stay out. As during the Napoleonic wars, the belligerents doubtless would try to prevent American merchants from trading with the enemy; should Washington aggressively defend American neutral rights, somebody was bound to get provoked. At one point, the danger of war grew so great that Roosevelt felt obliged to intervene diplomatically, urging the French and Germans to settle their differences (over Morocco, in this case) peacefully; the resulting Algeciras conference of 1906 lessened the tension but did not resolve the underlying troubles.

The situation in Asia seemed equally threatening. The vultures continued to hover over China's barely breathing hulk. As soon as one landed, it appeared, the rest would surely move in. Japan was the likeliest candidate for first on the ground. Since the Sino-Japanese War of 1894–5, Japan had continued to expand its influence on the Asian mainland. Japan's industrial revolution was under full steam; like the other industrial nations, Japan was looking beyond its borders for markets and sources of supply. The Japanese labored under severe domestic deficiencies of iron ore and the kind of coal needed for steel production, but there was plenty of both on the Asian mainland—hence Japan's desire for a sphere of influence there. Korea had been the logical first component of a Japanese sphere; the Chinese province of Manchuria seemed the second. Despite the modest success of a yen diplomacy analogous to what Americans were practicing in Latin America, the Japanese felt that their position in northeastern Asia was insufficiently secure; Tokyo intended to remedy the insecurity.

To this point, none of the Western powers with interests in Asia considered Japan a major threat. Worrisome, to be sure: Japan's quick defeat of China demonstrated that the Japanese were stronger than the Westerners had thought. But China in the 1890s might have been knocked over by a feather, and the Japanese army and navy had yet to clash with the forces of an industrialized country. Nor had Japanese troops shown that they could stand up to white men in battle.

The Russians, in particular, underestimated the Japanese. The government of Czar Nicholas had designs of its own on Manchuria and Korea. The Japanese until now had not much objected to Russian activities in Manchuria, but when the Russians tried a ruble diplomacy in Korea, Tokyo got testy. The Japanese offered Russians a deal: Japan would stay out of Manchuria if Russia would stay out of Korea. The Russians greedily and imprudently declined the deal, hoping to win both Manchuria and Korea. The Japanese took offense; Japanese leaders judged that the Russians, with a huge and undeveloped empire of their own in Siberia, were unfairly trying to bottle up Japan.

To break the bottle the Japanese struck out militarily. Without warning or formal declaration of war, they attacked the Russian Pacific fleet. Shortly thereafter they sent ground troops smashing into Korea. By the time St. Petersburg regained its balance, the Japanese had entrenched themselves in key positions throughout the Korean peninsula.

The American government had been watching the events in Northeast Asia with mounting concern. When the war began, the Roosevelt administration quietly applauded the Japanese, deeming Russia the bigger threat to the stability of the region. But the rapidity and completeness of the Japanese victories on sea and land alarmed Washington. The goal of American policy was balance, and an overpowerful and overconfident Japan would jeopardize the balance. Before the Japanese could add to their victories over the Russians, Roosevelt offered to mediate. He invited Japan and Russia to send representatives to America—to Portsmouth, New Hampshire—to talk peace.

The Russians accepted with a sigh of relief. Not only were they losing, but the military reverses had helped touch off a revolution that was rattling the china in St. Petersburg even as the Japanese were rattling St. Petersburg in China.

The Japanese accepted, too, though with a show of reluctance. In command of the situation on the ground and hoping for a rich peace treaty, they played hard to get. In their coyness, Japanese leaders led the Japanese public to expect a big indemnity, which would go far toward assuaging the pain of those who had lost loved ones in the fighting. Behind their hesitation, however, Japan's leaders were happy enough to stop shooting and start talking, for they were almost out of ammunition and money, and they wanted to settle before their shortages became obvious.

Roosevelt, aware of Japan's predicament, quickly let Tokyo's envoys know that a large cash settlement was unrealistic. Russia was down but not defeated, and if allowed time to mobilize its massive resources, Russia might make Japan wish it had been more reasonable. With a conspicuous lack of grace, the Japanese negotiators accepted Roosevelt's argument. They persuaded the Russians to consent to Japanese control of Korea and forced Moscow to pull Russian troops out of Manchuria, but they dropped their demand for an indemnity.

For his part in writing the Portsmouth Treaty, Roosevelt won the recently created Nobel Peace Prize. That such an admirer of war as Roosevelt should win the peace prize was only slightly more incongruous than that the prize had been established by the inventor of dynamite. The prize proved to be about the only thanks Roosevelt got for his pains. The Japanese especially complained about being coerced by the American president into accepting an unfair settlement. It was a classic case of buck passing: the Japanese government found it easier to tell the Japanese people that the Americans had cheated them out of their indemnity than to own up to the fact that the government itself had exaggerated the likelihood of getting such an indemnity. Fortunately for the government, but unfortunately for Japanese-American relations, the Japanese people channeled their disappointment and anger eastward across the Pacific.

The Japanese did have other, legitimate causes for feeling angry at America. In the first decade of the twentieth century, anti-Asian agitation again cropped up, again in California. In 1906 the San Francisco school board voted to segregate children of Asian descent from Caucasian children—on the model of what schools in the American South were doing to children of African descent. The Japanese considered this a slap in the face and protested vociferously to Washington. Across Japan noisy and sometimes violent anti-American demonstrations, which the government did nothing to discourage, became regular political events.

Roosevelt deplored the action of the San Francisco board—What did those yahoos think they were doing, meddling in foreign affairs?—but he had no constitutional authority to overturn its decision. Instead he invited the board members to Washington for a stern lecture on American national interests and on how those interests were larger and more important than the parochial concerns of San Francisco parents. Yet notwithstanding his expostulations and the prestige of his office, Roosevelt got results only when he offered the Californians something concrete. In 1907 the president negotiated a "gentlemen's agreement" with the Japanese by which Japan suspended most emigration to the United States in return for San Francisco's consent to rescind its segregation order.

The accord solved the immediate problem but left some ominous loose ends. Most disturbing was the tendency of politicians on both sides of the Pacific to use the other country as a scapegoat. Demagogues in California blamed the troubles of American workers on Japanese immigrants; demagogues in Tokyo blamed shortcomings in Japan's foreign relations on American obstructionism.

While this tendency—an amalgam of racism, xenophobia, genuine grievance, and cheap politics—came to constitute one of the hardiest features of transpacific affairs during the first four decades of the twentieth century, Roosevelt succeeded in keeping it mostly in check. In fact he negotiated some hardheaded and realistic agreements with the Japanese. In 1905 William Taft, then Roosevelt's secretary of war, traveled to Tokyo and met with Japanese foreign minister Katsura Taro. The meeting produced a memorandum outlining each country's acknowledgment of the sphere of interest of the other: the United States recognized Japanese hegemony in Korea, while Japan forswore any designs on the Philippines. The Japanese valued the Taft-Katsura agreement for ratifying their gains in the war against Russia; Americans liked it because it removed—if the Japanese could be believed—the primary military threat to the Philippines. The removal of the Japanese threat was especially important to Washington because American taxpayers were showing a reluctance to fund the Philippines' defense.

Three years later, the Roosevelt administration concluded another agreement with the Japanese. This agreement, the Root-Takahira Accord of 1908, followed a visit by the American navy to Tokyo. The voyage of the "Great White Fleet" (named for the color of the ships rather than the sailors) was a bold public relations maneuver by Roosevelt, who desired to remind the Japanese that the United States was a military power to contend with in Asia. The president sent all sixteen battleships of the American navy on a round-the-world cruise, with stops at strategic ports of call. Congressional critics charged Roosevelt with wastefulness and recklessness: the voyage was wasteful, the critics said, because it cost lots of taxpayer money; it was reckless because it placed all of America's largest naval eggs in one basket. Moreover, for a time that basket would be in the home waters of sneak-attack-specialist Japan. In an effort to prevent the voyage, Congress refused to appropriate necessary funds. Roosevelt responded by sending the ships halfway around the world with the funds on hand and daring Congress to let the vessels rust in the Indian Ocean. As Roosevelt guessed, Congress capitulated.

The show of force impressed the Japanese, contributing to a subsequent Japanese naval build-up; in the shorter term it encouraged Tokyo to conclude an accord with Washington further delineating the respective interests of the two countries in Asia. By the Root-Takahira agreement, the United States and Japan accepted the status quo in the region and reaffirmed respect for the principles of the Open Door in China. There was an implicit contradiction in the pact, however, for the status quo included a de facto sphere of Japanese influence in southern Manchuria and thereby violated the Open Door. But diplomats get paid for facility in elastic language, and the importance of this accord rested less in what it said than in what it symbolized—namely, an effort by the two parties to deflate the belligerent rhetoric between them and to accommodate the interests of both. The accommodation did not last, and the rhetoric eventually reinflated, yet the accord provided something of a breathing spell.

Wilson and the Mexican Revolution

The Republicans of the Roosevelt-Taft era had better luck bargaining with the Japanese and Russians than with one another. Not long after Roosevelt reluctantly retired at the beginning of 1909, biting his tongue for having said he would consider his first three years in office as a full term under the George Washington two-term rule, he and Taft, his hand-picked successor, had a falling out. The falling out gave rise to a three-way race for president in 1912 and consequently to the election of Democrat Woodrow Wilson.

Wilson had no experience in international relations when he was elected; but he did not think that the standards of human conduct in Afghanistan, Argentina, or Angola ought to differ much from those in his home state of New Jersey. Given the opportunity, he planned to attempt to enforce those universal standards.

Wilson got his first opportunity after a revolution erupted in Mexico. In 1908 Mexico's long-time dictator Porfirio Díaz fell prey to the illusion that often afflicts rulers who suppress dissent: he began to believe his own propaganda and think that the people actually liked him. Díaz asserted that Mexico was ready for democracy; he would allow the formation of an opposition party. Díaz's opponents took him at his word and organized to contest the presidential election of 1910. At first Díaz ignored the chief opposition candidate, Francisco Madero, but when it became evident that Madero had a large following, the dictator arrested him. Madero spent the election in jail, while Díaz declared himself the victor by an overwhelming margin.

Thinking Madero harmless, Díaz released him. Madero skipped across the Rio Grande to Texas, where he began plotting a revolt. He gathered supporters, denounced the recent elections as rigged and invalid, and bestowed on himself title of provisional president of Mexico. Returning to Mexico, he issued a call to arms against the Díaz regime.

The initial response proved disappointing, so Madero decided to go back to Texas for a while longer; but his example encouraged others to challenge Díaz. The most important challengers were Pascual Orozco and Pancho Villa in the northern state of Chihuahua and Emiliano Zapata in the southern state of Morelos.

Díaz was old—eighty years—and did not relish the prospect of fighting off several contenders at once. Judging Madero the least radical of his opponents, the octogenarian abdicated in Madero's favor and fled to Europe.

To this stage, the Mexican Revolution suited the American government well enough. Despite early friendliness toward American investment, Díaz recently had attempted to counter what he saw as excessive American economic influence in Mexico by favoring British investors over American in granting concessions and other commercial opportunities. The Taft administration, busy pursuing dollar diplomacy policies elsewhere in Latin America, saw events in Mexico under Díaz moving in just the wrong direction. Washington winked at Madero's revolution-organizing efforts in Texas, and American officials shed no tears on Díaz's departure.

But Madero turned out to be a disappointment. Although he was no radical—the real radicals were Zapata and his followers—Madero legalized labor unions and allowed strikes, which disconcerted American business interests. Worse, he failed to get a grip on the political situation in Mexico and lost ground to Zapata and the genuine revolutionaries. Washington began wishing Díaz had never left. The American ambassador in Mexico City, an ardent conservative named Henry Lane Wilson, actively conspired with Madero's right-wing enemies.

The strongest and most ruthless of the right wingers was General Victoriano Huerta, who staged a coup that toppled and then killed Madero. By this brutal deed, Huerta hoped to stop the revolution in its tracks. Instead he caused it to mushroom. Zapata's peasant armies intensified operations in the south; Villa's cavalry rode roughshod across the mountains and deserts of the north. A third Huerta opponent, Venustiano Carranza, also attracted a large following. Carranza's group called itself the Constitutionalists and demanded restoration of constitutional government.

It was at this point that Woodrow Wilson assumed the presidency of the United States. Although the other great powers had extended diplomatic recognition to the Huerta regime, Wilson refused. Standard—but not completely uniform—international practice had been to apply a simple, pragmatic test in determining whether to recognize a new government. Did the government really control the territory of the country in question? Aspiring governments were always claiming to be in control even when they were not; what other nations needed to know was whether a particular claimant could control what went on inside its territory.

A second aspect of the recognition test concerned obligations to other countries. When governments negotiate treaties, incur debts, and the like, they do so not simply for themselves but for their nations. Governments may change—by election, coup, revolution—but the obligations remain. (Differences on this point provoked much of the dispute between Alexander Hamilton and Thomas Jefferson regarding the appropriate American response to the French Revolution during the 1790s, particularly whether the Franco-American treaty of alliance of 1778 still applied.) If such were not true, other governments would refuse to make long-term commitments, and the better part of international relations would grind to a halt. (The worse part—war—would go on about as usual.)

Generally, governments had not concerned themselves about the methods by which other governments came to power or kept themselves in power. For the purposes of diplomatic recognition, moral or ethical tests had been the exception rather than the rule. There were two reasons for this agnostic attitude. The first had to do with the nature of the international political order. After hundreds of years of dynastic, religious, and ideological wars, the powers of Europe during the nineteenth century arrived at the principle that what happened inside a particular country was the concern almost solely of the government of that country and its people. Painfully and slowly, the powers agreed not to meddle in each other's internal affairs. If Britain wanted a constitutional monarch; France, a president; and Russia, a czar, that was the business of each country alone. The practice of recognizing governments on the basis of effective sovereignty and fulfillment of international obligations reflected this hands-off attitude.

The second reason was that judging the moral character of a government is a nearly hopeless task. What constitutes unacceptably immoral behavior in a government? Executing traitors? Waging war against small, weak neighbors? Suppressing dissent or preventing secession? Few countries, and none of the great powers—whose actions effectively established the rules for the rest—could bring a spotless record on such matters to the bar of international justice. For decades before the American Civil War, most governments of the world considered slavery inhumane and oppressive. The American government did not. Establishing moral standards for one's own country is hard enough; establishing them for another country, which may have an entirely different cultural background, is almost impossible.

But it did not seem impossible to Woodrow Wilson. The American president refused to recognize the Huerta government of Mexico, complaining that Huerta had seized power over the dead body of his predecessor Madero. It did not improve Huerta's prospects of gaining Wilson's favor that the Mexican revolution continued unabated. Although Wilson was hardly an agent of American owners of Mexican property, the president could not help being concerned about the future of a large amount of American foreign investment. Many of the property owners—along with Ambassador Wilson—advocated recognition of Huerta. But President Wilson was never very good at accepting others' advice, and he did not in this case. He shortly fired the ambassador.

The president did not content himself with denying recognition to Huerta. He actively maneuvered to have the general deposed. He pressured the British to withdraw their support from Huerta. London reluctantly did so. The chances of war in Europe were growing greater all the time, and as they had since the mid-1890s, the British appreciated their need to be on good terms with the Americans.

Britain's backing away undermined Huerta's financial position and thereby weakened his power base. Whereas leaders of popular uprisings can run low-budget revolutions (peasant guerrillas work cheap), right-wing movements require regular infusions of cash (to pay troops whose loyalty to the usually elitist reactionary leadership groups generally has to be bought). Huerta grew desperate for revenues and suspended payment on Mexico's large foreign debt. This further lost him favor with the British and other creditors and cleared the way for Washington to turn the screws still tighter.

Wilson did so by tilting toward Carranza in the ongoing civil war. Early in 1914 the president authorized shipments of American weapons to Carranza's forces. Huerta responded by looking for additional arms of his own. Germany, happy to make trouble for the British and their American friends, offered to supply such arms. When Wilson learned that a German ship bearing weapons was approaching the port city of Veracruz, the president ordered American marines to occupy the town.

The landing followed a fabricated, or at least much embellished, incident that already had Mexicans fuming at American arrogance. A handful of American sailors on shore leave at Tampico had tried the patience of the local authorities, as sailors on leave often do, and had wound up in jail, again as they often do. The men were detained briefly, and then released.

But instead of treating the affair as part of life on the waterfront, American officials acted as though it was cause for war. The American commander on the scene demanded a formal apology and a twenty-one-gun salute to the American flag. Wilson backed the demands, even the ridiculous second one. In addition, the president prepared Congress for war with a sermon on the need to insist on respect for the United States in relations with Mexico, especially with the scoundrel Huerta.

Wilson's highhandedness antagonized many Mexicans who otherwise had little good to say about Huerta. The American president's order to occupy Veracruz, an action that produced sharp fighting and hundreds of deaths, mostly Mexican, antagonized many more. Those antagonized included Carranza, who refused to be a pawn in Wilson's game and who in any event could not afford to appear less zealous in defense of Mexican honor than Huerta.

Wilson now realized that he might have gone too far. He agreed to a proposal by Argentina, Brazil, and Chile to stop the fighting between Americans and Mexicans and start talking. Yet the talking failed to find common ground between Wilson and Huerta, which was not surprising since Wilson's terms still included Huerta's ouster.

Carranza, also invited to talk, spurned the South Americans' offer. He wrapped himself in the Mexican flag and declared that he had nothing to say to foreign invaders of Mexican soil. Carranza could afford to stand on principle: the revolution was going his way. Indeed, by July 1914 Huerta was on the run. He left for Europe before the month ended—arriving just as the tension among European powers finally burst into war. In August, Carranza assumed control of the government in Mexico City.

Carranza's victory might have solved Wilson's Mexican problems if Carranza had managed to solve his own. In particular, Carranza had to figure out how to deal with the other revolutionary factions in Mexico. He failed, at least at first. Pancho Villa refused to accept Carranza's right to govern, as did Zapata. The two men led their troops against Mexico City and forced Carranza to flee. Ironically, Carranza took refuge in Veracruz, which Americans had evacuated just a few weeks earlier.

At the beginning of 1915, however, Carranza staged a comeback. His generals drove Villa and Zapata out of the capital. Villa retreated to the north, where he resumed his guerrilla campaign; Zapata headed south, back to his stronghold in Morelos.

After the outbreak of the war in Europe, Wilson had difficulty concentrating on events in Mexico. During the spring of 1915, the European war approached the United States, despite the president's efforts to keep clear. In May, the Germans sank the British liner *Lusitania* with more than one hundred Americans aboard. Under the circumstances, Wilson hoped to liquidate America's involvement in the Mexican revolution as quickly as possible. To this end, he extended de facto (informal) recognition to Carranza's government. The implication was that de jure (formal) recognition would soon follow.

Pancho Villa upset Wilson's plans. Villa realized that American support would probably make Carranza invincible, and he attempted to create a rift between the Americans and Mexico's new government. In March 1916 Villa launched a terrorist attack on Columbus, New Mexico. The attackers killed seventeen Americans and outraged public opinion across the United States. Wilson immediately ordered the American army to go after Villa.

Carranza initially acquiesced in the American border crossing; but as Villa danced about the countryside of northern Mexico, General John ("Black Jack") Pershing's expedition grew larger and more intrusive. Carranza came to believe that Wilson had something in mind besides punishing Villa: he feared that the American president wanted to undo various of the reforms of the revolution that threatened the value of American investments. Wilson *did* want to do precisely that, though how badly he wanted to remains unclear. In any event, Carranza warned the Americans back and sent troops to reinforce the warning. The American and Mexican contingents skirmished, with casualties in the dozens. A bigger clash appeared imminent. Villa looked on in delight.

Unfortunately for Villa's chances of displacing Carranza, the Germans chose just this moment to get particularly ugly. In January 1917 Berlin decided on war against American shipping in the North Atlantic. Once the new policy took effect, Wilson would have almost no choice but to declare war on Germany. For four years Wilson had tried to keep the United States out of war; now he certainly did not want to get America involved in two of them.

At the end of January 1917, Wilson announced that he was canceling the Pershing expedition. By early February, the American troops had left Mexico. A few weeks later the American government acquired a copy of the so-called Zimmermann telegram, which included a proposal by the German government to the Mexican government for an anti-American alliance. The scheme was almost absurdly unrealistic (a simultaneous offer to Japan to switch sides in the war from the British-French-Russian camp to the German-Austrian-Turkish had only a slightly better grip on reality), and the Mexicans were not seriously tempted. But Wilson did not want to take any chances. During the first half of 1917, his representatives mended fences with Carranza, and in August of that year Washington extended full de jure recognition to Carranza's government.

*   *   *

It was a measure of the importance and power of the United States that Germany went to improbable lengths to start a brush fire on America's southern border before attacking on the Atlantic front. A decade and a half into the twentieth century, the Germans recognized that American strength could well determine the outcome of the world war.

This recognition, and more particularly the reality it reflected, was something new in the history of American international relations. Through almost the end of the nineteenth century, the United States had been a regional power at most, gradually extending its control across the North American continent to the Pacific, and later spreading its influence throughout the Western Hemisphere, but having little impact on the world beyond. At the very end of the nineteenth century, America's horizon of power expanded across the Pacific, encompassing the Philippines. American officials proclaimed an Open Door for China, and during the early years of the twentieth century they undertook to prevent Japan from getting overly powerful in Northeast Asia. At the same time, Washington deepened its position in Latin America. The United States made a formal protectorate of Cuba and informal protectorates of most of the other countries of Central America and the Caribbean. America built a canal across Panama and stamped its mark on the Mexican revolution. But Europe, still the center stage of great-power rivalry, remained essentially beyond the area most Americans considered vital to their country's safety and welfare.

This opinion would soon change. In 1914 Americans were halfway (conceptually, not chronologically) to a redefinition of their international interests. At the time of their country's birth in the late eighteenth century, most Americans were happy to control merely their own small corner of the Atlantic world; by the middle of the twentieth century, they would consider the entire planet their bailiwick. At that latter date, a few Americans would look back fondly to the days when they had to worry about only North America or even the Western Hemisphere. But most would find the idea of global power irresistibly alluring.

Sources and Suggestions for Further Reading

The Spanish-American War and the events surrounding it have been the subject of scores of books. H. Wayne Morgan, *America's Road to Empire* (1965) is succinct; Frank Friedel, *The Splendid Little War* (1958), has lots of pictures; David F. Trask, *The War with Spain in 1898* (1981), is comprehensive. Other useful volumes are Ramón Ruíz, *Cuba: The Making of a Revolution* (1968); Louis A. Perez, Jr., *Cuba between Empires, 1878–1902* (1983); Lewis L. Gould, *The Spanish-American War and President McKinley* (1982); Julius W. Pratt, *Expansionists of 1898* (1936); David Healy, *U.S. Expansionism: The Imperialist Urge in the 1890s* (1970); and Ernest R. May, *Imperial Democracy* (1961).

On the Philippines, start with H. W. Brands, *Bound to Empire: The United States and the Philippines* (1992); and Stanley Karnow, *In Our Image: America's Empire in the Philippines* (1989). Then proceed to Stuart Creighton Miller, *"Benevolent Assimilation": The American Conquest of the Philippines* (1983); and Peter W. Stanley, *A Nation in the Making: The Philippines and the United States, 1899–1921* (1974). The opposition to annexation of the Philippines is detailed in Robert L. Beisner, *Twelve against Empire* (1968).

American policy toward China is the subject of works cited in the previous chapters, as well as of Thomas J. McCormick, *China Market: America's Quest for Informal Empire, 1893–1901* (1967); Charles S. Campbell, *Special Business Interests and the Open Door Policy* (1951); Michael H. Hunt, *Frontier Defense and the Open Door: Manchuria in Chinese-American Relations, 1895–1911* (1973); and Marilyn B. Young, *The Rhetoric of Empire: American China Policy, 1895–1901* (1968).

Regarding the Caribbean basin, Dana G. Munro, *Intervention and Dollar Diplomacy in the Caribbean, 1900–1921* (1964), is solid. David G. McCullough, *The Path between the Seas: The Creation of the Panama Canal, 1870–1914* (1977), is lively. David F. Healy, *The United States in Cuba, 1898–1902* (1963), examines the first American occupation of the island; Allan R. Millet, *The Politics of Intervention: The Military Occupation of Cuba, 1906–1909* (1968), examines the reprise.

American relations with Japan play a large role in Howard K. Beale, *Theodore Roosevelt and the Rise of America to World Power* (1956), which is also the best book on the inimitable Teddy as a maker of foreign policy. Akira Iriye, *Pacific Estrangement: Japanese and American Expansion, 1897–1911* (1972), looks at the growing friction between the two Pacific powers, as does another book by the same author: *Across the Pacific: An Inner History of American-East Asian Relations* (1967). Roger Daniels, *The Politics of Prejudice* (1962), discusses the anti-Japanese movement in California. Eugene P. Trani, *The Treaty of Portsmouth* (1969), recounts the negotiations that ended the Russo-Japanese War.

American troubles with Mexico are explained in Robert E. Quirk, *An Affair of Honor: Woodrow Wilson and the Occupation of Veracruz* (1962); P. Edward Haley, *Revolution and Intervention: The Diplomacy of Taft and Wilson with Mexico, 1910–1917* (1970); Larry D. Hill, *Emissaries to a Revolution: Woodrow Wilson's Executive Agents in Mexico* (1973); and Mark T. Gilderhus, *Diplomacy and Revolution: U.S.-Mexican Relations under Wilson and Carranza* (1977).

Index